THE OTHER
JAPAN

D0110228

THE OTHER JAPAN

Voices Beyond the Mainstream

DAVID SUZUKI
KEIBO OIWA

Fulcrum Publishing
Golden, Colorado

Fulcrum Publishing edition 1999

Library of Congress Cataloging-in-Publication Data

Suzuki, David T., 1936–
    The other Japan : voices beyond the mainstream / David Suzuki, Keibo Oiwa.
        p.   cm.
    Originally published: The Japan we never knew: a journey of discovery. Toronto, Canada: Stoddart, 1996.
    Includes bibliographical references and index.
    ISBN 1-55591-417-9 (pbk.)
    1. Japan—Description and travel. I. Oiwa, Keibo.   II. Title.
    DS812.S878   1999
    952—dc21   98-47560
                                                                                  CIP

Printed in the United States of America
0 9 8 7 6 5 4 3 2 1

Cover photographs: The cover is a composite of two photographs by photographer Natalie B. Fobes, copyright © Natalie B. Fobes. The background image is of an Ainu elder at a salmon ceremony in Sapporo, Hokkaido, Japan. The foreground image is of a young Japanese woman, also in Sapporo.
Cover design: Elizabeth Watson
Page design and composition: Andrew Smith Graphics Inc.
All photographs taken by the authors, unless otherwise noted.

Fulcrum Publishing
350 Indiana Street, Suite 350
Golden, Colorado 80401-5093
(800) 992-2908 • (303) 277-1623
www.fulcrum-books.com

The lives of our respective fathers,
Carr Kaoru Suzuki and Toshio Oiwa, were intertwined with
the Japan we never knew.

As we worked on this book, they spurred on our curiosity
about these people called Japanese.

They both passed on while we were embarked
on this voyage of discovery, leaving us with mysteries and
questions to ponder.

They live on in our memories and genes,
and this book is dedicated to them.

contents

INTRODUCTION

by David Suzuki

t HE year 1995 was a significant anniversary. It had been fifty years since atomic bombs were dropped on Hiroshima and Nagasaki, the Second World War came to an end, and the United Nations was formed in the hopes of ending war for all time. Not surprisingly, Japan was the focus of much of the attention and retrospective activity.

Over the decades, the image of Japan has gone from one of a rapacious military machine through duplicitous, sneaky enemy and vanquished foe, to one of economic superpower.

Japan's astounding postwar recovery, from massive destruction and humiliating defeat to a modern industrial society, has impressed friend and foe alike. The country's products, initially dismissed as imitative, cheap, and low quality, now set the standards for others. Japan has manufactured items that compete directly with those that other countries have excelled in producing — and won. They displaced Swiss watches, pushed German cameras aside, and outmuscled American automobiles, steel, television, and computers.

For the West, the Japanese people remain an enigma, which we westerners conveniently overlay with widely held stereotypes — they show little emotion, they work like ants, they are great at imitation but show little originality, they are obedient and polite, they are homogeneous in race, language, history, and culture. As with all generalizations, each of these notions contains a kernel of reality that is immediately countered by individual exceptions. Whoever the Japanese are, they arouse emotions in other countries. They are welcomed for their investments and tourist dollars, yet are feared and hated for their actions in the Second World War. Their products are admired and desired worldwide, but they are accused of unethical competition and business practices. They lead the world in energy conservation and efficiency, yet are condemned for pillaging the oceans and forests of the world. They are recognized for their economic clout, yet criticized for not taking a position of leadership in global politics.

Japan has always aroused a complex multilayered response in me personally. My ancestry is Japanese, so that even as a third-generation Canadian, I will always be identified by a hyphenated description, a *Japanese*-Canadian. While my physical features reflect my ancestry, the mind behind the face feels itself completely Canadian. So who are these people who look so much like me and my family and yet become completely alien the minute we attempt to communicate?

As a peace activist who has long opposed nuclear weapons, I have many times invoked the names Hiroshima and Nagasaki to conjure up all of the horrors of modern warfare. Japan has been a powerful symbol for the peace movement. For the past two decades, Japan has also become a symbol of the terrible ecological costs that accompany explosive economic growth. While Japan's postwar economic success has allowed it to carve out a major role in the global market and dazzled commentators in the Western world, environmentalists have become increasingly vocal about the country's dreadful ecological record. In 1972 at the Stockholm Conference, the whale became the main symbol for all endangered wildlife, and it has continued as the focus of concern. At the last meeting of the International Whaling Commission in Kyoto in 1994, the strong support for an immense Antarctic Reserve was opposed by Japan, which has been intent on increasing its quota of whales. Euphemistically called "research," Japan's whaling operation continues to supply whale meat for Japanese consumers.

Japan has also been attacked for its use of immense drift nets that scythe their way through the oceans, and for logging operations that strip ancient forests from Canada to Malaysia and Siberia to satisfy Japan's insatiable demand. Japan has actively supported World Bank funding for megadams and megaprojects in countries where Japan is anxious to exploit the resources.

I first visited Japan in 1968, and it had a huge impact on my life. I gained an insight into how much my identity in Canada was caught up in being physically different. In Japan, surrounded by people who looked just like me, I suddenly felt as if I had disappeared. And I found things that absolutely enthralled me — the food, the exquisite attention to detail and aesthetics, and samurai soap operas on television. I have returned to Japan more than a dozen times since, and because environmental concerns have come to dominate my life, my inability to arouse a sense of urgency and need for change among Japanese has increasingly angered and frustrated me. I always seemed to meet a uniform response either of incomprehension or disinterest in my concerns. Japan seemed monolithic, homogeneous, and conformist.

At a meeting in Kyoto of North American environmental activists and Japanese media people, I encountered the enormous social pressure that effectively enforces conformity. In one session, the American activist Randy Hayes, of the Rainforest Action Network, got up and announced that he had just got out of jail; he'd been arrested for protesting the logging of tropical forests in Hawaii. "My country has a terrible environmental record," he began, "and a lot of us are willing to go to jail in protest. But we also look on Japan as one of the worst nations committing environmental crimes." It was a sensational statement that had the effect of a grenade being lobbed into the audience. One of the journalists on the panel, an eminent Japanese television host, was extremely angry and dismissed Hayes's remarks as "Japan bashing." That's when I realized that a direct assault is ineffective in that country, because it immediately elicits a response of drawing up the bridge and defending against what is perceived as an attack on all Japanese. The question, then, is how can such a defence be penetrated?

Over the years I have met individuals who negate the Japanese stereotype — outspoken, critical, independent, and original. But their rarity only served to emphasize the overwhelming impression of uniformity within the population. In 1992 I attended a conference at Meiji Gakuin University in Tokyo held to reflect on the five hundred years since Columbus's arrival in the New World. It was there that I had my first inkling of real grassroots activism in the country. I encountered young students who were receptive, indeed hungry, to hear different perspectives. I gave a hard-hitting talk, the sort I delivered in North America, and to my surprise, the audience was receptive and enthusiastic. I watched their response to some of the powerful aboriginal leaders from North and Central America and was amazed to see professors stand up and support them. In fact, there was an almost idolatrous following of some of the aboriginal guests. At that meeting, I learned of the aboriginal people of Japan — Ainu, Okinawans, and Uilta. Here was a very different Japan from any I knew.

Travelling to Hokkaido after the conference, I met Ainu people like Mieko Chikkup, Koichi Kaizawa, and Shigeru Kayano, who were not pursuing Japanese assimilation but were determined to hang on to their Ainu identity. When we were taken to the dam being built on their sacred river, the Saru, the pain of the imminent flooding of sacred sites was palpable. And when Koichi took us into a forest to see the largest chestnut trees in Hokkaido only to discover they had been clear-cut, we were all devastated. Here was a group of people through whom we might be able to raise issues in Japan that could no longer be avoided or hidden.

It became clear that I had paid far too much attention to those who speak from positions of authority or power in Japan, that beneath those visible layers of position were individuals with radically different perspectives and priorities.

No one illustrated this hidden Japan better than Keibo Oiwa, the anthropologist who had organized the conference at Meiji Gakuin University and invited me to participate. Like many young Japanese in the 1970s, he had been radicalized by student activism and took part in demonstrations, which led to a stint in jail. He was expelled from university for his radical activity, which could have had enormous repercussions in later life. In 1977 he travelled to North America, where he enrolled at George Washington University; after two years he transferred to McGill University in Montreal. When he completed his degree in philosophy and continued on in anthropology at Cornell University, he wrote a PhD thesis on Jews in Montreal.

Keibo has an insatiable curiosity about people and is attracted to the unusual, the eccentrics, the individualists; he is fascinated by minority cultures — Jews in Montreal, African-Americans in Harlem. It is ironic, then, that all his life he had assumed he was Japanese, only to discover as an adult that his father was Korean. It opened a window into his father's life that he continued to explore while he did research for this book.

During the trip he had organized to Hokkaido in 1992, he issued a challenge. He told me there was a very different Japan from the popular image portrayed by the media. What I had to do, he said, was come to Japan and meet with grassroots activists in the areas of peace, human rights, and the environment. The challenge struck a responsive chord in me because, in my ecological activism in Canada, my attention has been increasingly focused on grassroots groups, where the real transformation must and is taking place. The environmental philosopher Thomas Berry has suggested that acting on the slogan "Think globally, act locally" tends to disempower by the immensity of the challenge. Instead Berry believes we must "think and act locally" to have any hope of having an effect globally. I took Keibo up on his challenge and discovered people as radical as any I have encountered in North America. I found a country with a diverse history and culture, people critical of Japan's war record and others searching for alternatives to the sterile consumption-driven values of global economics.

This was an uplifting discovery for me. Everywhere in Japan I have looked, I have found people working for profound change at the level of local communities. As a North American, I am working for similar goals that are rooted to a place. What I learned in Japan has been a treasure trove of experience that has much to teach us.

One of the most startling lessons of twentieth-century biology has been the discovery that *diversity* — genetic, species, and cultural — is a critical part of long-term resilience and survival. In a time of rapid environmental and social change, it is this diversity that provides the possibility of combinations that allow adaptation to the new conditions. We have learned from painful experience that *monocultures*, the attempt to create populations of one or a few species of highly selected genetic stocks, are vulnerable to new pests, disease, or environmental upset.

The astonishing diversity of culture and language our species has always had is rapidly diminishing this century under the twin assaults of global telecommunications and economics. From the forests of Papua New Guinea to the Kalahari Desert to the crowded streets of Shanghai and Rio, we can recognize the same singers and Hollywood actors and brand names on running shoes, soft drinks, and radios. Humanity is becoming monocultured as societies and their surroundings undergo explosive changes. But biologists know that this time of cataclysmic transformation is the very moment diversity is most important. We hope that the fascinating people you will meet in this book will provide insights and ideas that will expand, rather than shrink, your horizons.

part one

war and
peace

the Legacy of war

"The most striking feature of these records of that terrible summer is the silence of the citizens following the bombing . . . It was a cruel and complete silence, worse than any other, like a moan that cannot be voiced."

1994 NOBEL LAUREATE
KENZABURO OE, IN HIROSHIMA NOTES

tRAVELLING throughout Japan today, one sees no physical scars of war. But the Second World War will soon come up in conversation, for it is a touchstone, the ultimate reference point against which to measure today's events. For those who lived through it, the psychic and social scars are deep.

The year 1995 marked the fiftieth anniversary of VE-Day, the end of the war in Europe, the atomic bombing of Hiroshima and Nagasaki, VJ-Day, the end of the war, and the establishment of the United Nations. For North Americans born since the war, those events have little relevance. But Japanese, even the younger generation, are still coming to grips with Japan's role in the war and the humiliation of defeat.

The debate still continues as to whether Hiroshima and Nagasaki were the cost of a speedy end to war or symbols of war gone too far. Japan has come to be viewed by some as a victim of war, the only country ever to experience a nuclear weapon deliberately used on civilians. Yet a retrospective on Hiroshima planned for 1995 by the Smithsonian Institution received such a storm of objection from veterans' groups that the exhibition was gutted of its focus. Opinion seems to be split between anger at Japanese atrocities committed during the war and outrage at the bomb's introduction, which brought a new dimension to warfare.

What has caused such powerful revulsion for atomic weapons? It can't simply be the number of people killed. After all, more people were killed by the fire-bombing of Tokyo than by the atomic bombs. It can't be the manner of death. Instant incineration may be more merciful than the often protracted agonizing deaths from "conventional" weapons. Is it that radiation-induced mutations are passed on to innocent generations of the future? Yet this ability of nuclear weapons to imprint the future is shared by chemical weapons, such as mustard gases, which are strongly mutagenic.

Perhaps part of the reason nuclear weapons seem so terrifying is that they marshall the powers of the queen of all sciences — theoretical physics — to unleash the very energy of matter itself. Henceforth, no area in science has been beyond potential military application, and the connection between scientific research and weapons of destruction has remained tighter than ever. Henceforth, Dr. Strangelove is now as popular an image of scientists as Albert Einstein.

The fundamental explanation of nuclear weapons' exceptional horror may have been provided by Stephen Jay Lifton, Yale's famous psychiatrist. In the weeks following the bomb, Lifton recounts, a rumour spread through Hiroshima that nothing would ever again grow in the city. People were aghast; while we all understand that each of us will die, we are assured by our knowledge that nature persists. When it seemed that nature itself was ended, people felt that this was the ultimate horror. Only when new plants sprouted did people feel hope again. Now we know that nature can withstand those bombs, but in the years that followed the

Second World War, hydrogen bombs and a massive proliferation of weapons created a very real spectre of the end of nature itself.

A consequence of Hiroshima and Nagasaki was the birth of a strong antinuclear movement in Japan. Paradoxically, fifty years later, Japan has a vigorous nuclear energy industry and is accepting radioactive wastes from other countries for reprocessing. The Japanese understand war's true horrors, and they share a commonality of experience with all other victims of war. But as a defeated nation and as a victim of the most terrifying weapons, they also are in a unique position. Even half a century later, the Second World War is still close to the surface of their consciousness. And for those who bore a disproportionate share of the costs, the war continues.

The drive from Tokyo to neighbouring Saitama prefecture (a prefecture is a political area, like a large county) was long and hot, although our driver was skilled at navigating the frighteningly narrow roads and avoiding the traffic jams that are almost constant on most Japanese roads. Our destination was the home and museum of two important Japanese artists, Iri and Toshi Maruki, although Iri, then in his nineties, did not feel up to seeing us.

When we got out of the car, it was as if we had entered another world, an oasis surrounded by trees. On our left was the museum; on the right was the Marukis' home, and before us was the Iruma River, which glistened in the midday sun. As we admired our surroundings, one of Toshi's assistants greeted us. We followed her through a traditional Japanese gate into a garden with stone pathways, and then to an old house that had been converted into Toshi's studio. The interior was large and open, all the dividing walls having been taken out. Sitting on a *tatami* (straw matting) in the middle of the room, Toshi Maruki was surrounded by papers, canvases, desks, and different tools of her craft. We had seen photos of her murals depicting the horrors of war, and we expected Toshi Maruki to be intense, tough even, with little time for pleasantries. But the person sitting before us was the picture of softness and grace, and her manner was gentle and inviting. She asked us to sit on the *tatami* in front of her. When we asked about her experiences in the war, she answered quietly:

> The papers said it was a new type of bomb. Up until the atomic bomb, the papers always said Japan was winning. When we read about the new bomb, I sensed it was pretty serious because the language had changed.

The first atomic bomb was exploded over Hiroshima on August 6, 1945. Three days later, Toshi's husband, Iri, went to the devastated city to search for his parents. He eventually found them living in a makeshift shelter. They had lost everything. Iri sent a letter to Toshi, via a friend who was leaving the city, asking her to join him. She had no idea what to expect, since the Japanese media had been extremely circumspect about the effects of this dreadful new weapon. In Hiroshima, she found people hunkered down in pitiful holes covered with tin scrounged from the debris. There was no food. The annihilation had been complete.

Maruki paused in her story. Because there was no furniture in the studio, everything was scattered around on the floor. She reached for some dried flowers and put them beside a small doll that sat upright on a miniature chair. Not far from her stood a half-finished painting. "I've finished with the big pieces," she said, "and am now painting small pictures like flowers and dolls. I'm doing very different pictures now." Satisfied with the placement of the flowers beside the doll she continued her story.

> The war was over, but there was no food. Everyone had left. You couldn't tell one field from another. I went looking for food and found a pumpkin. One side was soft and the other hard. I picked it and washed it. I found rice that had been hidden in a barrel. So I cooked the pumpkin and mixed it with rice. I was very hungry, so I took a mouthful and thought it was sour, but decided to swallow it anyway. Then I had a couple more mouthfuls. Immediately, I got a pain in my stomach and had to rush out with diarrhea. The second

time, I began to bleed. I was very sick and lost a lot of weight. I had
no energy and thought I was going to die. So, while ill, I began to
paint the Hiroshima experience.

Sick with radiation poisoning, Maruki moved with her husband to
Tokyo, where she continued to languish. She thought she was going to
die and wanted to paint what she had seen of Hiroshima as a last testa-
ment. Looking at her smooth skin and pink cheeks, we could not imagine that she had been so sick. She was one of the lucky ones who
miraculously recovered, as if spared to carry out her mission.

A few months later, we moved to Katase. I had a mirror and modelled
for my own pictures. I began drawing Hiroshima. I'd draw on a piece
of paper about the size of a *tatami* mat. One day I hung the picture on
the wall and went to bed. In the middle of the night, I got up to go to
the bathroom, and on the way back, a breeze caused the picture to
move. It frightened me. With that fear, the sight of Hiroshima came
back to me, and I felt this fear had to be shared with others.

I called the first piece *Ghost*, and I exhibited it in a group
showing. At first I was advised not to use the words "atomic bomb."
So the title was changed to *August 6*. People came from all over.

And that was the beginning of a lifelong commitment for both
Marukis. Their murals of the war were exhibited throughout Japan.
Another turning point came when she took the Hiroshima panels for a
showing in the United States. There, a professor at California Institute of
Technology scolded Maruki. He said the Japanese used the bomb as an
excuse for the terrible things they had been responsible for, including the
infamous Rape of Nanking. Stung by that critique, Toshi and Iri extended their murals beyond Hiroshima and the bomb. Their passion never
flagged, but their vision changed from latent nationalism to a questioning of the very nature of the human heart. This resulted in the broaden-
ing of subject matter from Japanese Hiroshima victims (*Ghosts*; *Fire*;
Water) to Korean and American Hiroshima victims (*Crows*; *Death of
American Prisoners of War*), then to all Second World War victims (*The

Battle of Okinawa; *Auschwitz*), followed by all victims of man's inhumanity to man (*Minamata*; *Sanrizuka*) and finally to hell.

"There are many kinds of people," she said. "I hope there still are a lot who reject wars. I'm worried there might be another war." We asked her if it wasn't human nature to wage war.

> Not every human being has this nature to fight. I hope this memory will be somehow kept to teach us. It's been half a century since the atomic bomb. I think human beings are about to forget it. Those who have experienced it can never forget; it's too painful even today. But we are dying, and the next generation who have heard about it are getting old too. The third generation from us see Hiroshima as ancient history. I'm afraid they'll repeat the same thing again.

Now we were eager to cross the courtyard to the museum and see the murals for ourselves. As we walked, Maruki's description of the bomb's aftermath rang in our ears:

> People lost their feet or their hands. Their skin was burned and coming off. So they covered themselves with Mercurochrome and were red. When that ran out, they put on a white salve. Their eyelids and lips were like raw meat. Their eyes were all swollen and they couldn't see. They were called ghosts. Their eyes closed, their hands held out from the body, their clothes burned off and only rags left. They couldn't lower their hands because it hurt too much, so they held them out from the body. They walked in a line for two or three kilometres to where twisted houses were still standing. In the outskirts, people were afraid of the victims because they looked like ghosts. They closed the shutters and wouldn't come out to help. So the victims walked farther and farther until they lost strength and collapsed. After the bomb, winds swept dust and ash into the sky. Then black rain fell. If we were wearing white shirts, they turned black.

The museum where Iri and Toshi Maruki housed their murals was large. There were four galleries containing three or four murals each: two rooms of Toshi's solo work; a room of charming, cheerful primitive art painted by Iri's mother (the Marukis taught her to paint when she was seventy-five); and a room displaying personal items they had collected or were given during their travels. There were also relics — burnt bamboo, petrified wood — of Hiroshima. It was an intensely personal museum.

One of the contradictions of art is that there is a dignity in the portrayal of horrifying scenes. Using Chinese black and white ink, large wall-size murals show victims with burns, yet they are not grotesque but dignified. The Marukis' depiction of the madness of war and of our ability to be inhumane to one another shows us how complex and twisted the nature of war really is. The murals play no favourites. There are many victims: the Americans, the Japanese, the Koreans, the Okinawans. The images demand that the viewer reflect on the way we treat one another; the mute mouths scream at us to avoid such horrors forever. The Marukis believe the duty of the artist is to face human darkness and act as conduits of past pain so that others, especially the young, will understand these horrors and not repeat them.

> After drawing so many hells, I began to place women with their babies in the pictures, hoping that they might have a power to save. I drew many mothers holding children, and I also drew a woman giving a helping hand to a man. Watching me draw, Iri said, "Things don't work that conveniently." I thought he might be right. So I drew devils trying to tempt women and interfering with what they were trying to accomplish.

At the end of our visit Maruki presented us with a large picture book of her murals. The last page was blank. Maruki made a space in front of her, and dipping a brush into a pot of Chinese ink, she drew a picture of a peace dove. In the belly of the dove lay a mother and child. As we left Maruki's studio, a couple of young women were being let in. One of them was a Korean artist who was painting a series about "comfort women" (the thousands of women who were forced by the Japanese to serve as sex slaves). Her face glowed as she was introduced to Maruki. Like the Korean artist, we felt fortunate to have met Maruki. She is someone whose memory will live on in her stirring paintings.

Far away, on the other end of Japan in Okinawa, a younger generation still lives with the reverberations of the war and the American occupation that followed.

The origin of the Okinawans is unclear. The islands where the Okinawans live are closer to Taiwan than to the main island of Japan. The original inhabitants could have come from Taiwan and islands farther south. In medieval times, Ryuku, as Okinawa was called, was a kingdom that thrived as the crossroads for trade between China and Japan. Eventually it evolved its own unique culture, a blend of indigenous customs with those of their trading partners. It was in the golden age of its history and culture that Columbus "discovered" America.

The Ryuku Kingdom existed as an independent nation until it was annexed by Japan in 1879 and became Okinawa prefecture. The people were always treated by Japanese as second-class citizens, sort of "country cousins." They were kept in low status socially, economically, and educationally. Use of the Okinawan language and the teaching of Okinawan history were forbidden. The Japanese instituted the use of the word Okinawa, instead of Ryuku, the name the people called themselves.

By the time the Second World War began, many Okinawans considered themselves Japanese and were proud to pledge allegiance to the emperor. They were moved by the raising of the flag and sang the national anthem. In the final phase of the war, Okinawa was the entry point for American soldiers into Japan. For the Japanese imperial command, the islands represented the last line of defence. Soldiers and civilians alike were expected to fight to the death.

Author and former American soldier Harold Rickard translated Shoko Ahagon's book, *The Island Where People Live*, and described the relentless attack on Okinawa:

Aerial bombardment of Okinawa by U.S. forces began in 1944. The landings on the beaches began on Easter morning April 1, 1945. The cruel struggle continued until General Ushijima's suicide and the surrender of Okinawa on June 23 . . . the southern one-third of Okinawa was completely destroyed. . . . Almost one-third (62,000) of the civilian people died of wounds, starvation and disease. Many of them were elderly persons, mothers and children. Okinawans had been placed in the most dangerous battle positions by the Japanese officers. Many had been executed as "spies" because the Japanese military leaders did not trust their loyalty. Food and shelter in natural caves and tombs were taken from Okinawan civilians by Japanese soldiers, exposing them to death or wounds. Many Okinawan civilians committed mass suicide because Japanese propaganda had convinced them that American soldiers would torture, rape and kill them. High school girls pressed into service as nurses were not allowed to come out of a large cave, which served as a Japanese field hospital, to surrender to the U.S. soldiers. Most of them died by the U.S. infantry's flame throwers which filled the cave with fire and death. Small children were separated from their families. Many people took refuge in the forests and mountains of northern Okinawa.

Japan's strategy of deliberately using Okinawa as a sacrificial border where the Americans would be stopped was successful in the sense that American soldiers never landed on the main islands of Japan. But the suffering of Okinawan civilians was beyond imagining. The toll on all sides was horrendous, but the numbers tell who suffered most: 12,520 American soldiers were killed in Okinawa, compared with 244,136 Japanese soldiers and Okinawan civilians.

For more than two decades after 1945, Okinawa was occupied by the American military. It was a critical part of American hegemony in Asia, a gateway to China, Russia, and the Middle East. Like the Philippines, Okinawan bases were the distribution points of personnel and equipment. Today 75 percent of all the American military bases in Japan are located in Okinawa, which in area makes up only 0.6 percent of Japan. Twenty percent of the main island of Okinawa is used for bases, taking much of its prime agricultural land, which was confiscated from protesting farmers.

Since Okinawa reverted to Japan in 1972, 15 percent of the base area has been returned, but in the meantime there have been 115 aircraft accidents, including 34 crashes, as well as 129 forest fires caused by artillery practice.

Not surprisingly, there has been opposition to the American presence, but Americans have injected massive amounts of money into Okinawa's chronically underemployed and poor communities. Since the end of the Vietnam War, many Okinawans have adapted to the presence of the Americans, so much so that a sizable group actively works to encourage them to stay. Nevertheless, the Okinawans have longheld simmering resentments, and "incidents" with the military have kept the resentments alive.

We came to Okinawa city to meet Shoichi Chibana, a grocer and unlikely rebel. On October 26, 1987, he was in the stands of the softball field in Yomitan village, his hometown. He slipped off his shoes and looked across the stadium to where Masaru Hirose, president of the Japan Softball Association, was sitting in a place of honour. The stands were packed for the National Games, which were being played in Yomitan village for the first time. There, on top of the ten-metre wall enclosing the stadium, was the Hinomaru, the Japanese flag with its red circle on a white background.

Masaru Hirose had forced Yomitan village to raise the Hinomaru at the competition. If they had refused to raise it, Hirose threatened to change the venue. That would have been disastrous; the stadium was brand-new, built especially for the games. Everybody, including the mayor who was a friend of Chibana's, knew that Hirose's threats were to be taken seriously. There was nothing they could do but raise the flag.

To make matters worse, the day before, Hirose had been scheduled to visit the Chibichiri cave, where many Okinawans had died in the name of Japan. Chibana and many of his fellow citizens were enraged. Chibana felt it was his responsibility to stop the man who was forcing the Hinomaru on the people of Yomitan from entering the caves. When Hirose tried to enter the caves, Chibana blocked his way. Yoneya Fumi, an old woman who had lost five family members in the caves during the last days of the war, heard what Chibana had done and said, "That is good."

It was then that Chibana realized that for the sake of the dead and the living, someone would have to do something about the raising of the flag. Villagers had already protested against the Hinomaru and the proposed singing of the Japanese anthem, "Kimigayo" (The Emperor's Reign Forever). High-school band members refused to play the anthem. One girl dumped her school's Hinomaru in a ditch. Yet no matter what they tried to do, the flag and anthem remained a scheduled part of the events. Chibana spent that night talking to his wife about his plan. She was due to have a baby in the next few days but gave him her support nonetheless.

As he looked up at the Japanese flag, his heart pounded in anger that it had been raised here in Okinawa and in fear at the consequences of what he was about to do. He hurriedly scaled the wall, tugged on the ropes and brought the flag down. Awkwardly, he tried to set it on fire. When the flames finally caught, he raised the burning cloth for the stunned audience to see.

Then he climbed back down and wondered what to do next. An old woman handed him his shoes while another shouted, "You must flee!" He ran out of the stadium. He could almost hear the president of the Japan Softball Association, Masaru Hirose, yelling for the police. A friend pulled up next to Chibana in his car, congratulated him and asked if he had a getaway vehicle. Chibana said that he hadn't really expected to get away but that he *was* hungry. So his friend gave him a lift to the Kadena McDonald's where he had a hamburger. Finally he called a lawyer and turned himself in. In a country in which behaviour is tightly circumscribed by social approbation, Shoichi Chibana's act of flag-burning put him in the pages of history. It also put him in jail. While he was in prison, his wife gave birth to their child.

Despite the seriousness of Chibana's actions, we laughed when he told us the story. He met us in Birdy's Bar, his favourite watering hole, which also happens to be the preferred drinking establishment of the

Green Berets from the nearby American base. The Green Berets were in Somalia fighting at the time, and the talk in the bar was that eighteen of them had died two weeks earlier on a botched raid at Aideed.

Chibana's good looks and easygoing, charming manner belie his reputation as a radical and fanatic. But, as he told us, he had never expected to become a leader:

> I was born in 1948. The Americans were nice to me and gave me candy. I liked Americans. When I was a young boy, many Okinawan girls in our area were called "honey" or "only." I didn't know until I was older that these terms meant prostitute and mistress. It was then I realized our powerlessness. We made a tiny fraction of what American GIs made. They could buy anything they wanted. That's why I worked for Okinawan reversion to Japan, hoping we'd be better off.

Even after centuries of Japanese occupation, Okinawans knew they were different linguistically and culturally. Tokyo was a long way from Naha, and the local people chafed at being treated like second-class citizens. Nevertheless, two decades of occupation by the American military was perceived as worse than belonging to Japan. And so, when given the opportunity, Okinawans voted to revert to control by Japan. Chibana continued:

> I was pro-reversion. I waved the Japanese flag at rallies. Under the Americans, we didn't have basic human rights. We couldn't elect our own government, arrest American criminals, make our own laws. We were mad. American perpetrators of everything from traffic accidents to rape were tried by American military court and set free. We were frustrated and humiliated. The U.S. dollar was strong: it was $1 to ¥360. After graduating from high school, I worked at a steel mill. I was paid $50 a month. The chairman of the local government got $300. A low-level U.S. soldier got $200. An officer, $300 to $500. There were also many Vietnam War soldiers on R and R who had a good chance of dying in the very near future. So, of course, these

men spent their money freely and mostly on women. There was public prostitution. Americans could hire a "wife," a woman whom they would put in a cage [an apartment] and give $50–$100 a month.

Chibana stopped talking as the waitress put down another round of drinks. Then he resumed:

> Just because I was in the student movement doesn't make me special. Six hundred out of eight hundred students at the Ryukyu University would go to demonstrations. It was a time when the future of the island was being decided. That was the Okinawa of my youth. We were eager to escape all this by being incorporated into the Japanese Constitution. We thought it was beautiful, a real Peace Constitution.

In the central part of Okinawa's main island, an atmosphere of war still hangs over the area because of the ubiquitous presence of the American military — stores selling used army equipment, shop signs with flags painted on the front and the words "American-Owned" or "Welcome Americans," old dirty cars instantly recognizable as foreign-owned, military jets and huge helicopters roaring overhead continuously. Chibana motioned to the walls where lacquered

"Actually, I'd rather have American soldiers than the Japanese Defence Force because of what Japanese soldiers did to us fifty years ago."

SHOICHI CHIBANA,
GROCER AND ACTIVIST

posters of Cary Grant, Greta Garbo, and Humphrey Bogart smiled down at the Okinawan patrons. On the wall above the cash register hung the infamous picture of a doped-up Elvis shaking hands with Nixon. On the other side of that was a sign that read, "Welcome Military Personnel."

> It's not that I'm anti-American; it's their presence on our land. The Japanese Defence Force is the same to me. Actually, I'd rather have American soldiers than the Japanese Defence Force because of what Japanese soldiers did to us fifty years ago. I'm more afraid of the Japanese

than I am of the Americans. I know many people here feel the same way.

For many Okinawans, Japan's unique constitution, with its Peace clause, offers a model to the world, a renunciation of war forever. Imposed on a country humiliated by defeat , this remarkable document says:

> The Japanese people forever renounce war as a sovereign right of the nation and the threat or use of force as a means of settling international disputes.
>
> In order to accomplish the aim of the preceding paragraph, land, sea and air forces, as well as other war potential, will never be maintained. The right of belligerency of the state will not be recognized.

Under the terms of the Japanese surrender and its new Peace Constitution, Japan could no longer have a standing army. But an escape from this stricture was the creation of the National Police Reserve, rationalized as a kind of internal national police force like the FBI or RCMP. In 1954 the National Police Reserve was converted into land, air, and maritime forces, known as Jieitai (Self-Defence Force), whose existence allegedly does not violate the Peace clause in the constitution. In terms of ground troops, ships, and planes, Japan's military strength now ranks sixth in the world.

To Okinawans who remember the Japanese Imperial Army, which had cruelly used civilians as an integral part of the defence against the American invasion, the Self-Defence Force simply stirs up all those bad memories and loathing.

Chibana leaned across the table as if telling us a secret:

> In 1973 after the reversion, a Japanese naval member of the Defence Force walked through town in his uniform. He was attacked and beaten up. It's the presence of any kind of military personnel that we resent. I am ambivalent about what I want. I don't speak about separation from Japan.

Apart from our table, there was only one other person in the bar, an

Okinawan who was busy chatting up the bartender. Chibana smiled at us and turned to the man.

"Are you Japanese?" he asked.

The man, perplexed and slightly annoyed at being distracted from his conversation, answered tersely, "Yes," and then turned his back to us. Chibana leaned back into our conversation.

There are three types of Okinawans. One type answers, "Yes, I'm Japanese." Another answers, "No, I'm Ryuku." The third group says, "I'm both, but Okinawan first." I belong to the third group. If you consider the islands as Japanese, you will notice many Okinawan things. If you consider them Okinawan, you will notice many Japanese things. It's a strange place. Even more so after reversion. I'd love to say I am Okinawan but I'm in the Japanese economic structure. I carry a Japanese passport. I can't ignore that, but I'm not willing to accept it.

Chibana explained that this sense of ambiguity is shared by the people of his community and the other ordinary people of Okinawa. That assures him that he is with them, even though his actions, such as burning the Japanese flag, sometimes look extreme.

For me, the Hinomaru is not the national flag. Officially it's not the national flag. It's just the flag of the military during the war. Germany and Italy changed their flags. I didn't think burning the flag was such a big deal, but the response was shocking. It was so big. East Timorese, Puerto Ricans, American Indians all came to meet me for inspiration. I always answer, "Please don't consider me a representative of Okinawan dissent."

I didn't expect the response from right-wingers either. They tried to burn my store. I couldn't imagine that. But there was also unexpected support. In the past five years everything has surprised me. Sixty-five lawyers from as far away as Osaka and Tokyo have volunteered to defend me. I don't even know most of their names.

As we gathered up our belongings to leave Birdy's bar, Chibana had one final thing to say on the subject:

I am still explaining why I burned the flag. People think I am a crazy radical. But when they talk to me, they realize I am just a normal person. In the context of Japan, the act looks crazy, but in the context of the community, it was not so strange. If the customers at my supermarket thought I was crazy, they could go elsewhere. They didn't stop coming. Many felt my action was extreme, but they understood why I did it. I feel I am supported. I am very happy with this support. I'm just an ordinary guy who wants to be with my pretty wife and my friends and my kids and socialize.

The next day Chibana offered to show us the Chibichiri cave. That morning we left the Deigo Hotel in Okinawa city and drove past the Kadena base, the largest U.S. air base in Asia. Occupying forty-eight percent of Yomitan, it casts a wide shadow across the area.

Once outside the city, our route took us along the island's edge, past rocky shores and lines of rectangular shapes in the water that revealed extensive aquaculture. Eventually we reached Yomitan village, Chibana's home.

At the entrance of the village hall was a big sign declaring "nuclear-free village" and on the stone wall facing the street was a large mural. Article 9 of the Japanese Constitution was written on the mural. At the time of reversion, Yomitan had 32,000 people, which qualified it to be classified as a town. In Japan and other countries all over the world, people prefer to have their communities in cities rather than towns and in towns rather than villages. People who live in villages are disdained, considered hayseeds. The people of Yomitan deliberately chose to remain a village, a decision that is shocking in Japan, which worships the trend to bigger as better.

Tokushin Yamauchi, the mayor of Yomitan and a good friend of Chibana's, says, "The Earth is a sphere, so wherever you live is the centre. Whether you live in Hiroshima or Yomitan, you are at the centre of the world." This is a strong statement about relativism, denying the hierar-

chical view and affirming diversity. There are different things on the
Earth, there can continue to be, and there should be. In the hierarchical
worldview, you are required to identify yourself according to its order.
Refusing to be included in the hierarchical order, Chibana shows he is a
member of his community; that is where his identity lies.

In Yomitan stands the ruin of a sixteenth-century castle, and we met
Chibana there, arriving at the same time as three busloads of teenage girls
from a Christian school in Hiroshima, here as part of their peace studies.

In the light of day, Chibana, with his perpetual smile, actually looked
younger. He was dressed in a purple sweatshirt, blue jeans, running shoes,
and a cloth cap. Standing on a wall at the top of a hill, he greeted the girls
in the Okinawan dialect. In response to their shock, he explained:

> I spoke in my language to remind you that there are other languages
> than Japanese and to emphasize the need to respect other cultures. I
> want to talk to you about a tragic period when differences were
> denied and hated. In April 1945, 350,000 U.S. soldiers landed here to
> invade Okinawa. The fighting continued to September 1, even after
> the war had been officially ended on August 15. The landing here was
> intended to cut Okinawa into north and south parts. Before landing,
> the navy bombarded the shore. We estimate there were four bursts
> for every 3.3 square metres! We call it the Hurricane of Iron.

After Chibana finished his lecture, he took us down a narrow flight
of stairs to the Chibichiri-*gama* (cave). A creek murmured in the underbrush. Before the war, this was a popular picnic spot. After the war, it was
used mostly as a garbage dump. Next to the low, dark cave entrance was a
two-tiered sculpture, a plaster statue made to commemorate the eighty-
four people who died in the cave. Most of the main figures have been
defaced by right-wingers in retaliation for Chibana's "heinous act." The
vandalism shocked the villagers and the relatives of the dead, who said it
was like a "second death." After much discussion, it was decided to leave
the damaged sculpture to remind people of what had happened.

Immediately inside the cave mouth were garlands of colourful *origami* (paper foldings) cranes, symbols of peace left by visitors. Written on one of the walls beside the cranes was a short poem: "Please tell future generations of the sadness of war." On the other side was a small, candlelit altar where people paused and prayed before entering the main body of the cave.

For decades after the war, no one in the village had talked about what had happened in the caves. Then Tetsuro Shimojima, a nonfiction writer and artist from mainland Japan, started to investigate and he enlisted Chibana's help. When they first entered the cave after years of silence, they could hear the crunch of human bones underfoot. After Shimojima left, Chibana interviewed survivors and decided to act as caretaker and guide people through the cave. Up to 20,000 people visit the cave every year.

Chibana told us and the other visitors what happened. On April 1, 1945, the first day of the battle of Okinawa, 140 people from Yomitan village hid in Chibichiri-*gama*. American troops sent a message saying those who surrendered would not be harmed. But the Okinawans had been taught in their Japanese-run schools that surrender, especially to the barbaric Americans, was an unimaginable, shameful act. They believed that once captured they were as good as dead. They had no will to live. As the terrified people tried to decide what to do, two veterans of war in Asia urged everyone to commit suicide. When the two old men ventured to the mouth of the cave, they were shot by the Americans. As they were dragged back, mortally wounded, the rest of the refugees knew a barbaric fate awaited them if they were taken alive.

Chibana told us to turn off our flashlights. Instantly we were plunged into total darkness. All we heard was breathing and Chibana talking quietly.

In the dark of the cave, a very pretty teenage girl begged her mother to kill her. She resisted, but her daughter's frantic pleas finally overcame her maternal instincts and she complied by slitting her daughter's throat. The killing had begun. Parents killed their children, then themselves; a nurse injected her family with poison and then others who begged for it until she ran out. The remaining survivors decided to block the cave entrance with their futons and set fire to them, but the flames were smothered by three women who had just given birth and were desperate that their newborn babies should live. The next day, another attempt was made to start a fire. As they lit the flame, the Okinawans screamed, "Long Live the Emperor." Dying was not easy and some people didn't die in spite of their wounds.

In all, eighty-four of the 140 died, including forty-seven children. Some think the inhabitants of Chibichiri-*gama* were lucky because for them the war ended in two days.

Inside the cave, the ceiling and walls are charred from the flames of the burning futons and bodies. The floor has been worn smooth by the feet of visitors except near the spot where most of the people died. Here the cave has been preserved the way it was when it was first discovered. There are charred bits of false teeth, buttons from student uniforms, a scythe (probably the one used by the mother to slit her daughter's throat), a fragment of a comb, and, of course, human bones. It is an exceptionally disturbing place. Chibana finished his speech.

> Those children did not take part in the decision, so I say it was not just a mass suicide but a mass murder. Why would mothers go against their every instinct and kill their own children? They preferred to kill the creatures they loved the best rather than let them be captured by the enemy. That's what they were taught. Their humanity was transformed by their education.

Another cave, Shimuku-*gama*, was closer to the shore near a huge naval antenna called the Elephant Cage. There, 140 villagers hid out, but they all surrendered and none were killed. Why was there such a difference in the way people behaved at Chibichiri? Chibana thinks it is because in Shimuku there were two men who had lived and worked in Hawaii and knew Americans. They spoke some English and they negotiated a surrender. In Chibichiri, there were two ex-soldiers, who perhaps thought the Americans would be as cruel as the Japanese had been in Asia.

The human mind is an amazing thing. There is nothing extraordinary about the physical makeup of the Chibichiri cave, nothing in the geophysical features that distinguish it from any other cave on the island. Yet, knowing its history, we make it special. We do that with other things as well. An object that once belonged to someone special or was used on a special occasion is physically no different from any other of its kind, but because of what it was witness to, we instil great value on it.

Coming out of the Chibichiri cave, we were reminded of Shelley's famous inscription on the shattered statue of a past king: "My name is Ozymandias, king of kings. Look on my works, ye Mighty, and despair! Nothing beside remains." Fifty years after the Hurricane of Iron, there are no scars of war visible on the land, but psychic scars are seared into the hearts and souls of survivors.

Chibana is a modern-day shaman whose role is to remember the past. Like the Jews who say, "To remember is the root of redemption but to forget leads to holocaust," Chibana has taken on the responsibility to speak for the dead. Although he is busy with his life and businesses, the community has tacitly assigned him the role of caretaker. Collectively and through him, they remember the past.

Far from perpetuating the popular image of Japan as victim, two unlikely people, Toshi Maruki and Shoichi Chibana, have taken the significance of the Second World War to a deeper level. Atomic warfare is only another example of the human capacity to inflict brutality and horror on one's fellow human beings. As Toshi Maruki showed us, if Hiroshima and Nagasaki are to have long-lasting symbolism, they must represent all war and cruelty. Chibana's actions reminded us of the often unthinking violence that occupying forces inflict upon indigenous peoples everywhere. As East Timorese (Indonesia), Penan (Malaysia), aborigines (Australia), and Amerindians of North and South America know, there remains much to redress.

CHAPTER 2

remembering
the past

"There are two ways to deal with your pain over the loss of a beloved. One is by remembering and the other is by forgetting."

SAYING OF THE LAKHOTA PEOPLE

COUNTRIES and groups deal with the psychological scars of war in different ways. In North America, Japanese-Americans and Japanese-Canadians from the West Coast, who were uprooted and relocated to camps during the war, later struggled to become invisible and do well materially. As a group they are quite successful today. The generation that had experienced the evacuation from the West Coast and incarceration between 1942 and 1945 didn't talk about it much; they were too busy trying to be Americans or Canadians and affirming their worth.

During the campaign to gain redress for the wartime persecution, *sansei* and *yonsei*, third- and fourth-generation Americans and Canadians of Japanese descent, most of them born after the war's end, saw the relocation as the definitive event that defines what Japanese-Canadians and Japanese-Americans are today. The uprooting has been romanticized in the lore of their identity.

Fifty years is a long time in the life of an individual, but it's a mere flash in history. In Canada, the defeat of the French by the English on the Plains of Abraham more than two hundred years ago is still deeply embedded in the Quebecois psyche, and its ramifications fuel the current Canadian agony over the future of Quebec. In the United States, a recent PBS series on the Civil War rekindled the collective memory of the great trauma that occurred more than a century ago. The problems of Northern Ireland, the Palestinian question, the inhumanity of Bosnia, all these are merely current manifestations of historical events. Fifty years is but a moment.

While war remains omnipresent in Japan, one is struck by the Japanese syndrome of *forgetfulness*. War is everywhere, yet war is nowhere. Everybody remembers the war, but everybody has forgotten it. It seems that two forces in the society contradict each other, with the prevailing force being the ability to forget.

For Jews with a long collective memory of ghettos, pogroms, and the Holocaust, there is a powerful will to remember. On the cover of the series of booklets put out by the National Archives of the Canadian Jewish Congress is a quote from Baal Shem Tov:

Forgetfulness leads to Holocaust;
Remembering is the root of redemption.

In contrast to the way the Jewish community treasures its memories and survivors of the Holocaust, those who lived through Hiroshima and their families are often targets of discrimination in Japan. People avoid them and the subject as if they might catch their disease. And Japanese society often supports the attitude that victims are to be blamed. Many Korean *hibakusha* (bomb victims), who had been forcibly taken as labour to Hiroshima before the bomb, were excluded from pensions or compensations for which Japanese victims were eligible. But perhaps most importantly, most people seem to have chosen not to speak of the atomic bombs, obediently following demands of American censors. The Japanese government has a long record of editing textbooks to exclude the wartime Japanese history and its role as an aggressor.

As the fiftieth anniversary of the end of the Second World War approached, Japanese politicians faced the task of presenting a resolution to mark the occasion. Prime Minister Tomiichi Murayama, of the Social Democratic Party, proposed to "acknowledge the nation's militaristic past so Japan can become an 'honourable' country." But the process of drafting the statement stalled when the three parties that made up the coalition government couldn't agree on the wording.

Late on Friday evening, June 9, 1995, the resolution was finally passed despite the absence of Shinshinto, the largest opposition party. The ruling coalition rejected last-minute amendments suggested by the Shinshinto party, and in protest, the party's 171 members boycotted the plenary session in the Lower House. The Japanese Communist party attended the session but voted against the draft, declaring its contents too ambiguous. The resolution says:

> On the occasion of the fiftieth year since the end of the World War, this chamber of the Diet offers its sincere condolences to the war dead and to all other victims of the war throughout the world.
>
> We look back at the various instances of colonial rule and acts of aggression in modern history in the world and recognize both that we carried out such acts and that we brought suffering upon the citizens of other nations, especially in Asia, and express deep regret.
>
> This chamber, under the ideals of eternal peace enunciated in the Constitution, hereby expresses its determination to open a future of peaceful coexistence for humankind by joining hands with other countries of the world. We affirm the above.[1]

The angry response of Asian countries to Japan's reluctance to acknowledge its militaristic past underlines their deep suspicion that the country hasn't changed and bears no remorse. The number of cabinet members who, by denying Japanese atrocity or aggression, have raised the ire of other countries demonstrates the depth of historic revisionism in Japanese society.

As the only country ever to experience the deliberate explosion of a nuclear weapon in war, Japan has been a symbol for the peace movement. The memorials in Hiroshima and Nagasaki are powerful incentives to forswear nuclear war altogether. It is therefore ironic that Japan has become one of the leading users of nuclear power.

To be sure, Japan's energy-hungry industry makes demands that cannot be fulfilled by the country's own energy resources. Japan is therefore extremely vulnerable to the vicissitudes of economic, political, and social volatility in other countries and regions. Hence, the high percentage of nuclear power plants in spite of strong grassroots opposition to their presence in local regions. The power of the central government is obvious in the way the nuclear industry has been promoted and forced into communities that have opposed it.

Against considerable global approbation, Japan has welcomed the shipment of highly radioactive nuclear wastes for reprocessing into high-grade plutonium, the major fuel for nuclear weapons. To counteract the objection to Japan's nuclear involvement, the government paid for a promotional film made by the Power Reactor and Nuclear Fuel Development Corporation. In the film, Pluto Boy, a cartoon character, tells children that plutonium is a safe friend of human beings. Pluto Boy introduces himself in an innocent, baby voice: "I am not a monster. Please look carefully at the real me. I really hate war. I love working for peace." [2]

Pluto Boy then drinks water that has been contaminated with plutonium to show that it is harmless. This scene caused an international uproar. U.S. Secretary of Energy Hazel O'Leary sent a letter of protest to the president of the nuclear agency:

> Pluto Boy downplays the dangers of plutonium by asserting that even a child could drink water containing plutonium without harm. This approach to an important public-health concern is misleading. [3]

There are other reasons for concern about Japan's use of nuclear power. Japan is a mountainous series of islands with its population densely packed into limited habitable spaces. But as part of the geologically unstable "ring of fire," the islands are constantly subject to earthquakes. A Kobe-size tremor near a nuclear plant could prove disastrous. Another safety factor that can't be ignored is the risk of accidents. Also, there is no such thing as a foolproof technology for shipping and processing highly radioactive materials. No technology, including airplanes, computers, or cars, can ever be free of accident.

What's more, nuclear technology to generate power cannot be separated from weapons. The release of energy by atomic fission can be harnessed for peaceful or military purposes. There is no clear line that separates the two fates. In most countries, radioactive material flows freely between the energy and military sectors. As recent history involving Israel, South Africa, and India indicates, once sold, radioactive material gets lost, exploited in unexpected ways, or used illicitly, all of which are beyond control.

Nuclear weapons represent the undeniable link between dangers of nuclear power and modern warfare. The vast majority of scientists around the world carry out work for military agencies whose research budgets far exceed those for health, transportation, communication, and education combined. Modern weapons from napalm to agent orange, neutron bombs, Star Wars, Patriot missiles, and weapons that target specific ethnic groups were not dreamed up and created by military minds. It was *scientists* who conceived them.

War itself is always a massive experiment, a test of new weapons and theories whose consequences can be measured only after tests are performed. Once the atomic bomb had been created and tested by some of the greatest minds in physics, many just couldn't wait to see it used under the "real" conditions of war.

Edward Teller, the so-called father of the hydrogen bomb, has often stated that he hadn't wanted to have the bomb dropped over Hiroshima. Instead, he had recommended that it be exploded high in the sky so that Japan could see that a new weapon had indeed been invented. He believed Japan would then have surrendered. Most historians agree the second bomb over Nagasaki was superfluous — the Japanese had seen what happened to Hiroshima. But the fact that the Nagasaki bomb was based on a different mechanism supports the notion it was dropped as an experiment. As a victim, Japan ought to be sensitive to deep issues raised by nuclear technology and warfare.

We went to the lobby of a very grand hotel in the centre of Tokyo to meet with Katsuichi Honda, a famous journalist, and talk about such issues. A slim, modest man, unlike the swashbuckling figure one might expect, he wore a sloppy wig, not as an affectation, but as a disguise to hide his identity from right-wing militarists who act violently towards individuals like him.

It was raining hard outside, and Honda's umbrella spread water across the floor. In such a luxurious place, the three of us, in our casual clothes, looked like misfits. Honda is an extremely busy man, yet when he was talking to us, he was relaxed, soft-spoken, pensive. He gave us the impression that he didn't have anywhere better to be.

Honda is a rarity in Japan, someone who sees his own society and culture with remarkable clarity. What makes him even more exceptional is that, in a country where conformity and social equanimity are all-important, he doesn't flinch from delivering his blunt and often harsh critiques. Honda sees the military mentality as pervasive in Japan's unquestioning conformity and in its battles against Ainu (Japan's indigenous people), Koreans, Okinawans, and even nature itself.

What kind of a man is Honda? What made him such a severe critic of his own society? How has Honda established a journalistic reputation based on questioning some of the most deeply held assumptions of Japanese people? When they travel, most Japanese stay together in groups — Honda describes them as tight schools of *medaka* fish — yet he earned his reputation by undertaking adventures most Japanese would never think of experiencing alone. His audacious articles and his questioning of common assumptions and beliefs have made him a bête noire of right-wingers. His books have been bestsellers and he is well known and widely admired. A 1987 survey of Japanese college students revealed that Honda was the author they were most interested in reading.

Honda was born in 1932, in a small village in the mountains of

Nagano in the central part of Japan. It was his childhood that has shaped his outlook. He told us:

> In those days the rivers were full of fish and animals. Life was abundant. The rivers were all destroyed by the mid 1960s. I loved nature. My boyhood dream was to become a biologist. Later I got involved in mountain-climbing, but at first I did it mainly to be closer to nature.

As a college student, Honda joined a mountaineering club and went to the Himalayas twice. Although his first love was mountaineering, he couldn't make a living as a climber. Since he also liked writing, he chose journalism and began work for the *Asahi Shinbun*, one of Japan's largest newspapers. In 1959, he was assigned to visit Hokkaido, the country's northernmost large island, for three years. Like most Japanese, he wasn't aware of the problems of the Ainu, the indigenous people of Japan, although he did know that there was enormous prejudice towards them. Later, long before it was chic to do so, Honda became a champion of Ainu people and culture.

His big break, professionally, happened when thirteen Japanese climbers died in a mountain-climbing accident. Honda hired a helicopter to drop him near the accident. As an experienced climber, he was able to reach the accident site before any other reporters and give an on-location report. It was a major scoop and his reports electrified the public. As recognition of his initiative, Honda was given the freedom to cover whatever he liked.

Honda travelled to exotic remote places and somehow tapped a Japanese vicarious enjoyment of such areas. In 1963 he lived with the Inuit on Canada's Melville Peninsula for three months; Japanese readers were riveted by his reports. Then, over a six-month period, he made a number of trips to Irian Jaya, the Indonesian part of the island of New Guinea, to live for a month with the native highlanders who were then considered Stone Age people; again, a big hit with Japanese readers. Honda told us:

I went to Arabia and lived with the Bedouins. Then the Vietnam War heated up. By 1966 I had done northern Canada, New Guinea, and Arabia. I had formed my own ideas about what journalism is. So I decided, instead of going to exotic areas, I should look at the biggest problem facing us — Vietnam.

Honda's reporting from Vietnam rode the wave of anti-Vietnam War sentiment in Japan. He saw the war as one in a long line of invasions by the United States.

Up to 500,000 American soldiers were already in Vietnam. I noticed that photographers went to the front, but journalists didn't. So I decided to visit villages at the front lines and see how the people lived. I witnessed Americans committing atrocities on villagers and I reported it. [My reports] created a sensation.

In postwar Japan, a victorious United States had imposed the constitution, which stood as the ideal of a democracy defending freedom and opposing discrimination. But what Honda saw in Vietnam didn't fit his image of Americans, and he began to seriously question what the U.S. really represented. His reports from the battlefields reflected his scepticism. Wishing to know more about Americans, he went to the United States, where he learned that Japanese had acted in similarly barbarous ways during the Second World War.

In 1971 Honda visited places in China where Japanese soldiers had committed atrocities during the Fifteen-Year War.

What did Japan do to China between 1931 and 1945? It was nothing but aggression and invasion. However, the mass media never used these words, referring instead to "war," as if both sides were to be equally blamed for the conflict. The Fifteen-Year War was a classical case of colonial invasion by Japan.[4]

According to Honda, five main components make up an "invasion": murder; physical violence such as pillage, arson, and destruction; rape; enslavement; and economic exploitation. Graphically and without softening his words, he bluntly defined Japan's attack on China as an invasion.

At that time little was known publicly of the Nanjing Massacre (Rape of Nanking), which was perpetrated by the Japanese Army against the Chinese of Nanjing in 1937, The Imperial Army started an intensive attack on Nanjing on December 10, 1937, and killed at least 200,000 people over the next six weeks. Honda said the atrocities were not the result of a sudden killing frenzy but began from the moment the Japanese troops landed. To people accustomed to politeness and government propaganda, his descriptions were shocking.

One was a report of an incident on November 22, 1937, when about one hundred soldiers entered a village of twelve households and forty-nine people. Thirty-eight were caught and the horror began.

There were two young women: one, a seventeen-year-old; the other, a pregnant woman. The two were separated from the other prisoners, and many Japanese soldiers raped them. The women who were raped were dragged to the garden as other soldiers were setting houses on fire. Soldiers thrust a bamboo stick in the seventeen-year-old's vagina; she died as swords pierced her. The pregnant woman was also disembowelled as soldiers gouged the embryo from her body.[5]

Honda went on to document men being locked in houses that were then set on fire so they burned alive. A two-year-old began to cry in fear and he was torn from his mother and thrown into a burning hut. Most of the remaining prisoners were forced to jump into a ditch where they were shot.

Honda's description was based on an interview with a Chinese man who miraculously survived the terrible incident. He also found a Japanese man named Tanaka who had been one of the soldiers who herded Chinese villagers into a river and began shooting them. Honda reported how Tanaka was haunted by the image of prisoners trying to escape the bullets by climbing on top of each other in a gigantic human column. The order was to kill every Chinese to avoid international coverage and condemnation. But not all died.

A fifty-seven-year-old survivor of Nanjing who was seven at the time gave Honda intimate details. He described how the Japanese soldiers, upon entering his home, shot his father and a neighbour. The boy fled to the bedroom and hid under a blanket. He heard his grandfather being shot, then the blanket was pulled aside and he witnessed a scene from hell:

> There were many soldiers standing there. My grandmother came to protect us; she was immediately shot. I could see the white brain spurting out of my grandmother's head. I fainted so I didn't see what happened afterward. After some time, I regained consciousness as my four-year-old sister was crying. It was still bright outside. She was crying under a blanket. . . . On the same bed, one of my sisters [thirteen years old at the time] lay dead. Her lower parts were naked and both legs were thrown on the floor. In front of the bed was the corpse of my grandmother. Near the door was my grandfather's corpse.[6]

But if these stories merely corroborate the brutality and inhumanity of war, Honda does not excuse the Japanese.

> The fundamental difference between Japan and others is the ways in which the Japanese take responsibility for the atrocities. . . . The problem is not in the past, but rather in the present. Twenty years after the war's end, most Japanese still do not know what the Japanese did in China. . . . There is nothing to be gained from apologizing for past militarism. A true apology is to prevent the rise of militarism today.[7]

Based on his wide travel outside Japan, Honda suggested that, in spite of Japan's attempt to portray itself as a *victim* of atomic weaponry, the rest of Asia has not accepted this image. All over Asia in places like Nanjing, Singapore, Corregidor (the Philippines), Chungjing (China), and Panmunjom (Korea), people remember Japanese brutality.

Pointing out that Japan also violated international law by using chemical weapons in China, Honda hammered at the fact that his country has never pursued war criminals on its own initiative. Japan's failure to face up to its guilt is a theme Honda has returned to again and again in his writing:

> On the fortieth anniversary of the German surrender, West German President von Weizsacker made a memorable speech about the need to

remember and recognize past war responsibility and guilt. What did the Japanese prime minister do on the fortieth anniversary of the war's end? Nakasone publicly worshipped at the Yasukuni Shrine — the shrine that honours war dead, and in particular, war criminals — an action that earlier prime ministers had avoided. This is like going to the grave sites of important Nazi leaders in Germany. . . . However, the Japanese government's actions were predictable for those who understand the Japanese behavioural pattern. In Japan, a Class A war criminal, Kishi Nobosuke, became prime minister; a major war criminal like Kodama Yoshio becomes a key figure in the Lockheed scandal [in which the American warplane manufacturer gave multi-million-dollar bribes to Japanese politicians], and no one pursues the Emperor's war guilt. The Japanese people are irresponsible. Hence, it is to be expected and consistent that Prime Minister Nakasone should honour war criminals. Postwar conservative regimes have not changed at all; in this sense . . . the Japanese have been ruled by a single-party dictatorship since the Meiji Period.[8]

"Our beautiful and verdant village has become silent because of the terrible poisoning of our mountains and farms."

KATSUICHI HONDA

JOURNALIST

There was very little difference ten years later at the fiftieth anniversary, although what Honda called "a single-party dictatorship" began to collapse in 1994. In the heated debate over the Fiftieth Anniversary resolution by the parliament, the opposition group expressed an anxiety that many Japanese have felt: Do those of us who were born after the war have to keep accepting the burden of guilt? What are we responsible for? To these questions, Honda answered:

Our generation has no obligation to apologize to the people for the Japanese invasion. However, we must recognize Japanese war guilt. We must not let the prewar symbol of militarism re-emerge or let the prime minister revive Yasukuni Shrine as a public institution. As long as we let these things go on, we become responsible, and pass on our crime to our children's generation.[9]

During the period Honda was most intensely engaged in activities in Vietnam, he also investigated a new kind of war — against the destruction of the environment. In 1973 he wrote movingly about his childhood memories and how his village had changed in the intervening years. When his father died, Honda took a leave from the newspaper and returned to his village in Nagano prefecture to help his mother and sister. One of his happy childhood memories was of catching tadpoles, which he would put in the pond in his backyard. Tadpoles represented the peace and serenity of the village. So Honda walked to the swamp where he had netted tadpoles. Instead of a swamp, he found rice paddies.

> Nonetheless, that alone should not have prevented me from finding tadpoles. As in the past, water still flows and tadpoles can live in a rice paddy. But pesticides have wreaked havoc — I could not find a single tadpole. Except for eels, all the fish that used to be so plentiful have disappeared. From my childhood memory and play, I know very well which type of fish live in which part of the small river. Therefore, it didn't take me long to realize that there were no tadpoles in all the swamp.
>
> Without my parents, my village is a lonely place. If the rivers were still filled with shrimp and tadpoles, if the fireflies still flew into the house, if the frogs still cried all night long, our village would still encompass the images and smell of my parents. Such a place would evoke my home. But our beautiful and verdant village has become silent because of the terrible poisoning of our mountains and farms. With my parents' death, nature has also died. Not sadness but anger dwells within.[10]

What Honda saw in Japan was in striking contrast to what he had observed in wartorn North Vietnam two years after his mother's death. Walking through the villages, he observed paddies and rivers full of shrimp and small fish. The farmers were using fertilizers that didn't kill other forms of life.

As I was looking at the small fish in the paddies, I wondered who was being destroyed. North Vietnam is daily being bombed and destroyed. However, the country that is being more fundamentally destroyed is Japan. My village can be seen in North Vietnamese villages. With the plan for the renovation of the Japanese archipelago, what will happen to our nature and environment? In my hometown, new highway construction is in progress. People even discuss a new high-speed railway system. I wonder if the villagers will really find happiness in all this.[11]

In 1989 he wrote passionately to his fellow Japanese in words that should be heeded in North America:

People who grew up in the countryside should go back and observe the mountains and rivers of your youth. People who grew up near the ocean, observe your favourite beach. People who grew up in a city, revisit a rural area you visited several years ago. You will then understand the continuing destruction of our environment. Yet the present is better than the future. . . .

I visited the Shiga Highlands near my hometown recently. The mountains have become bald from all the ski slopes. Even the last bastion of nature, the national park, is threatened with "development." Tourist companies, including Seibu, are lined up with development plans. Furthermore, construction is paid for with public money as corporations negotiate favourable financial arrangements. My hometown is being invaded.[12]

What is the meaning of progress in this seemingly prosperous country? Honda asked angrily. The forestry department was cutting down old-growth forest in national parks, and the Ministry of the Environment supported plans to destroy the last remaining coral reef to build an airport in Okinawa, while what was called the "resort plan" was supposed to turn twenty percent of Japanese land into golf courses and other types of leisure development. As early as 1974 Honda wrote an article entitled "Development as Invasion":

So far, no one has bought up the atmosphere. Yet it is possible to enclose a particular area and claim all the air within. This is no longer a matter of fantasy; that is precisely what is happening to water and land.[13]

By using the term "invasion," he deliberately superimposed what was happening in postwar Japan on the wartime Japan.

> Some argue that the Japanese value nature, but I have my doubts . . .
> the people who live on the land are, sadly, devoid of any desire to be
> grateful for, and prevent the destruction of, nature. There are only
> 20,000 people in birdwatching societies, but over 300,000 people have
> licences to shoot these birds. Japan is populated by some of the most
> spiritually impoverished people in the world.[14]

Since retiring from the *Asahi* newspaper, Honda has worked as the publisher and editor-in-chief of a new weekly magazine called *Kinyobi* (Friday), which offers a forum for critical and investigative journalism largely lacking in mainstream media. His outspoken opinions have led to threats of physical violence from right-wingers. Several years ago, the Kansai branch of the *Asahi* newspaper was attacked and one person was killed. One of the right-wing organizers said, "If someone had to be killed, why wasn't it Honda?" Ever since, Honda has disguised himself whenever he appears on television or attends public events. Yet Honda seems to be everywhere — at a remote Ainu village giving the eulogy at an elder's funeral, or in Okinawa lecturing on ethnicity — and all the while, his books keep on coming. Whenever he is asked to attend a rally, concert, or conference, he seldom refuses.

In 1990 Hitoshi Motojima, the mayor of Nagasaki, publicly affirmed Emperor Hirohito's war responsibility. Shortly afterwards he was shot in the back at point-blank range by an assassin. The mayor survived and Honda raged:

> The barbaric murder attempt serves to let the whole world know of the
> irrationality, the lack of ethics, and the premodern state of
> consciousness of the Japanese who have not changed at all since the
> Second World War. It can be said that the assassin played an extremely
> unpatriotic role.[15]

Honda has repeatedly argued that true patriots are those who risk their lives by criticizing the wrongdoing of their country. He told us that he wanted to write a book called "What You Should Not Learn from Japan" for people outside the country. "To expose shameful aspects of our society, that's my patriotism," he said quietly.

The key concept of such a book would be "*medaka* society" (*medaka* are small fish that have been a favourite research animal for Japanese scientists). In our interview, he explained it as follows:

> I call Japan a *medaka* society, where thousands of little fish are in one school all going in the same direction. There is no leader, no common logic. They just watch what their neighbour does. If he turns, they all turn. Neither theory nor logic nor ethics underlies or informs Japanese behaviour. Quite simply, a Japanese looks around and does what others are doing; that is the principle of action. That's why Japanese have trouble with theory, logic, and ethics; they cannot argue or debate. Particularity, idiosyncrasy and individuality are hated and discouraged. That and Japanese environmental problems are closely related.

In a 1991 article he redefined the term and applied it to his analysis of *ijime* (student bullies), a major sociological problem facing Japanese society in recent years.

> The *medaka* society is a product of the Ministry of Education. It is, of course, easy to administer a society of *medaka*. In order to create a *medaka* society, the Ministry of Education defines education as regurgitation. The Ministry of Education decides what is good to think, while denigrating individual opinion. Individuality is punished, and no one is encouraged to think on one's own. And things are getting worse. . . . Recently the problem of *ijime* — students bullying other students — has become serious in elementary and junior high schools. The root of *ijime* is that some students are harassed and beaten up for being different from the majority . . . anyone who is different becomes the target.[16]

Earlier, in 1986, Honda berated Japanese for their unthinking conformity.

A reporter from National Public Radio in Washington, D.C., described Japanese behaviour in the following way: once a problem is solved, the Japanese immediately start running in the same direction.

In general, Japanese behaviour is based on the principle of emulating the majority. This is one of the causes of the Japanese soldiers' atrocious behaviour during the Second World War. When other soldiers were engaged in a massacre, no individual would dare stop it. On the contrary, everybody simply participated in the inhumane act.[17]

We asked Honda what is peculiar about the Japanese political structure. He replied:

> *Tetsu no sankakukei* — the iron triangle — refers to bureaucrats, corporations, and politicians. I'd add to that, the mass media. Individuals or groups that do something different feel strong pressure. There is an inertia that resists change. If we had had a national referendum on the Nagara River issue, we would have won. [He was referring to one of the two remaining wild rivers in Japan, which developers wanted to tame with dams and concrete walls to prevent flooding. Environmentalists and fishermen fought against it, and the opponents grew into a major grassroots environmental movement. They lost, but the experience signalled the potential power of grassroots action. Soon after the development was completed, negative effects on fishing were detected.] But there is no system like that and no grassroots movement to create such a system. We have nothing equivalent to a citizenry formed by autonomous individuals. In Japanese history, there is not one example of a grassroots movement changing the power structure. The *medaka* society has a long history.

We commented that Americans and Europeans have destroyed nature too. Isn't the problem more a consequence of modern life rather than a specifically Japanese problem? we asked.

Yes, but in the West, there was always resistance. Look at
Japanese rivers. They're all straight and enclosed in concrete.
In Europe there is a movement to remove the concrete.
There are many examples of Europeans moving against
environmental destruction.

We suggested that urbanization and the global economy have disconnected us from the factors that once stabilized communities and gave
a sense of place. Honda replied:

Being separated from nature, we are now experiencing some
strange things. Many kids exhibit strange behaviour. They are
locking themselves in their rooms and refusing to come out for
years. They are killing their parents. There are lots of examples like
that in my article "Revenge of the Children." When we study it
closely, aberrant children all have something in common — total
alienation from nature.

As we wrapped up our conversation, we asked Honda where he finds
hope. He first said, apologetically, that he was not an optimist but then said:

We need a revolution to overthrow the establishment. And it has to
come from the grassroots. We will need help from outside. We must
create a solidarity with people outside. By being supported and
endorsed from outside, people and groups within Japan have a better
effect. Nagano, the minister of justice who said the Nanjing massacre
didn't happen, would have got away with it, but there was a massive
protest from China and Korea. So he got fired.

In his humble way Honda expressed a hope that he'll play a role in
the grassroots revolution. "Opinions are not enough," he said. "We need
facts to support our struggle. That's where our work as journalists would
be expected to play an important role."

We asked whether he was encouraged by the fact that he had a lot of
readers. "Yes, I am, but it's still far from enough to cause change in the
whole structure."

There are others who have actively criticized and opposed the military activity of Japan and its complicity in such activity with other countries. A remarkable thinker and critic is Shunsuke Tsurumi, the author and editor of numerous books and a former professor at a number of universities. Tsurumi, one of Japan's leading intellectuals and activists, began his life as a rebel early on. He was born in Tokyo in 1922 and, as a child, watched his father, Yusuke, a major liberal political force, become powerless in the face of increasing Japanese militarism. As Japan entered the period of the Fifteen-Year War, Tsurumi spent most of his youth hiding behind books, cutting class, and getting into trouble.

By the time he was fifteen, Tsurumi had been kicked out of many schools and was becoming a serious embarrassment to his father. Tsurumi was sent to live in the United States. Miraculously, once he left Japan, Tsurumi became a wonder student. He quickly mastered English and, at sixteen, gained admittance to the philosophy department of Harvard.

One day not long after Japan had launched the war against the United States, police came to Tsurumi's apartment and asked, "Are you an anarchist?" Tsurumi replied, "I can't say no to that question." He was promptly jailed and scheduled for deportation along with other prisoners of war. While in jail, Tsurumi completed his thesis and graduated from Harvard. Since his deportation, he has chosen never to re-enter the United States.

Upon his return to Japan, Tsurumi served in the navy in Indonesia. After the war ended, he organized a group of brilliant thinkers, including his Princeton-educated sister, Kazuko, and put out a magazine called *Shiso no Kagaku* (Science of Thoughts), which celebrated its fiftieth anniversary in the spring of 1996.

Tsurumi is more than just an armchair intellectual. He has been an active organizer for decades. He was a major force behind the "Peace in

Vietnam" sit-ins and demonstrations during the Vietnam War. He says with a smile that during that period he spent more time sitting on the road than on a chair. He has also always been active in Korean issues. In the 1980s Tsurumi and some friends published from his house a magazine called *Koreans* to force the government to get rid of detention centres designed for illegal aliens and used exclusively for non-Westerners.

We met him in Kyoto, where he has lived since the 1960s. Like Honda, Tsurumi sees the continuation of the prewar mentality into contemporary society of Japan, and he views the past with some regrets. During the war, like most Japanese he was helplessly swept up in the tide. After the defeat, the Allied occupation forces imposed progressive social reforms that the Japanese could not have accomplished. Tsurumi's great regret is that the Japanese couldn't institute the reforms on their own. Japanese had a great opportunity to contemplate the meanings of war and peace and determine their future, but in their haste to build a new life something important was missed. He told us:

> When the constitution was proposed to the people, Japan lay in ruins. That was the landscape that surrounded the Japanese and the Americans from the occupation force. And the ruins were not only in Tokyo, Yokohama, Nagoya, and Osaka, but also in Okinawa, Hiroshima, and Nagasaki. It didn't end there. It

"By looking at the future and acknowledging the potential ruins that wait there, we can see more clearly the path we are walking today."

SHUNSUKE TSURUMI,
AUTHOR AND FORMER
UNIVERSITY PROFESSOR

was all over in China, Philippines, Burma, and other places. Many Japanese failed to face the ruins that existed beyond their limited world. Both Japanese and Americans failed to see the ruins in Okinawa and the ruins in Hiroshima and Nagasaki.

Tsurumi reminded us that we must see the imposition of the constitution in its context, set in a landscape devastated by the war.

We need to see that wartime landscape in order to see our future. The prevailing view in contemporary Japan is that the ruins are in the remote past. By looking at the future and acknowledging the potential ruins that wait there, we can see more clearly the path that we are walking today.

The constitution seemed to hold out the promise of a new beginning in a devastated country. In this fact, Tsurumi sees hope for the Japanese. "If we wish, we now may be able to understand the meaning of our experience better than the Americans of fifty years ago and even better than the Americans of today."

While Tsurumi has been able to reflect on Japanese from within the country, others have been kept on the margins of society. They can therefore see with the objectivity of outsiders. Still others, such as Honda, have acquired a perspective from having travelled extensively in other parts of the world.

Another top Japanese journalist, Hiroshi Ishi, specializes in environmental topics and has visited every continent on the planet and more than seventy countries. While on sabbatical from the *Asahi Shinbun* newspaper to work with the David Suzuki Foundation in Vancouver, he described in his typical straightforward style the militaristic nature of Japanese society and its ultimate impact on the environment. To support his viewpoint, Ishi pointed out that Japanese boys go to school in militarylike uniforms and short haircuts.

Japan is a military society based on war. Every ten to twenty years the country experienced a major war. After the Second World War, the Americans prohibited arms or the means to war. But Japan didn't lose the military mentality. Instead, it was transferred one hundred percent to the economy. Today Japanese media refer constantly to the trade war. Japan's business community *invades* countries and *wins* by destroying industry. For example, Japan destroyed the textile industry in England, watches in Switzerland, cameras in Germany, high tech and automobiles in America.

Japan's workers are like soldiers. That explains why they can tolerate the terrible conditions they live and work under. It is a state of war. Often the company provides the workers with homes that are analogous to barracks. The soldiers travel, uncomplaining, in jam-packed subways to reach the battlefront where the officers (bosses) tell them what to do. When the battle is finished at the end of the day, then the men confirm their solidarity and fraternity at the bar. Finally, late at night, they return to the barracks where all they do is sleep. This is a country in which war dominates the psyche.

Ishi also applied his notion of militarism to Japan's economy and finances.

Japanese companies are often not interested in profit as much as they are in market share. By capturing the market, the war is won. The salaryman [corporate executive] is often referred to as a corporate warrior. *Karoshi*, the sudden death of an apparently healthy person, has been recognized to be the result of overwork. This is the equivalent of death in the battlefield. *Tanshin funin* is service performed for a company abroad or in a remote part of Japan: often the worker is sent alone to spend long periods away from home and family. It is a disruptive service in the name of the company.

The wartime frame of mind has been preserved and applied to the postwar nation building, Ishi believes.

During a war, the industrial machines increase their production capacity to pour out weapons and material of war. Once the war ends, the industry is overproducing and must seek a market for its products. One way is to embark on another war, and for the West, that was the Cold War. But the Cold War didn't use the products. What could be done is to create new markets, for example, with

Third World dictatorships, and embark on hostilities [Korea, Vietnam]. Another way is to diversify, produce modified products, and create a market by encouraging overconsumption. The Japanese are a perfect population for that — overproducers, overconsumers, throwaway. Even the destruction of urban centres in Japan during the war worked as an advantage, because the country could rebuild from scratch and build the most modern, efficient factories.

Ishi's invocation of "battlefields" and "warriors" provides another way to view the activities of major industries in the global economy. But the economic miracle of postwar Japan has impressed the international community, many of whom would like to emulate the country's record. Yet even as a culture of militarism may underlie the business agenda, Japan's leaders have actively promoted an image of their country as a victim of atomic warfare, while denying their country's record of aggression and atrocity. But as such thinkers as Tsurumi and Honda point out, until Japan faces up to and renounces its past, the country cannot take a place as an equal among the community of nations.

CHAPTER 3

Life is the treasure

"When we saw the atrocities of broken heads, hands

and feet torn off, intestines scattered about,

innocent children slaughtered, and the spectacle of

mountains of dead bodies more than the eye

could take in, we thought that neither God nor

Buddha were in this world, but only the Devil."

SHOKO AHAGON

In war, it is often said that "might is right" and "to the victors go the spoils," implying that right and wrong are irrelevant. However, many see the Second World War as the last great battle between the forces of evil and virtue, or fascism and democracy, which the good guys won.

Half a century later, when the raw passions of hatred and pain have faded, the line between good and evil is not so clear. Films may romanticize acts of heroism, compassion, and generosity that undoubtedly do occur during battle. But in war we are all losers. Even the conqueror must gain his victory by acts of brutality and murder.

For the survivors of the Hurricane of Iron, the devastating bombardment and invasion of Okinawa as the war drew to a close, the end of war did not end the suffering and grief. Buildings and villages were flattened, the land torn apart, and friends and relatives left dead or wounded. "Peace" meant a continued struggle for survival and turned out to be merely a prelude to a second invasion of American troops.

For Shoko Ahagon, the American occupation and confiscation of farmers' lands was a galvanizing call to action and led him to question deeply the consequences of war. He became a leader in the call for an end to American occupation, which he believes will "rehumanize" all of us. He is an inspiring beacon of peace, a farmer and peace advocate many regard as the Okinawan Gandhi.

To meet him, we travelled by bus two hours north from Naha, the capital of Okinawa, then took a thirty-minute ferry ride to Iejima, a small island of 5,000 people with a large U.S. military base. From the ferry we could see Gusukuyama, a hill of 172 metres, looming out of the centre of the flat island. It had once had a beautiful shape, reminiscent of Mount Fuji. During the war, however, American shells destroyed a cave within it, and today, Gusukuyama's silhouette reveals jagged gouges, its lovely symmetry cruelly disfigured by that relentless bombardment. It is a constant reminder of the ravages of war.

We were met at the dock by Ahagon's two assistants: Hiroko Yamashiro, a cheerful woman of thirty, and her aunt, Etsuko Jahana, a woman in her mid-fifties who uses crutches to walk.

"Did you come all the way from Japan today?" Jahana asked us. At first the question startled us with its implication that Japan was a foreign country.

When we asked Jahana to tell us about Ahagon and his Wabiai no Sato (Village of Forgiveness and Peace) complex, she explained that it was from there he wrote, taught, and demonstrated the power and value of peace, education, and dialogue. Originally planned as a place for the elderly and disabled to live and learn, the complex was part of Ahagon's overall plan to build a school for farmers on his land in the Maja district of the island, which is now occupied by the American base.

Shoko Ahagon was born in 1903 in Okinawa, just across the bay from Iejima. He was one in a large farming family of seven brothers and sisters. Because he was physically the weakest, he chose not to become a farmer. At eighteen he decided to become an elementary-school teacher and left home bound for Tokyo. But while in Osaka he read of the great Tokyo earthquake, which had recently occurred, and decided instead to go overseas.

He spent five years working in Cuba and five years in Peru. In Cuba he found a land completely controlled by landlords. It became clear that if he stayed there, he would be a slave all his life. So he went to Peru and worked for a barber, thinking that a barber is an honest profession. He was saving money to go home when his close friend got sick and said he wanted to die in Okinawa. Ahagon gave him the money he had saved.

He slowly worked his way back. Panama, Mexico, San Francisco, then home to Japan. Since he had studied the Bible extensively, Ahagon decided to become a minister. He went to see an internationally known minister in Tokyo who advised him to go back to Okinawa and be a farmer. Undeterred, Ahagon went to Kyoto to visit Tenko Nishida, who had a well-known spiritual retreat. But he also advised Ahagon to go back to his farm roots. "I am physically weak," Ahagon replied. "I have no experience, no talent, no land. Could I still farm?" Professor Nishida told him those things were not important. If he went back and worked hard, all those things would be provided. So he married the daughter of a man who owned a big farm. She was knowledgeable about farming, and with her help, they farmed and raised their son, who, they hoped, would also be a farmer.

Ahagon wanted to build a school for farmers. Because farmers knew little about politics and the world in general, he felt it necessary to bring

them out from under the control of ignorance and oppression. He wanted the farmers to have pride in themselves. He wanted his son to help
him establish the school and to go out into the world to spread his message. Then the war began.

We asked Jahana how she came to work with Ahagon.

> I was sick in bed for eighteen years after the war. I had been living with
> my grandfather, and then he died. Without him, I didn't think I would
> be able to survive. I was completely paralysed. I couldn't move and
> socially I was very isolated. Nowadays you can see handicapped people
> everywhere, but it was different then. I was ashamed to be seen. I was
> extremely shy. One day Ahagon said, 'Whether you are rich or poor,
> beautiful or handicapped, we all end up the same white bones, so there
> is no reason to be shy or ashamed.' He took very good care of me. Just
> after the war many people who were suffering would go and talk to
> him. Many people were saved by him, especially war orphans. I was
> handicapped by the war, so I decided to dedicate my whole life to the
> cause of peace. I have been working here thirty years.

We pulled up to Wabiai no Sato, and Jahana took us first to the small
museum. On the outside wall, facing the courtyard, were the following
inscriptions in Japanese: "Those who take up the sword shall perish by
the sword"; "Countries that have bases will be ruined by bases"; and
"Nations that have nuclear arms will be ruined by nuclear arms." On a
plaque over the entrance was "Life Is a Treasure," written in English.
Jahana explained:

> Peace means to respect the lives of human beings. In this house you
> will see the remains of a war that destroyed human lives like insects.
> Also the prayers and wishes of people who seek the value of life and
> who don't make the mistake of treating life lightly.

The one-room museum was divided into three by two tables that ran
nearly its whole length. On the tables was Ahagon's personal collection of
war relics. Deprivation and desperation were mutely apparent in articles

made by survivors after the war: shoes made from tires, a crude *sanshin* (an Okinawan three-stringed instrument) cobbled together from tin cans and pots from ammunition shells. Next to a display of clothes made from army sandbags and flour sacks was a sign that read, "Those who want weapons should first wear these clothes." There was an astounding collection of shells, grenades, parachutes, uniforms, pictures, and a wide array of memorabilia we might have been tempted to write off as junk. For Ahagon, the display was a demonstration of a kind of insanity and a plea for peace. On the walls were banners of support, photos, and written material. One was a set of guidelines entitled, "How to Talk to American Military." It read:

1. You should sit when speaking and keep your hands empty.

2. Short tempers, lies, and slurs are not allowed. Please remember that as a human being, a farmer is superior to a soldier (we grow and they destroy). Talk with reason as if speaking to a small child.

3. Remember that our problem is the result of a war that was caused by Japan. We, too, are responsible. Remembering all of the above, refrain from doing things that cause unhappiness to American people.

Jahana took us to meet Ahagon. Topped by short white hair, almost like a monk's cut, Ahagon's weathered face was handsome and full of dignity. A man with a formidable presence, he was seated on the floor in front of a low table in the middle of a *tatami* room. On the table were a magnifying glass, a newspaper, a scrap of paper with our names written on it, and an article by David that Keibo had edited. Ahagon had read the article and said he was very excited about discussing some issues with us. He had a very keen interest in Canada, he told us, because its stability doesn't seem to depend on a militaristic power. He remarked humbly that he hoped to learn from us.

Ahagon treated our interview almost like a ritual. As we talked, Jahana and Yamashiro served us tea, took notes, translated, and helped interpret when Ahagon had trouble understanding our questions.

Soon the conversation turned to the war, and Ahagon recounted his experiences at the end of the war. For many, defeat was unbearable and they chose death. For the living, war's end meant psychic devastation. As schoolchildren, the Japanese had been fed several beliefs: national wealth and military strength; to die on the *tatami* [at home] is to die a dog's death; if you die on the battlefield for the emperor, you will be enshrined in the Yasukuni Shrine and become a God. Ahagon explained:

> The emperor was considered a living god. He was supposed to love all his subjects as he loved his own children. I was taught to believe that. The lower god under him was the schoolteacher. We used to say, "You can't even approach his shadow." No one ever imagined that the schoolteacher could be wrong, especially about the emperor. Until the end of the war we still believed it. The Japanese as a whole believed it. Japan was the divine nation that must conquer the world. Unless we did that, the world would be unhappy. To us, it was a holy war to make the whole earth happy.

The British and Americans were seen as less-than-human barbarians to be attacked and killed. "Japan started the war," Ahagon said. "For the peace of the world, soldiers could make themselves into bullets and *kamikaze* [divine wind] would protect them." He lifted an old newspaper from his small desk. "This says, 'We go [to war] because we love peace.' How could human beings be so stupid? Could Japanese be the only ones?"

Ahagon stopped and turned to Yamashiro to make sure she'd been taking notes. For Ahagon this meeting was all about learning and he wanted to be able to refer back to it later on. He believed the solutions had to come from education, communication, and lots of dialogue. Modern minds may easily dismiss this ritualistic, old-fashioned man, but he truly believed in the individual meeting. Sitting in the centre of his world, the complex he had built around himself, he believed he was talking to the whole world.

"At the beginning of the war," he said now, "Japan seemed to be doing pretty well, but in 1944 we realized Japan was losing." He put down the newspaper and held up a well-worn book.

This is a book about the atrocity committed by the Japanese Imperial Army occupying Nanjing in 1937. It was an orgy of violence. One person could torture and kill hundreds of people. They got pleasure from it. I realized that human beings could be lower than devils. This was the reality of the divine army, the army of gods. If the soldiers of the emperor are this bad, what could you expect from the Americans, the devil-soldiers? Not only murder and rape but worse.

One month before the Americans landed, Okinawa was surrounded by warships. There were more than 500,000 American soldiers ready to invade. "Can you imagine?" Ahagon laughs. "At that moment, everyone, all of us, no exception, was insane."

To the consternation of the farmers, the Japanese government had expropriated land on Iejima before the war began. A large air base was built on the fertile soil. To the amazement and disgust of the Iejimans, the base was then ordered destroyed before the American invasion. The farmers couldn't believe the waste. On April 16, 1945, Iejima was the first place the Americans came ashore on Japanese soil, and the battle was quickly over five days later. The Iejimans suspect that the Japanese military knew the battle would be lost and destroyed the base to keep it from falling into American hands. Yet the islanders had been forced to resist to the death, and they suffered terribly as a result.

"Japan was the divine nation that must conquer the world.... To us, it was a holy war to make the whole earth happy."

SHOKO AHAGON,
FARMER AND PEACE
ACTIVIST

When Ahagon emerged from the caves, he told us, he found his island flattened, without a standing tree and only one building, badly damaged, which is preserved as a memorial today, like the one in Hiroshima.

When we saw the atrocities of broken heads, hands and feet torn off, intestines scattered about, innocent children slaughtered, and the spectacle of mountains of dead bodies more than the eye could take in, we thought that neither God nor Buddha were in this world, but only the Devil.

On this tiny island, 4,300 people died during the invasion: 800 American soldiers, 1,500 Japanese soldiers. Two thousand civilians were killed and many more wounded. Children, women, and men; husbands, wives, and grandparents — gone in one paroxysm of madness.

We had been hiding in the caves. The caves were infested with fleas and lice, and finally we had to leave. When we came out, we saw 4,000 dead bodies. We few survivors became POWs, and the entire population of Iejima was shipped by the Americans to Kerama Island. At that moment I didn't know whether it was better to be dead or alive. On Kerama we saw bones of suicide victims everywhere. Family members had killed other family members. Those who received bullets from the military to kill themselves rather than be captured by the Americans were the happiest because they knew what to do. Other people didn't know how to kill themselves.

In 1947 Iejima farmers were granted permission to return to the island. A dismal scene greeted their arrival — nothing green, no houses, just mounds of rubble. The only roads led to U.S. military installations. The returnees began to clear some land and gather the bones of the dead, which had been stacked in piles like cordwood.

Ahagon went into a deep depression after the war. He and his wife slept under tin sheets leaned against a wall. Finally, desperate for a better place to live and to get Ahagon out of his depression, his wife went to the village and asked the villagers for a house. They came and built them a beautiful home. It was the return of the community spirit that helped lift Ahagon out of his depression:

Once before the war, a man accidentally burned down his house.

When that happened, people in the village came, brought their own tools and food, and rebuilt a house that was even better than the one that was burned. In the old days, land was owned communally. Every nine years, the village would come together and assess how well the land was used and what new needs had developed, and distribute the land accordingly.

By 1950 funds had begun to trickle in to support construction of houses.

When the Americans came, that spirit of cooperation united us. But then money came to the landlords, and there was an ideological debate between communists and socialists, which split us up. I refused to let the land be rented to the military. I thought there was none worse than those who made war. When Japan lost the war, we thought it was good. If Japan had won, there would be war again. We thought because America won the war, there would never be war again. We wished for nothing more than an end to war. We thought that if we could work peacefully under the sun, we would be satisfied. And we believed in America and cooperated with the American military.

Ahagon stopped speaking, his eyes filled with an incredulous look at his own naïveté.

In 1951 Harold Rickard, whom we mentioned earlier as the translator of Ahagon's book, *The Island Where People Live*, landed on Okinawa as a member of the U.S. military and found the evidence of war still omnipresent. In his introduction to the book, he wrote:

When we landed, we found an island which still showed the terrible scars of the incredibly bloody battle between Japanese and American forces six years before. Japan did not fight the Battle of Okinawa to defend the Okinawan people, but used Okinawa for its last-ditch stand in defense of the Japanese mainland. Okinawa became an "island of sacrifice."[1]

Fewer than ten years after the end of the Second World War, and only a few years after the people had finally succeeded in rebuilding their simple homes and farms, the U.S. military came ashore at Iejima to take the land of the farmers at gunpoint.

The entire island had been placed within the "red line" of the U.S. military's master plan. The purpose was to construct an air-to-ground missile practice range for the U.S. Air Force. This second invasion came as a shock to the farmers who had worked so hard to recover their fields and regain a measure of stability and domicile on their home island. Ahagon describes the sense of duplicity and betrayal.

> When the Americans came to Iejima in 1953, they said they were conducting an investigation. The people therefore cooperated with the authorities. At the end of it, the Americans said the people would be paid for their help and asked them to put their seals on paper. It was a trick. They had signed their approval to evacuate the land. It was only the next year that they realized what they had done when the Americans demanded that they move off the land. Only four households were officially asked to move, but the authorities guaranteed everyone would be safe, that there would be compensation. No one would lose their livelihood.

The farmers held a meeting and demanded that none of the land be taken and refused to hand over their farms. The next year — on March 11, 1955, at early dawn — more than three hundred armed soldiers invaded the island. It was like the war all over again! The company captain for the Americans read the following notice and handed it over to the mayor:

> The Army of the United States of America is a peaceful and friendly corps. If the citizens peacefully accept being evacuated, you have much to gain. Should your citizens protest moving peacefully, you will lose much, and bring great damage upon yourselves, causing much unnecessary suffering.

Ahagon went on:

Then there was a lot written about receiving aid. He said that if we moved, trucks would haul our garbage, they would give us land for our houses, and farm fields would be given to us. He said, "You will receive some other person's fields." Although he spoke of giving us other farmland, *there was no other farmland.* It was as though he was saying, "If you people of Tokyo move, we will give you Osaka." How absurd!

The Captain continued, "Because this island was captured from the Japanese Army by the blood of American soldiers, you have no authority whatsoever over it. You must evacuate whether you agree or not!"

Ahagon protested against this shocking chain of events, but to no avail. He and two other men were arrested and jailed.

They inflicted violence upon us farmers who placed our hands together in entreaty. They tied us up with rough straw rope and even wrapped us in blankets — threw us like pigs inside chain-link fences, and after accusing us of the three crimes of agitation, violence, and public disturbance, set fire to thirteen houses. Then they demolished our buildings with bulldozers and drove us out, put up wire fence around our fields and used them as a practice range for mock nuclear bombs. Of course, we concluded with grief and sorrow, "The Americans are devils!"

The occupation was carried out in the brutal way of the conqueror. Pleas to leave some structures, to have consideration for the sick and elderly, were ignored as the soldiers went about their jobs with ferocious efficiency. As Ahagon was taking part in a sit-in protest in front of the Government of Ryuku (GRI) building in Naha, soldiers set fire to his house. When his neighbour pleaded with them to wait until Ahagon returned, they stopped setting fire to the roof and instead brought in a bulldozer and levelled his home.

Yamashiro Ume, a fifty-nine-year-old war widow who had

single-handedly brought up her fifteen-year-old son and four younger children, cried out, "Isn't there one sympathetic American soldier?" They entered her house, shouting, "Mama-san, give us a match! Mama-san, give us a match!" and went around hunting for matches. Seeing Ume-san crying out in confusion, "Stop it! Stop it!", they set fire to the house and cheered as the flames engulfed her home. In this way, one after another, our thirteen homes were destroyed by the bulldozers and fire.

The sit-in continued until April 13 when it was forcibly broken up.

At that time we, the farmers, decided that even if the Americans were devils we would act as human beings. We knew that the problem being caused by the American military then had originally been caused by Japan's attack on Pearl Harbor. We decided that we could not do anything that might cause a second war. We pondered how we could make a peaceful world. To study that and to secure the return of our land, we, the farmers, erected, near the missile practice range, a Solidarity Hall where we reflected on peace and war and studied many designs of history and society from ancient times. We investigated the way of peace taught by Confucius in his "Constitutional State under Peaceful Heaven"; Buddha's "Life of No Killing"; and Christ's teaching, "They that take up the sword will perish by the sword."

Ahagon and his fellow farmers also looked into opposing notions such as that of Alexander the Great, whose credo was: "The nation is glorified by armaments." They also studied Napoleon, who stated confidently, "In this world, nothing is impossible." They considered the history of Japan and Okinawa's civil wars; they looked into Hitler's suicide and General Tojo's execution by hanging.

Ahagon has come to understand that war is dehumanizing, transforming otherwise rational men into devils. One can never push out all devils; when one leaves, others come in. The challenge is to change devils back into human beings.

Ahagon's recipe for change struck us as charming, simple, and unique. With his mixture of naïveté and electrifying insight, he reminded us of the child who could see that the emperor was wearing no clothes. He believes in trying to show his opponents the benefits of change as a way of luring them towards ultimately improving everyone's condition. For example, he points out to right-wingers devoted to the emperor that, should a nuclear bomb drop, the emperor would be killed as well. If they want to protect the emperor, they should therefore fight for disarmament.

Ahagon also told us of his concerns about how life has changed on the island. "When we were children," he began, "frugality was what we were taught. Now it's consumption. There is no care for things. So the human mind is diminishing. We've got to regain the mind." Education, he said, has lost its direction, and this must be corrected, or society will lose its sense of direction. He went on:

> To be honest, for us ignorant farmers, it is difficult to know the contents of what is being taught today. I have a suspicion that education is getting worse and worse every year. Look at the intellectuals and scholars. They are so specialized they don't know anything outside their own field. In order to be a human being, we have to study everything related to being a human being. Children have to study to get diplomas, but there's a more important thing. They have to study to be a human being. Instead, schools teach gambling, winning and losing, beating and defeating. Those who win are good. By grading and competition and selection, we are teaching gambling in the schools.
>
> I wonder what kind of education is being given to our children. I think that in order to wage a nuclear war, it is necessary to create human beings who are so cold-blooded that they could use nuclear weapons. After all, education is managed and run by those who make weapons.

Finally we came back to a recognition of the powerful influence of economics and the way materialism and money seem to have overridden past values.

> Once the war was over, the rule was "Consumption is a virtue." Now our priorities are "Eat, drink and be merry." Now we realize that in wartime, when people said, "If you die for the emperor, you will become a god," it was actually to make the capitalists rich. Now we say, "Eat, play, throw away," and the capitalists profit. "Follow the latest craze! Use up things and throw them away quickly! Consumption is a virtue!" Once again, we are being deceived. The prewar and postwar rules really haven't changed.

Although Ahagon prized dialogues and meetings like ours, we could see he was getting tired. The grim look on his face told us that it wasn't easy dredging up painful memories of the past. Also we could see from the look of concern on Jahana's face that it was time to take a little break. We excused ourselves and went for a walk on the beach.

Yamashiro told us that the waters just off the beach are famous for coral, but that since commercial flower farming came to the island, the coral is dying. When it rains, the top soil washes into the ocean, killing the coral.

There is a deep sense of isolation on the island, which matches Ahagon's. He is an old man completely convinced of his mission, and although his supporters, who once numbered in the thousands, have dwindled to a few hundred, his hope never seems to lag. Each meeting is crucial to him because he believes that each person he meets adds to an accumulation that is taking him towards his goal.

As far as the media are concerned, he is nothing but an eccentric old man. Nevertheless he has continued to chip away, and his message is beginning to be heard. People have come from around the world to hear him and they have taken his message home. Like Socrates, he believes in old-fashioned dialogue and that the exchange of ideas can change the world.

We walked back into the central courtyard of Ahagon's complex and were surprised to see hundreds of small shoes outside the big hall where people stay and Ahagon gives lectures. We poked our heads into the hall and saw that it was filled with schoolchildren; up to three groups visit each day. Ahagon was sitting in a chair at the front of the room, and instead of teaching by invoking terrible images of war, he tried to relate the insanity of conflict to their daily lives. He began by saying, "I am just an old farmer who can talk only from personal experience. There will be mistakes and contradictions. I hope this will be the beginning of a respectful exchange and learning." He then told children that playground bullying is a type of war, and from there he built towards a deeper understanding of the nature of conflict. Ahagon's humility and respect riveted the children, who listened attentively. There was no difference between the tone he used with us and the one he used with these children. He was as polite, respectful, and straightforward with them as with any adult. "I am sitting here to learn from you," he continued. "And what I say to you might sound like old-fashioned, meaningless talk, but I hope that even in that there is something you can learn."

As he talked, two hundred young eyes were riveted on him. With us at the back of the room was one of their schoolteachers, and as he listened he shook his head. "At school we have a hard time keeping the kids quiet, yet look at them today — not a sound."

The major characteristic of Ahagon's philosophy is his belief in nonviolence and in dialogues that benefit both sides. In a country in which keeping face is so important, this attribute of seeing legitimacy in both sides is a crucial point. Without it, an adversary is left to fight without options. Ahagon told the children:

> When I was sixteen, I got sick. To cure the problem, I was sent to a
> hot spring in Kyushu. There, a Christian neighbour introduced me to
> the church and I became a Christian. When I came back, I lived as a
> Christian. Even during the war I prayed to God. I believed that after I
> died, I would go to heaven. When I came out of the cave, I saw

mountains of dead bodies. Houses and trees were burnt. I realized there was no God or Buddha in this world. If there were, why would this happen to innocent children? I believed that only politics could solve the problem. I went to Tokyo and visited the American Embassy and in vain tried to meet Prime Minister Sato. Instead, I met his representative. We argued and I realized arguments, slurs, and bad words weren't the way to make peace. Instead of harming the opponent, one must try to enlighten him and bring him towards change that way.

I also want to speak to the Japanese people and politicians. You sacrificed war criminals and a lot of people who were killed. But now you've forgotten and are arming with the help of the U.S. This is a mistake. Look at what we have — a constitution that says we gave up arms and the right to fight. We should not just keep it but spread it. The security treaty between U.S. and Japan is more dangerous than the treaty between Japan and Germany. It can ruin both Japan and the U.S. We must get rid of it. We can create a neutral nation.

Ahagon went back to religion, not the organization or the words but the spirit of Jesus Christ, Buddha, and Confucius. He discovered that the only hope was for love and compassion. He began to study and teach young people from his experiences and humbling insights. When Ahagon spoke of the past, we didn't feel any sense of attachment or nostalgia; his words were not clouded by overloaded personal feelings, but his stories shed a clear light on positive issues. At the age of ninety, he still looks towards the future, yet throughout the conversation it was clear that what he did was firmly based on the tradition of a communal way of living.

Ahagon was always an environmentally conscious farmer. He sees an essential link between war, destruction of human lives, and destruction of the environment. People whose humanity is lacking are the ones who take up weapons. The best way to create inhuman people is to destroy the nature that surrounds them.

Modern warfare is becoming such that we cannot distinguish between destruction of humans and destruction of nature. One just has to look at the Gulf War and the huge destruction of the environment. Look at the nuclear bomb-testing sites in the U.S. deserts and Pacific islands, which continue to contaminate the atmosphere.

As Ahagon himself admitted, it's very hard to destroy Satan or to make everyone godly. The challenge is to control the human impulse to be selfish. We need to create a sense of a higher self, what people get from family and in traditional communities. One's sense of comfort, well-being, and meaning come from belonging to family and community. Community becomes an extension of that self.

As we said goodbye, three youngsters from Kyoto arrived. Jahana ushered them in as Ahagon endlessly and tirelessly repeated his message that war is a form of madness and inhumanity that destroys those who wage it. Jahana, who adored Ahagon for having saved her from her bedridden existence, pulled out a pair of tattered gloves that have been repaired over and over with different-coloured threads. Ahagon explained that we needed books more than anything else because they contained seeds of knowledge vital to human beings. He therefore repaired his gloves to symbolize that the money saved could be spent on education.

"Modern warfare is becoming such that we cannot distingui[sh] between destruction of humans and destruction of nature."

Shoko Ahagon

(Photo: the only building left standing on Iejima Island, Okinawa)

The next day, Jahana took us on a guided tour of the island. We drove by sugarcane fields and commercial flower beds. There were relics of the war everywhere: a monument to Ernie Pyle, the humanist war correspondent; a cave where more than a hundred islanders committed suicide during the battle; a cliff overlooking a rocky shore off which islanders had thrown themselves to escape the fighting; and, of course, the U.S. bases. Through the U.S. Marines' fence we could see the land Ahagon still hoped to use as a school. We saw the Japanese and American flags flying proudly and a big sign that said Keep Out. Jahana pointed out the area that went down to the ocean and told us that it belonged to Ahagon. He still talked of the day he'd get that land back and open his school for farmers.

Halfway down a stunningly beautiful cliff we saw one of the few fresh-water sources on the island. It was being used by the military to water their runways in the summer heat. Islanders were forced to have their water piped in from the main island.

We visited the Sacred Cave in which a thousand people were said to have hidden. Jahana's father fought for six years in China. When he returned to Iejima, he saw the military buildup and knew there would be a war. He forced the people of his village to move to the main island, where they survived. On the other side of the island, the villagers believed they would be protected by the Japanese soldiers. Everyone trained with bamboo spears. During the invasion, they fled to caves and were all killed. Jahana could hardly speak when she recalled what Iejima was like when they returned two and a half years later. Amidst the devastation, they couldn't even tell where homes or land had been.

The last place she took us was Ahasha-*gama*, where 150 people, including her uncle, died.

As Jahana drove us back to the ferry, she told us that the Americans had already returned fifty percent of the land, and she was confident that they would soon return the rest. Ahagon, Jahana, and Yamashiro tirelessly work and plan for that day.

And in the twilight of his life, Ahagon's unswerving opposition to the dehumanization of war remains an inspiration to the world.

part two

japan's
diversity

a sense of place

"*Women were coming out of a sacred place,* utaki,

wearing a wreath of leaves around their heads.

They came down to a sacred rock, formed a circle

and sang divine songs for many hours. No one

was watching. Tanigawa and I were in a hut down

the road and watched through a crack in the

door. I was shocked. My image of a festival was not

like this. At that point I realized there was

something profound here, a key to understanding

questions of what is life, who am I, what is Okinawa."

YASUO HIGA

KINDAI, or modernity, is a belief that what is new is best. The converse is that what is old is not as good. The remarkable "success" of modern science is seen as proof of the benefits of modernity. People have become so intoxicated by the brute muscle power of science

and technology and their contribution to global economics that we seldom ponder weaknesses or limits of science and technology. Scientists
themselves often forget what makes science such a powerful way of
knowing and how it differs from other ways.

Traditional bodies of knowledge, often called worldviews, embody
the sum total of knowledge, observations, history, and speculations of a
people. In a worldview everything is interconnected — the past, present,
and future, the stars, forests, animals, and people. Science provides a radically different kind of knowledge. Scientists focus on parts of nature,
attempt to isolate and control the pieces, and thereby gain powerful
insights into that fragment of the world. Because scientists seek discover-
ies that are universal, independent of time and space, the knowledge they
gain is fundamentally disconnected from the context that makes the
piece they're studying of interest in the first place. As well, our scientific
knowledge base is so minuscule we have almost no ability to anticipate
the consequences of applying those insights through technology. Thus,
while scientific concepts allow us to create powerful technologies based
on restricted views, the ramifications extend far beyond the limited scope
of what we see through microscopes. Most people in industry, government, medicine, and the military don't yet comprehend this fatal limita-
tion to modern technology. Instead, they continue to trumpet the
endless wonders that flow from science. Nowhere is that more obvious
than in Japan.

Modernists see Japan as a remarkable success story, a success often
referred to as a miracle. Japan did indeed make a radical transformation from a rural, traditional society to the leading edge of twentieth-
century technological culture. Many people in the developing world
look at Japan as a model to emulate. The West has mixed emotions;
while admitting a certain admiration for Japanese diligence and excel-
lence, they also feel threatened by Japan's economic clout. Everyone,
however, has focused on Japan's technological, industrial, and economic achievements. Few remember that this "progress" was made by

real working men and women. Only in recent years has a darker side of this achievement surfaced. The Japanese are now beginning to face the adverse environmental effects, as well as the mental and spiritual void left by years of neglect and abuse.

●

Among those leading the search for new inspiration to fill this void is the photographer Yasuo Higa. According to him, despite sweeping modernization, some pockets within Japan have been overlooked, including the remote islands of Okinawa. Learning from these remnants of the past, he feels, is becoming more and more crucial to society as a whole. So he has dedicated his life to this pursuit.

When we first met Higa in Okinawa city for a late-evening dinner, his warm, lined face seemed laden with wisdom. Higa ordered a plate of wonderful tidbits — slices of pig's ears, fresh mackerel, a pig's foot. (Okinawans have been derogatorily called "pigs" by Japanese because they enjoy eating them.) His initial reserve soon broke down as he warmed to the subject of his obsession, studying and photographing the female shamanistic tradition that lives on in some of the islands of Okinawa.

The purpose of our meeting was to discuss the trip we would take together to Miyako Island. Higa had brought a couple of his award-winning photography books to show us. In his black-and-white photos, he tries to convey the whole complexity in portraits of faces. He finds that traditional people reveal themselves in their faces whereas city folk hide behind masks.

As so often happened, the minute we began to probe Higa's life, the Second World War loomed as his seminal experience. Yasuo Higa was born in the Philippines, the son of Okinawan immigrants. During the war in the Pacific, the Japanese military forced General MacArthur and his American army out of the Philippines. Higa told us:

Since most Filipinos were pro-American, we immigrants who were living among the Filipinos and had been their neighbours and friends suddenly were the enemy. When the Americans returned, as MacArthur had boasted they would, the Japanese soldiers retreated to the mountains. Since we immigrants were now the enemy too, we had to follow the soldiers. The mountains were the main targets of the Americans. It was hell. There were dead bodies everywhere. My father was taken to fight and died. We hid in the tropical jungle. I was the eldest, so I had to take care of my two younger siblings and carry our load. I lost my younger sister. We were barely surviving day by day. I didn't think about who to blame. We were there for months. I was seven years old.

Although they weren't even aware that the war was over, out of desperation, Higa and his family came down from the mountains on August 16, 1945.

After we surrendered, we were put in a camp. My father's brother's family were there. Within a week they all died from starvation and exhaustion. When we were put in a U.S. military car and Filipinos threw stones at us, I understood that we were hated.

In 1946, after spending some time in a camp in mainland Japan, Higa and his remaining family were able to return to Okinawa. He remembered being sprayed from head to foot with DDT by the Americans. After months of detention in camps, his family was finally allowed to return to Koza, his parents' village. Two years later, his mother died from the stresses of the war years, and Higa was raised by his grandmother.

Postwar Koza was called the "City of U.S. Bases." Higa watched it mutate from a farming village into a city whose sole purpose seemed to be servicing the American military.

We were poor. Everybody was poor, but we were even poorer than the poor. I had to beg my grandmother to let me go to high school. At that time, going to senior high was like going to university. I had good marks. Not being able to go to senior high would be a shame. But I never dreamed of going to college.

School was strictly Japanese, and although it was the American era the teachers were the same ones who had taught Imperial education before the war.

They would punish us for using Okinawan; we were always urged to speak Japanese — good, standardized Japanese. But I didn't think much about the Okinawan situation. My college friends did, but I had no way of going to college so I became involved in judo. I was pretty good, and I went to tournaments.

In Koza Americans were everywhere, and so were their racial problems. Center Street was for whites. The area around Higa's high school was for blacks. There were always incidents involving the soldiers: blacks being arrested by military police (MPs) and people fighting.

It was unthinkable to have American friends. Our lifestyles were completely different. Our neighbours worked as house maids for low-ranking soldiers. I never felt close. The difference was too great. I tried not to think about it. I absorbed myself in judo. I joined the police force because it meant I could continue my judo.

The Americans occupied but did not directly rule Okinawa. They introduced laws and set up the structures, but the local police enforced them. Americans were completely outside the local system, and Okinawan police had no right to arrest or detain them. All they could do was report incidents to the MPs. Higa patrolled the area right in front of the Kadena base. Okinawans and Americans were like oil and water, interacting but never mixing.

At night, MPs would come to the police box and patrol alongside us. We walked together but we wouldn't talk. Neither of us spoke the other's language. We didn't like or dislike them. It was a necessity. We had to patrol together. Again, they were so different from us. The power they had compared to the power we had. The money they had compared to the money we had. It was two different worlds.

In the 1960s, local workers and students began to stage anti-occupation, pro-reversion demonstrations. A few wanted outright independence, but most simply wanted reversion. There were frequent rallies and demonstrations. Higa said:

> As a policeman I became the oppressor. I was sent in uniform to demonstrations and ran into my cousins. I got married to a woman who was an elementary schoolteacher. The teachers' union was a strong force in the reversion movement, and my wife got involved in it. I was forced to think about this crazy situation. I was no longer able to pretend it didn't exist.

At this time, the Vietnam War was also intensifying. The B-52s that bombed North Vietnam were based across the street from Higa's workplace.

> From my police station, I could see them going out and coming back. I knew the schedule. One night, I was on duty and I saw a big mushroom cloud. I thought the Kadena ammunition depot that housed nuclear weapons had exploded. I thought it was all over. I thought my family and I would die. Later I learned that it was just a B-52 crashing. After ten years as a policeman, I quit. I realized the time had come to pull myself out of this chaos. My wife was happy that I was quitting.

As a detective, he was assigned to the photography detail. "I had seen a lot of pictures from the Vietnam War," he told us. "That made me want to become a photojournalist. I wanted to chronicle Okinawa. I wanted clear pictures, literally, of the chaos."

After he left the police force, Higa went to Tokyo for two years to learn photography. His family remained in Okinawa. His wife supported them through her teaching. On his return to Okinawa, Higa opened a coffee shop, then a chain of *soba* noodle restaurants. The restaurants were quite successful and he still runs them today. His wife was able to retire. "All the while, I kept looking at Okinawa, not through the eyes of a journalist, but through my own eyes. It was just before the reversion, so there were many photojournalists in Okinawa."

In 1974, Higa was hired by Ken'ichi Tanigawa, a well-known ethnologist who specialized in Okinawan culture and who was beginning a new magazine. For twenty days Higa travelled with him around remote Okinawan islands.

When I was in Miyako, we saw a festival called Uyagan. It was a shock. All the gods and ancestors coming down, late at night, to where people live. The gods, all women, form a circle and sing the songs of gods. I had never seen anything like this. It had never even occurred to me that such a thing could exist. My brain had been a jumble, occupied by the Americans, politics, and history. I couldn't believe this type of thing existed right here in Okinawa.

"The gods, all women, form a circle and sing the songs of go[ds]. I had never seen anything like this. It had never even occurred to me that such a thing could exist."

YASUO HIGA,
PHOTOGRAPHER
(PHOTO: SHAMANS ON
MIYAKO ISLAND)

In Okinawa, human bone remnants go back 15,000 to 18,000 years. On Miyako Island, the records go back almost as far. Miyako is the fourth-largest island in Okinawa, after the main islands of Okinawa, Iriomote, and Ishigaki. Two hundred and fifty kilometres southwest of Naha, it has a population of 60,000 and one city, Hirara. People of the island have a distinctive dialect and physical appearance. It was this island we planned to visit. We wanted to see the world that so enchanted Higa.

We spent the night in Hirara, then took the 7:30 a.m. ferry to nearby Irabu Island to see the women's festival, called Hidagan-Nigai, similar to Uyagan. From the boat we could see a group of women sitting in a semicircle in a small park facing the water. Not far away was another group of about sixty women sitting in the parking lot surrounded by stores and houses. They were facing the slip where boats were launched into the sea. The people in this fishing village believed the sea was a god. Women prayed to the god to give them a prosperous life and to protect their family members at sea.

Half the parking lot was filled with small trays, all placed neatly in straight lines. The size of the offerings reflected the size of the family's boat. The trays carried rice, two bottles and cups for *sake*, salt, and dried fish. Some had a pack of cigarettes. The women faced the lines of trays. Most were middle-aged or older. They were dressed in kimonos except for a few who wore western clothes. At the front were two women. One, around fifty years old, wore a white gown over her kimono. Her face struck us with its intensity and exotic beauty. Sitting beside her was a woman known as a leading shaman. Her look was less intense and more relaxed. In front of the women was a pile of sand in which massive amounts of incense burned. Behind the curtain of smoke a pig's head sat on the ground. The ritual had begun before we arrived with the sacrifice of the pig on the beach. To the left a group of men and women surrounded a huge woklike pan in which pork was being cooked. Here the men cooked and remained in the background while the women took centre stage.

Something bothered us about the setting. The sacred ceremony was taking place in the midst of concrete. On the ground were lines showing cars where to park. There was even a car parked right in front of a sign asking people not to park there for the ceremony. Higa's pictures of this place, taken fifteen years ago, show the women facing a sloped runway to the beach for the boats. Now the beach was not visible. A road and wall had been built between it and the parking lot. Sensing our discomfort, Higa explained that the women deal with the invisible world of spirits, the nonphysical world, and these changes in the material world were of no concern to them. The shaman began to sing a hauntingly slow and beautiful song, a recitation of the gods through the ages.

Higa then explained that the woman in the white gown, meditating alone in front of the others, was the leader of the ritual. Every three years, a new leader is chosen. Names are placed on pieces of paper, then mixed up and drawn. The first woman whose name comes up three times is the chosen one. Usually she is shocked and depressed at the news because the job is a demanding one. She attends all rituals and ceremonies of which there may be forty or more a year. She has to perform them carefully and lead a pure life, not leaving the island even to go to a major hospital if she gets sick. She is forbidden to sleep with her husband. Sometimes the woman's marriage does not survive.

Later, Higa told us more about the meaning of the rituals.

The way of thinking represented by the rituals is indigenous to the island, but the form was imposed by the fifteenth-century rulers of the Ryuku Kingdom. The forms look different in each village, but there is a commonality to all native people.

What is common? A belief in souls and eternity.

These indigenous communities have a long history, one going back to hunter/gatherers. For centuries they had a relatively high level of material and spiritual life. Then, in the fifteenth century, the Okinawan lords established the Ryuku Kingdom. They imposed a hierarchical and centralized structure with each community integrated into it, but the new system did not affect the people's daily lives or the framework of *shima shakai* (island society). *Shima* literally means island and refers to an isolated, self-sufficient space.

When Satsuma, the powerful clan of southern Japan, took over in the early seventeenth century, it didn't try to change the *shima* framework either. But finally, in the late nineteenth century, the Meiji Imperial regime imposed its structure over Okinawa through education, religion, and Japanese language and writing. Then the *shima* structure was affected. Only on remote islands has the premodern way of life survived. Higa explained:

For the people to have the premodern elements of the *shima* society they must know where they are coming from. By knowing the beginning, it is easier to see the path. It is also easier to understand from what point modernization begins, and to know where societies like Japan and the United States stand on that path.

Higa understands the dangers of *kindai*, or modernization.

Modernization means ceasing to recognize nature for itself and simply considering what it can do for human beings. Once human beings deny nature the right to exist, the only result can be destruction. While nature is being destroyed, human beings believe that it is an evolution and improvement. The whole Earth is now in danger.

We commented on the separation between science and spirituality that has taken place in western thinking. Once nature was seen as intertwined with spirits and as such was felt to be stronger and larger than our existence. Even at the time of Francis Bacon science was inseparable from spirituality. Bacon was a very religious man, and he considered his science as praise for God's creation. But since then, we have severed science from a sense of divinity. We now believe that we can know and control everything. We think that as long as knowledge is tied to spirituality, it is primitive and inferior thinking. Higa responded:

Judeo-Christian tradition is monotheistic, and it became universal by removing itself from a particular place. And losing the sense of place was the fate of all the religious traditions that tried to become universal. In the ceremony we saw this morning, the people were dealing with the gods from that place. To me this is the fundamental difference between the modern world and the *shima*.

To Higa, *kindai*, which results in the loss of the sacred sense of place, is also one of the fundamental problems of North American civilization. When Europeans arrived five hundred years ago, they lacked affection or respect for the land they called the New World, to say nothing of respect for the people who were already there. Since then they have never belonged to the land. The land was seen simply as real estate, as opposed to sacred earth. They bulldozed it for dams while completely ignoring the indigenous people, who said that this was holy ground where their ancestors rested. To this Higa replied:

> Yes, that's what *kindai* is. Okinawa is no longer free of modernization. But luckily we still have some clues that point to alternative ways of living. Whereas *kindai* insists on going in a straight line towards destruction, *shima* society grows in cycles. *Shima* society is based on the cycles of all lives.
>
> On the other hand, science and technology create a speed and power that are just overwhelming. I have a television set, but I have no idea how it works. I fly in a jet plane, and it is amazing that such a huge thing can fly through the air, but I have no idea how it works. So if we don't understand how the things we use work, how can we see where we are heading?

Higa's observations led us to reflect on science and its limits. Scientists attempt to observe objectively, detached emotionally from the object of their interest so that their experiments, observations, and conclusions aren't influenced. But in distancing ourselves from the object of study, we no longer care about it, losing any sense of the sacred or loved. Scientific insights imply an understanding of an object free of influence from its surroundings or period in time. But nothing we know exists in a vacuum free of its surroundings or its history. What scientists acquire can only be called an *artifact*, an aberrant description of nature that is created by the experimental conditions under which it could be observed. The great danger is that society often assumes such bits and pieces of knowledge provide an explanation of the workings of the entire universe. Or if not that grandiose, experts claim to know enough to "manage" or "control" forest ecosystems, whole populations of fish or mammals, or the quality of soil for agricultural production. It is a flawed belief based on a lack of understanding of what science is.

There are other ways of knowing that are every bit as powerful and far more profound than the growing body of scientific information. These other ways have been acquired over thousands of years of observation and thought. The gatherers of this knowledge never separated themselves from what they observed; rather, they were deeply embedded within it. They looked with wonder, awe, and passion, and what they acquired was critical for their very survival. That, of course, is the knowledge base of countless indigenous cultures around the planet, some of which Higa has encountered in Okinawa.

Higa took us to a park facing the ocean. We walked carefully down the steep, rocky cliff. At the bottom we came to a cave known as Sen'ningama. After walking through a narrow entrance into the darkness, suddenly we came to a large, bright cavern, with a sand floor. Rays of sunshine shot through a small opening and mixed with the mist of the shadows. We climbed a set of steep rocks and looked out through an opening onto the ocean.

Higa speculated that this was one of the early dwellings of the island's original inhabitants. The coral lake that surrounds the outer rim of the cave was a productive "garden" where the people gathered seaweed, fish, and shellfish. He believed that in those days the people lived in a matriarchal society in which men remained marginal.

It is not possible for us to go back to the original state of being. But at least we can acknowledge the primacy of nature and womanhood. I try to imagine what the human mind was like in its original state. Mind, nature, gods must have all coexisted inseparably. The mind echoing nature.

Nature is circular with its birth, growth, aging, death, and birth. And at the centre of this circle, Higa sees women.

The centre of *shima* society was women. We can see the traces of that time in many of the rituals we still have on remote islands. The sacred places, called *utaki*, are still found all over the islands. To me these are what is left of the sacred forests where women-gods lived.

So today men are still forbidden to enter many of the *utaki*, and the gods who appear in the rituals are women. It is clear that in the ritualistic tradition, the people have believed they are worshipping women and the matrilineal order.

Higa suggested that women symbolize darkness, night, moon, chaos. Men are light, sun, day, order. Modernization was an effort to conquer and eliminate darkness by light. But it is from darkness that imagination and creation come. Higa also identified two forces: centripetal and centrifugal.

> I believe women represent the force that pulls in, whereas men represent the force that tends to push away. Women, with their reproductive cycle, are more self-sufficient, just like the earth itself. So we can also say that they are cyclical, whereas men are linear. In that sense, science is very much masculine in principle.

"I try to imagine what the human mind was like in its original state. Mind, nature, gods must have all coexisted inseparably."

YASUO HIGA,
PHOTOGRAPHER
(PHOTO: SEN'NIN-GAMA,
IRABU ISLAND)

We told Higa about anthropologist Helena Norberg-Hodge's observations over a twenty-year period in Ladakh, a Himalayan kingdom in which people lived rich, full lives in geographic isolation. She said that once a road from India reached the capital city of Leh, young men began to abandon villages for city lights, and the traditional self-sufficiency quickly fell apart. Higa agreed.

> That is exactly what happened to our *shima* societies. But to begin with, men were always out fishing while women stayed on the island. It is women who see the men off and pray for their safe return, embracing them on their arrival. And in this process I see something fundamentally natural. It is just like a magnet. Somehow in the traditional world, the balance between the

two forces was maintained. But since modernization, we must have lost much of our magnetic power. Those who leave never come back again. But on these remote islands, women are still here, praying towards the ocean, communicating with the gods.

That night, Higa showed us videos of a remarkable festival that takes place every twelve years in the Year of the Horse on Kudaka Island. It is an induction into shamanhood of every woman over the age of thirty on the island. Inductees are purified and wear their hair down. Those who are already shamans have their hair tied up in headbands. The men help build two grass huts connected to the outside by a bridge and a walkway. Ashes representing the ancestors are taken from an elder's pot and put into a pot for each inductee. The women dance and repeat everything seven times. The inductees are put into the huts, which represent each village, and stay there for three nights. On the third day, they tie their hair up.

Because of this festival, Kudaka Island has been considered a sacred place all over Okinawa. However, there has been such a migration of young people off the island that, in 1990, there wasn't one woman who qualified, and the event was cancelled. When the Okinawan musician and activist Shokichi Kina learned of the cancellation, he felt the tradition should be continued, and decided to hold a concert to encourage the Kudaka people to hold the initiation event anyway. Higa, however, believed it was up to the people of Kudaka. Of course the tradition is dying and people are sad, he said, but in the future, something else may be revived. It will be different, but at least it will be theirs.

The future of the festival on Kudaka Island is not clear, like the future of many of the rituals in Okinawa. In 1995 Higa lived on Miyako Island chronicling all the rituals that happen throughout the year.

Higa continued with his analysis of the rituals.

In many rituals, ancestral spirits that have gathered in the mountains come down through the hills into the valleys. The purpose of the ritual is to express where the villagers are all coming from. The higher up the mountain, the older and more revered the spirits are. The entire landscape is used as a map indicating the history of the *shima* society from the mythological past.

So every ritual is a reconfirmation of where you have been and who you are.

David told Higa:

Ever since my children were born, I've kept albums for each of them. They are filled with souvenirs, such as the hospital wristband when they were born, their first baby teeth to come out, their first drawings, letters I wrote to them, birthday cards. They are a record of their lives. To me, those albums are priceless, but if I ever tried to sell them, they would be worthless in the marketplace.

Higa understood immediately and replied, "*Shima* people's land is their album. As they move and sing, they are tracing their album. The land is my album."

Like so many people in the world, Higa has had his eyes opened to the radically different values and perspectives of indigenous and traditional people. Universally, the key to those perspectives is rootedness to the land, a profound sense of interconnectedness with all animate and inanimate objects around. And in seeing through new eyes, Higa has recognized the destructive consequences and rootlessness of the dominant culture. In Japan, Higa is not alone by any means.

●

Among those remarkable people was Seishin Asato (1913–1982), respected as one of the forefathers of Japanese environmental philosophy.[1] On the main island of Okinawa, Asato waged a battle against environmental destruction of his native land by the American military occupation. This battle was based on an ecological philosophy born out of tradition. He once said:

Our struggle has been based on our belief that the ocean and myself are one. We are nurtured by the sea. I heard some people analyse the structure of the Chinese character for ocean and break it down literally into "water mother of humans." To me, this interpretation is so natural. At low tide, we used to go down to the tide pools and collect seaweed, sea urchins, crabs, and all kinds of shellfish. I was brought up like that; when you were hungry, you would go down to the sea. You would go there empty-handed and just stand in the sand. With your heel, you would dig a line into the sand and like that, a bunch of shrimp would come up with shining eyes. Sometimes, there were so many of them I got scared and ran away.

Asato tried to convey the way local people relate to their immediate surroundings.

There is a local word for ocean: *uramutu*. I translate it as "the ocean of treasures." Some local people call one area of the bay *jingura*; that means safe or treasure chest. I remember one old fisherman used to say the ocean is a bank. He would build a house and his bank was the ocean. It never occurred to him that he might borrow from Mitsubishi.

To Asato, the crucial place along the sea is the interface between land and water.

I see the tide land as the place where energy and life are concentrated in the ecological system. Today, ecology books teach us that the little shrimp that grew up in the tide land will go out to the ocean and their offspring will come back to our tide land; and bigger fish will live on these smaller ones. Thus, nature revives itself and maintains itself. That whole system and our lifestyle based on that system are now all gone because of the Crude Oil Transfer System [a massive development that allows oil supertankers to unload their cargo in a deep-sea port built in the bay]. The artificial road in the ocean cut off the tide current, so Kin Bay is no longer alive. The tide and the current of the sea are like an artery to human beings; what happens if you cut the artery? What happens to the children when you cut the artery of the mother?

Of course, the notion of nature as a mother is widespread among aboriginal people in many parts of the world. And as the eminent Rockefeller University scientist René Dubos once wrote:

> The statement that the earth is our mother is more than a sentimental platitude: we are shaped by the earth. The characteristics of the environment in which we develop condition our biological and mental being and the quality of our life. Even were it only for selfish reasons, therefore, we must maintain variety and harmony in nature.[2]

The idea of the ocean as mother has also been the central theme of Japanese writer Michiko Ishimure, who started her writing career with a series of stories chronicling the disastrous history of Minamata, where mercury poisoning caused so much illness (see Chapter 9). Like a painter she has brought out vivid colours on an otherwise bleak landscape. She revealed the eloquent voice of Yuki Sagami, one of the Minamata disease victims, in her book, *Paradise in the Sea of Sorrow*.[3]

> At times like that I would think of the sea. It was great to be out on the sea. At the end of spring and the beginning of summer, lots of flowers were blooming on the bottom of the sea. No garden planted by man could match the beauty of the sea then. . . . Even we fishermen who've spent years at sea still notice that unmistakable smell the sea has in early summer. It's a helluva lot different from the stinking water that comes out of the factory, I'll tell you that!
>
> The sea flows like a river, too, you know. It sort of oozes along slowly, but it flows just the same. It rolls on along, and all the shellfish, sea anemones, and seaweed move right along with it.
>
> Those old pine trees hanging off the cliffs with their branches practically touching the water — why sometimes their roots come

right up out of the water, and the cliffs are so windy that their branches take the shape of stair steps that run right back up to the top!

And there's nothing more beautiful than the fish! Those sea anemones open right up just like one of those pom-pom chrysanthemums in full bloom. There's one kind of kelp down there that looks just like a snowball plant. Another kind grows thick as a bamboo forest.

Just like on land, you can always tell the seasons, spring, summer, winter and fall down there in the sea. I believe there really is a palace at the bottom of the ocean, too, just like they say in the fairy tales. I bet it's beautiful as a dream. I could never get enough of it . . . the sea.

Even the smallest island has a crack in a rock somewhere under the water, from which a spring of pure fresh water gushes forth. When the spring-water and the sea-water meet, you'll always find sea-lettuce, that lets you know it's spring. Out of the smells, the smell of sea-lettuce warmed by the sun at ebb tide was my favourite.

We used to pick this sea-lettuce off the rocks and pluck the oyster shells from under it. We'd boil the oyster shells together with the sea-lettuce and soy sauce and make it into a soup. Townspeople don't know anything about delicacies like that. We don't feel like spring is really here until we have burned our tongues with this piping hot soup.

I want to have two strong legs to stand firmly on the ground. I want to have two strong hands with which I can work. With these hands I want to row my own boat and go gather fresh sea-lettuce. It makes me want to cry. I want so much to be out on the sea again . . . just one more time.

We found a deep sense of "rootedness to place" on Iriomote, a remote island in Okinawa. There, Akiko and Kinsei Ishigaki exude pride in where they live (you will meet them again in Chapter 8). On the last night of our stay on the island, they threw us a party at Akiko's weaving workshop. Her looms were lined up on one side. The old windows and doors were open, letting in a cool breeze. The trees and plants around the building, many of which Akiko uses in her weaving, filled the air with a rich scent. We sat on reed mats. Akiko's textiles, hanging from the ceiling, swayed in the breeze. On the table were raw fish, wild vegetables from the hills, raw boar meat, and *awamori*, a strong local liquor that Kinsei calls medicine for longevity. With his *sanshin*, a local three-stringed instrument, on his lap, Kinsei sat cross-legged and began to sing folk songs. He started quietly and slowly, and as the music built, Akiko stood up, put on a beautifully woven head-band, and began to dance. The years fell away and she became young and sensual once again. Takeo Shigeki, our friend and Okinawan specialist who accompa-nied us, picked up a pair of drumsticks and began to play along.

For them, nature and culture are intertwined and inseparable. Kinsei told us with his characteristic confidence:

> The reason we work to protect culture is that culture is the basis for protection of nature and our livelihood. When culture is gone, everything is gone with it. The festivals are our prayer for a good life. By destroying nature, you can never have a good life. In our tradition, we have all kinds of wisdom that tell us how to receive wealth from nature.
>
> Festivals promoted by governments are festivals without gods. When the emperor died, all over Japan events were cancelled. Our biggest festival was scheduled a week after his death and we went ahead and held it. For us, our gods are above the emperor.
>
> We have festivals to tell us how to live with mountains and sea and river. The wildcat is the god of the mountain, so we protect and care for them. When we go to sea, we say, "Please give us our share." Even when we cut the trees, we say, "Let us have our share." We never take more than we need.

"The reason we work to protect culture is that culture is the basis for protection of nature and our livelihood."

KINSEI ISHIGAKI,

ARTIST

As the evening continued, we were filled with a sense of wholeness. Even the darkness had substance with sounds, textures, and smells. Nothing seemed to be lacking or superfluous. Removed from our daily lives in the city, where we feel constantly driven, never satisfied, and obsessed with our wants and needs, we felt that everything was perfectly balanced.

CHAPTER 5

the ORIGINAL
peopLe

"Despite the 'assimilation policy' as rendered by the

Japanese government, we, the Ainu, have

maintained our ethnicity as indigenous people in Japan.

We have the right of self-determination.

We, the Ainu, have our culture, religion and customs

which no one can violate. The Ainu have never

given up these rights. Thus, the Ainu still firmly

possess the rights of culture, religion, language

and customs."

UTARI ASSOCIATION SUBMISSION
TO THE UNITED NATIONS, GENEVA, AUGUST 1987

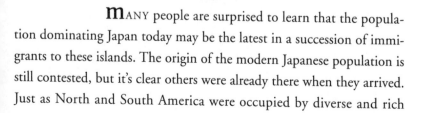

MANY people are surprised to learn that the population dominating Japan today may be the latest in a succession of immigrants to these islands. The origin of the modern Japanese population is still contested, but it's clear others were already there when they arrived. Just as North and South America were occupied by diverse and rich cultures before the arrival of Europeans five centuries ago, the Japanese archipelagos were inhabited by many aboriginal groups when invaders from the continent arrived probably from the Korean peninsula.

At that time, more than 1,500 years ago, the powerful state of Yamato (from which the Japanese state evolved) emerged in the western part of Honshu, the main island of Japan, and began to extend its reign to the south and north by conquering and assimilating the aboriginal groups. The people believed to be the ancestors of the Ainu inhabited the northeastern part of Honshu and Hokkaido, the island north of Honshu. Numerous military campaigns and conflicts in the northern part of Honshu against native groups were recorded throughout the ancient and medieval history of Japan. However, flourishing cultures of Ainu in Hokkaido were virtually untouched until well into the fifteenth century when Japanese started to establish a foothold in the southern tip of the island to engage in trade and plundering. There are records of two major armed rebellions by Ainu against Japanese maltreatment in 1456 and 1669.

During the Edo Period (1603–1867) under the rule of the Tokugawa Shogunate, exploitation of the Ainu was intensified by the land-lease system, in which Japanese merchants were granted leases and were free to use land and natural resources and enslave the people.

Takeshiro Matsuura, explorer and chronicler of the late Edo Period, wrote compassionately about the plight of the Ainu. It is believed that by that time, the Ainu population was decimated by disease brought from Honshu and brutal mistreatment, both of which seriously damaged the fabric of their culture and society. However, it was only after the new Japanese government of Meiji was established in 1868 that the massive migration of Japanese and colonization of Hokkaido started.

First the land-lease system was abolished, and the Hokkaido Colonization Commission was established. Under the assimilation policy of the government, use of the Ainu language was forbidden and the culture suppressed by force. In 1873 the central government promulgated the Land Tax Revision Act, according to which Hokkaido was classified as "ownerless land" and assigned to the Imperial household. The

Hokkaido Colonization Commission became the Hokkaido Agency in 1886 as the tide of colonists settling into Hokkaido multiplied, pushing the Ainu off the land and forcing them to move into undesirable and mountainous areas.

At the turn of the century came the new Former Aborigines Protection Act. It revealed clearly the Japanese attitude towards the Ainu: this aboriginal people had been assimilated and "they no longer exist."

After many centuries of conquest and terrible oppression, however, the Ainu do still exist. And they are fighting back against the ongoing invasion of their territory using every possible public arena to demand respect and recognition of their existence and rights to the land.

For Hiroshi Tsurumaki, a Japanese history teacher in Hokkaido, studying local history has always been more than a professional duty. For him, understanding Hokkaido history and the history of native peoples is part of a search for his own identity. And it was through his activities in the local history group that he met a family belonging to the Uilta people, one of the aboriginal inhabitants of Sakhalin Island, directly north of Hokkaido. Meeting them became a turning point in his life.

While staying with friends in Akan, we called Tsurumaki to ask him to set up a meeting with Aiko Kitagawa, one of the last-known Uilta in the country. We had met Aiko Kitagawa before, in the fall of 1992, at Tokyo's Meiji Gakuin University. We'd been attending a conference on the implications of the five hundred years since the arrival of Christopher Columbus in the New World. It attracted a large audience of students, academics, human-rights activists, and minority groups. On the second day of the meeting, a minor sensation occurred when Kitagawa rose and proclaimed publicly that she was a Uilta. Once wrongly called Orokko, Uilta are one of many native peoples inhabiting the northeastern part of the Asian continent. The Uilta had long overlapped geographically with two other main indigenous peoples — the Ainu and the Nivkh.

At first Tsurumaki had difficulty locating her, since at that time of the year she spent days in the mountains, picking vegetables and wild berries. But finally Tsurumaki was able to track her down. To meet Kitagawa and Tsurumaki, we drove to Abashiri, at the northeast end of Japan, facing the sea of Okhotsk. Most Japanese know this city only for the notorious prison it houses. As we pulled in, Tsurumaki came out smiling from the Jakka Dufuni (the House to Store Precious Things), the Uilta documentation centre that overlooks the Abashiri River. He greeted us warmly. Aiko Kitagawa was waiting in the building. As she saw us, she smiled shyly and apologized for being so hard to reach. We asked her whether she found a lot of vegetables and berries in the mountains. As she nodded, Tsurumaki explained that for her just being in the mountains was the important thing.

Kitagawa is still surrounded by the spirits of the earth. In the summer months much of her time is spent roaming the mountains. In her daily life she continuously communicates and praises nature. When she travels to a new place, she makes sure to pray at crossroads and bridges that span rivers. Kitagawa revealed this when she reminisced about the meeting where we had first met.

> When I attended that event at Meiji Gakuin University, we were going onto campus when we had to drive around a giant ginko tree. Suddenly my legs felt like lead and I couldn't move. When we were returning by the tree, I suddenly got cold and started to shiver. The next day I asked for a cigarette and candy and went up to the tree. I looked around to make sure nobody was watching, because I felt shy. I put the offerings down and said a prayer. I felt better right away.

With the help of Tsurumaki, whose Japanese is better than hers, Kitagawa told us about her brother, Gendanu, who was the founder of the Uilta Association and the documentation centre in which we sat. Gendanu (Japanese name is Gentaro Kitagawa) was born in 1922 in south Sakhalin and was adopted by the shaman and community leader Gorgoro Dahinneni (roughly meaning north river, which translates as Kitagawa in Japanese). He lived on a reservation built for the Uilta and Nivkh in 1925.

Since the end of the Russo-Japanese War (1904–1905), the southern half of Sakhalin was ruled by Japan. Across the border in the northern half of the island were the Russians. The occupation by Japan meant severe treatment of the indigenous people of the island, especially of the Uilta, whose traditional lifestyle was nomadic, following the reindeer. The Japanese policy of putting them in reservations was devastating. As children, Gendanu and Aiko were put in a school for native children and forced to change their names. They also had to learn Japanese and were prohibited from participating in their Uilta culture. Under the policy of assimilation they received an Imperial education. This extreme discrimination made Gendanu wish to become a full-fledged Japanese, so when the Japanese military came to recruit him as a spy, he accepted the opportunity.

In 1945 after the bombing of Hiroshima, Russia knew the United States was in a position to take all of Japan; wanting to grab a share for themselves, they crossed Japanese borders into Manchuria, Sakhalin, and Kuriles. People resisted; some were killed and many were captured. Most of the Japanese soldiers quickly escaped, but Gendanu was seized, tried in a military court, and condemned to a heavy sentence as a Japanese spy. He served nine years and six months of hard labour in Siberia. After his release, he chose to go to Japan. He settled in Abashiri in 1955 and received his Japanese citizenship in 1956. Tsurumaki explained to us what happened then.

"The next day I asked for a cigarette and candy and went up to the tree .... I put the offerings down and said a prayer. I felt better right away."

AIKO KITAGAWA, ONE OF THE LAST KNOWN UILTA. (PHOTO: INAU, AN AINU LAKESIDE OFFERING)

We applied for compensation and benefits on Gendanu's behalf for his military service and imprisonment, but were turned down because the Japanese said he didn't qualify. To us it was an obvious case of discrimination and injustice.

Tsurumaki and others were so outraged by the decision that they organized a movement to redress the wrongs done to Gendanu and his fellow Uilta. Even the Abashiri town council joined the fight. A member of the Diet who was a Communist argued for Gendanu in parliament. And it wasn't just about Gendanu. A lot of minority groups in Japan and overseas were in the same position. "We began to see the dimensions of the problem," Tsurumaki said, "but we concentrated on Gendanu."

In the Diet, members of the upper military testified. They said that they had recruited Gendanu during the war and that he had served in intelligence near the border, but the Department of Health and Welfare rejected the application on the grounds that Gendanu wasn't a Japanese citizen. They said that the Japanese couldn't recruit a noncitizen. It was a catch-22 situation. Gendanu had been recruited by someone up in Sakhalin, but because Japan legally couldn't recruit noncitizens, this wasn't recognized as even possible. Tsurumaki went on:

> So who drafted Gendanu? We found out that it was the Nakano School of Intelligence, which trained spies. They decided *dojin* [primitives] might be useful because they could tolerate cold, had a good knowledge of geography, and moved very fast. So they were trained as Japanese soldiers. They knew well that young native men would feel it was an honour to be an Imperial soldier and readily join up.

Tsurumaki did not give up even after the decision.

> The government knows we're still here. They also know that although it's a small case, it would open up other cases of Koreans and Taiwanese. Gendanu always said it's not about money, it's about the heart of the government to apologize. The government must express it in some way. The Japanese attitude seems to be to eliminate them, to wait for the problem to disappear. It's a small group, but it survived for thousands of years and it was a wonderful culture. Somehow we've got to help them survive. It's not just for them. I feel it's also for us all.

Quietly Kitagawa leaned forward and began to talk.

> Japan is my home. Sakhalin was my native land. I was born in 1928. When I first went to school, my classmates were Uilta, Nivkh, and

children of other groups. The school was set up just for *dojin,* but I didn't know then that it was racism. Every day we were taught in Japanese and told to become Japanese. In town wherever I went people despised me, calling me *orokko* [a derogatory term for Uilta]. I thought Mother was responsible for this and hated her for it. I still remember that.

When I turned seventeen, I began to work in a tannery and fish cannery under contract to the Japanese military. At the end of the war the Russians came, and young native men who had worked for the Japanese military were arrested and taken to Siberia. Many died there, but some came back years later. In the meantime we women, children, and old people were left behind. At nineteen I got married to a young man from another native group called Kilin. But six months later he was arrested as a war criminal and sent to Siberia. I realized the war makes innocent people so unhappy. War is terrible. I also realized that the Japanese education was a lie. When I was working for a factory in Poloneisk, I threw myself in the river, but I couldn't end my life. I felt betrayed, and I decided that from then on I would be tough like a devil to survive.

In 1952 I married a Korean man. Like many other Koreans in Sakhalin, at fifteen he had been kidnapped and blindfolded by the Japanese and forced to work in the mines. After the war, abandoned by the Japanese and stuck in Sakhalin, he worked for a fishnet factory.

Then one day, my first husband came back. My second husband said I should go and talk to him, and if I preferred, I could go back to him. So I went to see my first husband. He said we didn't separate because we fought, it was just the war. And now that I had children, I should stay with my husband and he would go away. So I stayed with my second husband.

After I had my third child, we finally received a letter from my brother, Gendanu, telling us he was going to Japan. Our family decided to join him in Japan. That's how we came to Abashiri, my new home.

Although the Kitagawa family had been betrayed by the Japanese, they still hoped to receive official recognition of Gendanu's service for Japan. When they settled in Abashiri, the city saw them as an asset and fabricated a tourist attraction called "Fire Festival of Orochon" (*orochon* is another derogatory word for Uilta). Aiko Kitagawa and her father, Gorgoro, who was on welfare and living in public housing, agreed to participate in this humiliating show out of a sense of indebtedness. Tsurumaki and his group felt responsible and decided to help Gendanu in his effort to preserve their culture.

Before Gendanu died in July 1984, he achieved all three goals he had set for the Uilta Association he formed with the support of Tsurumaki's group. In 1978 a museum was built. In 1981 a group was organized to go back to Sakhalin to visit relatives and friends. And finally in 1982 a monument was built on Tenzan Mountain overlooking the Sea of Okhotsk to console the souls of Nivkh and Uilta who died in the war. The inscription on the plaque reads:

Rest in peace
We will not let your death be meaningless
Praying for Peace . . .
   May 3, 1982
   The Uilta Association

Before we left, Kitagawa folded some paper and then cut a detailed traditional pattern free hand and presented it to us as a gift. This form of cutting is the Uilta art of *irga*. Aiko and her sister are the only two who still practise the various Uilta folk arts. Much of the art in the documentation centre is Aiko's. *Irga* embroidery on clothing, bags, and shoes, Uilta woodwork, containers made of birchbark and animal skins with arabesque embroidered patterns, are all exhibited alongside traditional tools made by Gendanu.

It is believed there are about three hundred Uilta still on Sakhalin, which is now in Russian territory. In Japan, there are probably only a handful of Uilta left. Kitagawa is the only one who admits her heritage publicly. Her sister, who spends much of her time with Aiko, has yet to declare herself a Uilta. Kitagawa's children wish to live as Japanese and be assimilated into Japanese society, although they support their mother's decision to live as a Uilta.

Most Japanese have never heard of the Uilta. Those who have heard of Kitagawa assume past injustices have been dealt with and the case is closed. After all, how can one person represent an ethnic group and culture? In a society of more than 120 million people, there would seem to be little reason to worry about such a small group as the Uilta. But Kitagawa feels that when she dies, something immense and irreplaceable will be lost. And we feel that if nothing is done, the Japanese will have missed the opportunity to better understand their past mistakes and to create a more humane society in which diverse cultures can coexist and enrich one another.

●

At the end of 1992, after the conference aforementioned at Meiji Gakuin University, we went to Hokkaido with four conference participants from the Americas: one Mohawk and two Cree women from Canada and a Mixquito woman from Nicaragua. Accompanied by an NHK (Japan's national network) television crew, we travelled from Sapporo towards the eastern part of Hokkaido. Our trip had two objectives: to visit the Ainu communities scattered around the island and to observe the degree of environmental destruction.

We stopped in the village of Nibutani, which is the only place in Hokkaido where the Ainu are a majority. Nibutani is known as the hub of Ainu culture and features an Ainu museum and cultural centre. Koichi Kaizawa and Shigeru Kayano agreed to be our guides. Kaizawa was a farmer and a native of Nibutani. He practised organic farming, growing rice, potatoes, and various other vegetables on the farm he inherited from his grandmother. Kayano was the best-known Ainu elder in Japan and overseas, and had a vast knowledge of Ainu culture. Born in Nibutani in 1926, Kayano was in his late sixties when we met him and he spoke with the sort of dignity and wisdom that comes from experience and pain. His Ainu identity is his entire existence. Kaizawa told us that Nibutani has a population of about five hundred of which eighty percent are Ainu. The Nibutani Ainu are a part of the Saru Ainu, who make their livelihoods along the Saru River. They are traditionally hunters and gatherers, and salmon is their staple food. In his book, *Our Land Was a Forest*, Kayano writes about his early years:

> This Nibutani, where I was raised in material poverty yet with spiritual wealth, is in the town of Biratori, located in the Saru region of Hidaka county, Hokkaido. . . . The Saru River flows near here and rice paddies abound. In the past, salmon were plentiful in the river, and in the nearby mountains there were deer and hare. The Ainu had settled long ago in the Saru River region, with its mild climate and rich supply of food, dotting the landscape with their communities. I believe it is to the Saru that Ainu culture can trace its origins, for the *kamuy yukar* state that the river is the land of Okikurmikamuy. This is the god who taught folk wisdom to the Ainu: how to build houses, fish, raise millet, and so forth.[1]

Kaizawa, an experienced woodsman, took us to the end of what used to be his property. It had been taken over in the past century by one of the Zaibatsu (a powerful financial group) known as the Mitsui Corporation. As we walked he told us the story of his aging father who had expressed a desire to see a chestnut tree before he died. This area was the northernmost range of chestnut trees. Since his father was very ill, Kaizawa set off to find a chestnut tree he could videotape. He walked a long way into the forest and eventually found one. Kaizawa was happy to be able to fulfill his father's dying wish.

As we walked farther, Kaizawa decided to show us the chestnut tree he had videotaped. It was one of the largest in the area and would give us an idea of how big the original trees were before the Mitsui Corporation began logging. It was a tough, long hike over several high hills and through dense bamboo underbrush. We hiked along the spine of hills so steep that we could have plunged over the edge on either side by taking a single step off the trail. Because they don't have such mountainous regions on their land, the two Cree women had a hard time with the terrain.

After an hour of heavy slogging, Kaizawa picked up the pace. He excitedly told us the tree was just over the next ridge. But on reaching the top, we discovered the entire valley, from the top of the hill to as far as we could see, had been clear-cut! The chestnut tree was gone. Kaizawa stared in shock and anger, unable to speak. The hillsides were completely shaved of all vegetation. Logging roads had cut a wide ribbon into the earth, and there were large pockmarks where the slash had been raked and burned. Once they used horses to skid the logs out on the frozen ground in winter. Now they needed wide roads so the bulldozers could get in. It was as if a battle had been fought here. We knew that on the steep slopes, once the rainy season started, the topsoil would quickly slide off the hills.

While we stood there on the ridge, Kaizawa broke away and walked down into the clear-cut. He spent a good deal of time looking over the land, not speaking. When he returned to the group, there was an awkward moment as we searched for the right words to express our sorrow. He broke the silence by saying, "I'm glad my father died before this happened."

Many Canadian environmentalists have accused Japan of logging forests in other countries in a way they would never do with their own forests. The for-

"Until a few years ago, Japan was telling the world they didn't have any ethnic minorities... Once there is recognition of Ainu, Japan has to recognize other ethnic groups."

Koichi Kaizawa,

Ainu farmer

est near Nibutani proved the critics dead wrong. Big corporations everywhere seem hell-bent on liquidating the forests under the mistaken conceit that they know enough to regrow them and the belief that it is a waste to leave a merchantable tree standing.

Koichi Kaizawa was born in Nibutani in 1946. His name — "*ko*" means "to cultivate" — was given to him by his grandfather who wanted his grandson to be a farmer. Living in a time of forced assimilation, his grandfather believed becoming a farmer and abandoning the traditional lifestyle of hunting and gathering would be the only way for the Ainu to survive and be full-fledged Japanese.

Even though the Ainu are a majority in Nibutani, discrimination still exists. "But there were more Ainu, so when there were fights, we could win," Kaizawa told us with a wry smile. But outside Nibutani, his grandfather understood who was more powerful.

My grandfather was an assimilationist. He believed that by abandoning his Ainuness he could overcome racism and become Japanese. So he consciously prohibited speaking Ainu at home, refused to observe the customs and ceremonies. My grandmother was not Ainu, but she had been abandoned as a child and adopted by Ainu, so she grew up as an Ainu. It was she who loved the Ainu culture and kept the habits. We were influenced by her.

Probably influenced by his father, my father was also an assimilationist and didn't know much about Ainu culture or the language. He believed in being Japanese. He was recruited for the war as a Japanese, but once in the army he realized that discrimination against Ainu was still widespread. In China, he found five ethnic groups coexisting in Manchuria and northeastern China. He saw the harsh way Japanese discriminated against Koreans. He realized the Ainu had to have their own culture. You can't escape from what you are. When he returned from the war, he wasn't the same person he had been before. That was the beginning of the Ainu movement for him.

Kaizawa's father, Tadashi Kaizawa, was one of the founders of the Utari Association of Hokkaido; with its 25,000 members it is the largest Ainu organization. He was especially concerned with the welfare of the Ainu people and the recognition of their culture. In 1899 the Former Aborigines Protection Act had simply extinguished the rights of Ainu. Under the guise of protecting the impoverished people, the act was instrumental in further destroying their cultural and economic base and accelerating the process of assimilation. Tadashi Kaizawa played a central role in the movement to push for an Ainu New Law (Counterplan to the Proposal for Legislation Concerning the Ainu People).

Kaizawa told us he bitterly remembers the 1972 Winter Olympics in Sapporo when an NHK television announcer said, "It's been one hundred years since Japanese pioneers came to this no-man's land." Koichi snorted.

Until a few years ago, Japan was telling the world they didn't have any ethnic minorities. But we have been making progress slowly but surely. I think we have had an impact. Once there is recognition of Ainu, Japan has to recognize other ethnic groups.

In August 1987 the Utari Association delivered a paper to the United Nations in Geneva. In it they asked the U.N. to investigate their situation as an indigenous and ethnic minority within Japan, stressing the following three points:

1. Despite the "assimilation policy" as rendered by the Japanese government, we, the Ainu, have maintained our ethnicity as indigenous people in Japan. We have the "right of self-determination."
2. We, the Ainu, have our culture, religion, and customs which no one can violate. The Ainu have never given up these rights. Thus, the Ainu still firmly possess the rights of culture, religion, language, and customs.
3. The Ainu have the right to demand the establishment of a "New Act" which should replace the discriminatory "Hokkaido Former Aborigines Protection Act."

Another achievement of Tadashi Kaizawa's was his trip to China to obtain recognition of the existence of the Ainu as an ethnic group within Japan. He managed to get an invitation from the Chinese government for an Ainu delegation. Koichi Kaizawa added,

During the eighteen years since the first visit, we have been invited three times, and sixteen Ainu have visited the country. In his will, my father instructed that we go to China and officially thank them on his behalf. I did that this year.

What Tadashi Kaizawa, his son, and their fellow Ainu saw on their visits influenced them greatly; in the Chinese system, small ethnic groups have a guaranteed place. The Ainu suddenly had a broader perspective. Like aboriginal people in North America, the Ainu community had a range of views about their relationship with the dominant society. Some would like to separate completely, demanding land and political autonomy over it. At the other end of the spectrum are many who have already assimilated and disappeared into the Japanese mainstream. Kaizawa told us how the visits to China had affected him.

> When I first went to China sixteen years ago, I had a separatist view and I expressed it. One of the Chinese officials said to me, "I understand you want independence, but after you get it, what happens then? It might cause a third world war. Hokkaido being such a hotspot, the Chinese, the Russians, the Americans won't be silent. So you can imagine what might happen. Do you still want independence?" And I had to say no. The Chinese man said, "Wouldn't you prefer establishing rights and then peacefully coexist with Japan?"

Koichi Kaizawa's motivation had always been anger and a desire for a place where the Ainu could be left alone to live their lives and practise their culture. That did not change. He was still angry about the way the Ainu have been treated, but his approach became more moderate and rational.

> The highest goal would be an autonomous state within Japan. I understand the Japanese cannot accept the idea that we would take all of Hokkaido and that the Japanese would have to leave. Although we say clearly that northern Honshu, Hokkaido, and the Kuriles were once our territory, we do not tell Japanese to go away. We want to avoid unnecessary bloodshed. Taking up arms will just make enemies. We prefer to talk, and that's more appropriate because it's part of Ainu tradition called *ukocharanke*.

Kayano explained to us the meaning of the term *ukocharanke*:

> *Uko* means "mutually," and *charanke* means "to let words fall"; the compound word *ukocharanke* thus refers to the Ainu custom of

settling differences by arguing exhaustively. It also implies that the Ainu do not solve disputes by violence. *Charanke* requires the talent to argue with logic and the physical strength to sit in debate for days. Kaizawa continued:

I understand the Ainu world is evaporating quickly. We are now witnessing the last generation of Ainu. Their rich cultural background is dying out. In the meantime Japanese scholars have been collecting material about Ainu. When we are ready, we will be able to get it back with the help of the Japanese knowledge of Ainu culture. It's sad but that's the reality. First Ainu must know what being Ainu means. And then we must have the Japanese recognize the Ainu as indigenous people.

Nibutani is known for its excellent Ainu Cultural Museum. It was Kayano who collected the Ainu cultural items while working as a forester, and it was he who eventually founded the museum. He took us on a tour of the museum, which was now housed in an impressive modern building.

Shigeru Kayano was born in 1926. As a child he learned the Ainu language from his grandmother. After graduating from elementary school, he became a labourer working in the mountains. Only much later, when he realized the importance of the culture he absorbed in his childhood, did he begin to work consciously for the preservation of Ainu culture. Besides founding the museum, he started an Ainu language school in his backyard, which has since spread to a dozen communities in Hokkaido. As an ethnologist he has written dictionaries, collections of mythology, legends and folk tales, and books of essays.

Kayano and Koichi Kaizawa's father, Tadashi, were close friends and considered each other partners in the same struggle for the Ainu. Kayano was in charge of cultural matters, and Kaizawa, Sr., was in charge of political matters.

The history of the Ainu in Hokkaido echoes the experience of North and South American Indians. Although the Ainu at one time occupied all of Hokkaido, Japan simply took over the mountains as national or corporate property, and the rivers have gone to the Ministry of Construction and Fishery Cooperatives. In the 1960s it was decided to create an industrial park twenty kilometres from Nibutani. The land was confiscated and a huge port built and dredged. But with the oil crisis in the 1970s, the economy began to sputter, and the land has never been developed. Nevertheless, construction has begun on a huge dam on the Saru River. Already the muddy water has interfered with the fish runs. The amount of electricity generated by the dam will be trivial — 3,000 kilowatts — enough to light one building. The real function of the dam, it was said, was to provide water for the factories, but now that the building of factories seems remote, the rationale has shifted to the need for water for irrigation and to use the dams for flood control. Clearly there is no valid need for the dam, but construction continues. The construction companies are well connected with the government, and the jobs inject money into the local economy, giving an illusion of prosperity. So it will continue, and another piece of an indigenous culture will disappear as yet another fragment of an ecosystem is modified and biodiversity lost.

Kaizawa and Kayano took us all down to the Saru River. There we climbed into two dugout canoes. The water was murky, and on the opposite bank, bulldozers were digging out the soil in preparation for the day the whole area would be underwater. Kayano stood on the stern of the canoe and, with a long pole, pushed us along the river. He was enjoying himself out on the water.

In a country renowned for its love of nature, it is strange that even here in Hokkaido most rivers have been "domesticated." They have been straightened and dammed, their banks lined with concrete and rock. One part of the riverbank filled in with concrete is now called Ecological Park by the municipality. In his book, *Our Land Was a Forest*, Kayano recalled:

> I cannot begin to imagine how many salmon in the old days swam up the Saru River, then called the Sisirimuka. The *kamuy yukar* that my grandmother used to sing for me described the salmon as swelling the

water surface like a seismic wave as they swam against the current, "the backs of those swimming near the surface being scorched by the sun, and the bellies of those swimming near the bottom of the water nearly scraped off by rocks."[2]

It wasn't until we were almost at the construction site that Kayano told us that we were going to travel "illegally" under the huge dam. From the bank an official from the construction company watched our two boats through binoculars. In front of us the huge concrete structure of the dam loomed. As the current flowed faster, the boats picked up speed, and together the two canoes shot under the gate neck and neck almost as if we were racing. Kayano's brother pushed his pole against the concrete dam. At his symbolic act of defiance we all cheered. But at the same time we were shocked to see the imposing, monstrous structure already standing on this once idyllic river. We realized with heavy hearts that the struggle Koichi Kaizawa, his father, and Shigeru Kayano have been waging was on the brink of defeat.

When his father was alive, Kaizawa was reluctant to get too wrapped up in the struggle. Tadashi had always been extremely busy with little time for the family. As a farmer Kaizawa knew that there was nobody else who could take care of his farm.

My father asked me if it was okay to oppose the dam. I told him to go ahead, and promised, after he died, I would take up the cause. When he began to protest, I knew it would take ten to twenty years. But I didn't know my father would pass away so soon.

Kayano and Tadashi Kaizawa owned pieces of farmland that were to be flooded by the dam. For both of them the issue was far greater than the fate of their small plots. Out of thirty thousand rivers in Japan only two hadn't been either dammed or modified in some way. To them the fight had an added symbolic significance, because it was also about the survival of the Ainu. For the Saru Ainu who live on the river, destroying the river meant the destruction of their livelihood and culture. Nibutani, as it is described in the legends and mythology, is a sacred Ainu place.

From the canoe, Kayano pointed out various sacred sites. At one, we were shocked to see bulldozers moving and destroying the earth. Kaizawa explained:

> Kayano and I are suing the people who expropriated the land for the dam. Once we started the case, the state decided to join the side of the expropriators. This is good because it puts us in direct discussion with the government. We are forcing the state to listen to us. I now realize that this is what my father was doing. The judge recently ordered the state to give a clearer statement on its position about whether the Ainu are Japan's indigenous people. So it's getting interesting. What we want is a policy statement on the distinction between indigenous and ethnic minorities. Without recognition of us as indigenous people, our culture and history will not be recognized.

Recently Koichi Kaizawa's son, Taichi, wore an Ainu outfit to his college graduation, an event that attracted wide coverage in the media. But Kaizawa hopes for the day such things will not be considered news. Kayano gave copies of the newspaper reports on the graduation to his students in language class. They were very impressed and remarked how courageous the boy was. When we talked to Taichi later, he said, "It wasn't courageous. It was normal. But young people now are so conservative. They ask me, 'Why are you causing problems? Why can't you be satisfied with what you have?'"

His father said the Japanese in and around Nibutani keep asking the same thing.

> "We get along. Why are you stirring it up? It's about culture, isn't it? We're helping you protect that." A writer once wrote, "The Roman Empire died out, but its culture thrives." So the same could be for the Ainu. But that would mean the elimination of the Ainu. The culture would be preserved, but the people would be erased. And we refuse that.

We asked what Kaizawa thought was the most important challenge facing the Ainu. He replied:

I guess it's pride. How to bring that back. The Japanese state has to recognize us. Then they have to write a true history of what happened. By knowing the facts, both Japanese and Ainu will have a different attitude. Racism will decline and mutual respect will thrive. It may take three generations, so if we don't start now, the Ainu will disappear. I think probably every indigenous group is in the same situation. They have been pushed to the limit. But once they recover their pride, they'll take everything back.

Just before Tadashi Kaizawa died in early 1992, he wrote an appeal to the president of Mitsui Corporation urging him to return the Ainu forests and mountains that they owned. Tadashi knew that his life was coming to an end. He asked his son to have an Ainu-style funeral for him and asked Kayano to read a farewell prayer in the Ainu language. And so, Koichi Kaizawa organized the first Ainu-style funeral that had taken place in many years. Tadashi's body was surrounded by piles of chrysanthemums. Facing a picture of his dear friend, Kayano asked the Ainu gods for his safe journey to their world. Under Kayano's guidance a traditional marker was carved out of wood and placed at the grave on a hill overlooking the family farm.

While still working as a farmer, Kaizawa was also involved on two battlefronts. His fight against the dam continued. He and Kayano had thirteen volunteer lawyers with expertise in different areas who were ready to prove the Ainu are indigenous. He was also involved with the National Trust Movement, through which he hoped to regain the mountains behind his farm. The National Trust, which is headquartered in Osaka, collects supporters and funds to buy back land in small increments until it co-owns a significant area. It had been Kaizawa's father's dream to regain the mountains; Kaizawa's dream is to use them as a stronghold in the resurging Ainu culture, as the Ainu and Japanese friends would demonstrate an ecologically viable way of living by applying the wisdom of the elders. Kaizawa explained:

> Hundreds of people have listened to me, understood our cause, and now each one of them is giving the message to many others. That's how things get better. It seems to be a slow process. But in fact it is the fastest way. This is the Ainu wisdom of *ukocaranke*.

In August 1993 Kaizawa was the main organizer of the Nibutani Forum, in which he was able to involve not only his Ainu community but the municipality of Biratori, with its Japanese majority. The forum received wide coverage from the national press and was attended by native people from fifteen different countries. Many participants expressed their support for the Ainu's fight against the dam.

In the summer of 1994 Kayano became the first Ainu to be elected to the National Assembly. In his first speech to the Diet, Kayano spoke his native Ainu language, which is not officially recognized. As he spoke, an unusual quiet descended over the assembly, and there was a mixture of excitement and embarrassment. Switching his speech to Japanese, he said he was there to sit with them and engage in a fruitful *ukocharanke* until they came to a mutual acceptance and respect.

After our visit with Kayano and Kaizawa we travelled to the eastern part of Hokkaido, where we were reunited with some Ainu friends: the Takiguchi family of the town of Akan. Facing Lake Akan, the town with its hot springs was a popular resort destination for Japanese tourists from the mainland. At the edge of town there was a section called Ainu Kotan, which means Ainu Village. The village was set up for the Ainu by a wealthy local landlord and is primarily a tourist attraction. The main street goes up a small hill and on either side are stores with colourful facades, selling everything from highly artistic sculptures and crafts to cheap plastic souvenirs. Many salesclerks dress in traditional Ainu costumes and wear embroidered headbands. At the top of the slope is a large thatched hut where groups from the community perform traditional music and dance at regularly scheduled times.

The Takiguchis own a small craft store on this street. In a way, the couple is symbolic of the future of the Ainu. Yuriko, an Ainu woman originally from Tokachi, is an artisan practising traditional embroidery and knitting and is also active in various communal cultural activities. For our arrival, she had collected all kinds of mountain vegetables and filled the table with incredible dishes. In spite of her limp, she bustled about her house to keep us plied with food and drink, her large, friendly eyes promising to break into laughter. Her husband, Masamitsu, a deaf mute Japanese sculptor, was born in Manchuria. Slim, with a short ponytail, he actively joined in our conversation with a mixture of sounds and sign language that his wife understood and translated for us. For his work on large wood sculptures, Masamitsu rents a house in the countryside of Teshikaga. The Takiguchis let us use it as a base of operations. The hot springs heated the whole house and there was a warm natural bath outside.

A good friend of Yuriko's, Kiyono Nagane, an elderly Ainu woman from Ashoro, joined us to tell her story. Her vision was so poor she had to peer at us through very thick glasses, and most of her teeth were gone, but she talked loudly and animatedly. She had all of us roaring with her raucous delivery and sense of humour. She began:

> I was born in Hokkaido in 1924. Until I was five I lived in the mountains. Then we moved to Obihiro, a city in the southeastern part of Hokkaido. The kids called me Ainu, but I didn't know what they meant. They would harass us for being Ainu. So my father would go to the kids' homes, but that only made things worse. Of course the children learn these things from their parents. I just worked harder until I became like a boss and could order other kids around.
>
> When I was twelve or thirteen, I loved dancing and being part of the celebrations. There were lots of occasions — people going to war or getting married. Everyone, old people, young people, huge people,

would get up and dance in a circle. They would drink homemade sake.

My husband was very handsome, but I didn't like him very much. In fact, I tried to get away from him by taking a job as a maid in Sapporo. He kind of deceived me. I thought that he was a fisherman or something, but he was a hunter. He hunted birds at first. He brought a bird to me to be plucked. I had no idea what to do, so I began to pull one feather out at a time. He came over and asked me what I thought I was doing. He pulled the feathers and they came off so cleanly.

He was such a good shot that if he spotted a fox, he would wait till it was joined by a second one and then kill both of them with a single bullet.

But mostly my husband, Genjiro, was a bear hunter. He killed 134 bears. He would sell the gall bladder. It was worth as much as gold. It's very bitter. When you hold it up and look through it, it is a clear yellow. Some people add blood to it to increase its weight, but then it becomes brittle and brown and you can tell. We would sell the teeth, the skin. The paws tasted so good, the best meat of all. Bear meat is only good at certain times.

My husband and I are both half Ainu. We lived where there were only Ainu. If there was intermarriage, it was because Japanese would come to be with us, not because Ainu would go out and find a Japanese partner. My husband and I didn't speak Ainu, but as we got older, I called him names in Ainu and he answered back in Ainu. I have been writing down the words. My husband knows a lot of the names of animals and hunting language.

I never had my children in the hospital. My mother-in-law would come and help. I had my first child when I was twenty-two and I was scared. My mother-in-law was very hard on me. I had the last two babies by myself. I would get an *obi* [sash] and hook it around my feet so I could pull against it. My eldest daughter was there and I told her to help me. When the baby came out, I couldn't bring myself to look, so I told her to look at it. She fell down in a faint. I told her to go and boil some water, but she said she couldn't move her legs. Even now, she doesn't like babies.

My husband said if the children looked like him, they would be beautiful and wouldn't have to worry. If they didn't, then it was my fault.

The sun had set. Although it was chilly outside, the hot springs running under the house kept us warm. Yuriko Takiguchi poured more tea and added more dishes to the already overloaded table. As Kiyono Nagane showed no signs of tiring, we asked her what she thinks of the way the Japanese have developed Ainu land. She replied:

I think it's contradictory what they say and what they do. I worked for the forestry department, and they taught me about the water cycle. Yet even in national parks, they're cutting trees like mad. They cause landslides. Then they build dams.

It's a vicious cycle. They know what effect the dam will have, but they build it. They know the effect of cutting trees, but they still log. Then when the bad effects happen, *we're* the ones who have to move out. So I'm against the dam at Nibutani, but once it's built, what can we do?

The Japanese built dams and destroyed the fishing. They built a munitions depot for the Japan Defence League. I joined the opposition, but they built it. Now they propose a development for the military and I oppose it. But people like it. They think it will bring money into the region, that the soldiers will spend money. But they can buy things cheaply on the base. Even with all the opposition, everything gets built, so it's useless. People are thinking only of money for tomorrow.

The forestry department said if they clear an area of trees, then plant new ones, there will be trees again in seventy to eighty years. But I won't be around then. It doesn't make sense. The same people who are cutting are planting. Now we never see a big tree anymore anywhere. When the forest is cut, the animals disappear. We don't know how long it will take for everything to grow back.

Foresters claim to have expertise and science. But Nagane made so much more sense. The illusion that modern science and technology can provide all we need to carry on with our destructive ways is dangerous and foolish.

The only place where there are big trees left is in the national parks, and they want to cut those too. Wherever I go, I see naked mountains. People speak of the Earth being sick. They mean this. My generation is almost over, but children today . . . I don't know how they're going to survive.

Walking on asphalt, you don't feel good. It's hot. Urban people with children are surrounded by concrete and now want to get away from the concrete so they can walk on earth.

Masamitsu Takiguchi motioned to us that he'd like to say something. We communicated through lipreading, gestures, and sounds he made with his throat. The strangeness of communicating in this way faded quickly as we became used to it. He told us:

When we cut trees, I feel bad because it hurts them. That's why I prefer to use driftwood and bogwood for my sculptures. Look at the way we cut the trees. We just cut more and more. We cut the old oak that the owls and other animals need, and they disappear right away.

In Washington, Oregon, and British Columbia, spotted owls and marbled murrelets are found only in old-growth forests. When those trees are cut down, the birds disappear. Yet this connection is still disputed. This artist saw with clarity what the "experts" still debate.

Masamitsu Takiguchi was born in 1941 in Manchuria, the northeastern part of China, where Japan had set up a puppet regime during the Second World War. Living conditions were very rough there, thanks to the war, and he developed pneumonia when he was three years old, resulting in his loss of hearing and speech. After his family returned to Japan, he entered a school for the deaf and eventually took up crafts, which have become his lifelong passion. When he was twenty-two, he travelled to Hokkaido, where he met Yuriko, fell in love, and eventually married. Since then, eastern Hokkaido has been his home. As a wood carver, he has earned many prizes and given exhibitions in both Hokkaido and Tokyo. He told us:

> I work only with wood because it has a *tamashii* [soul]. Each tree has its own personality. I can tell by the texture, hardness, and colour. A tree strives to grow, twists and turns in its struggle. To slice it straight is sad after it tried so hard to grow for many years. If it is crooked there are reasons for it. So each curve is important. When I look at it, I see life and try to imagine why it went like that. When I see the flow of the grain, I could see the wind in it. The series of sculptures I did called "Kaze" [Wind] was inspired by the wind I saw in the tree. I also see a prayer in the tree. The tree has life. The tree is quiet but it is praying quietly. Maybe I am crazy, but I do believe a soul is there.

"When we cut trees, I feel bad because it hurts them. That's why I prefer to use driftwood and bogwood for my sculptures."

MASAMITSU TAKIGUCHI, SCULPTOR

To him, dead wood was not really dead. He demonstrated by carving a piece for us. His work never imposed on nature; rather, it helped nature express herself. One of the most common images in his pieces was a fairy-tale-like woman. Just like the Chinese folk tale in which a baby girl emerges from a bamboo tree, the faces on Takiguchi's figures spring forth from the natural grains and shapes of the weathered driftwood. He would take a large trunk of a dead tree, but would carve only a small section of it. But as he showed us, his conservative strokes returned a beauty and depth to the wood.

I live in Hokkaido because I like to be surrounded by trees. But, of course, they're cutting them down here, too. I'm shocked daily when I pass by a place and think, "Oh, they've cut that, too." They cut even small ones for paper. Science and technology are very destructive because they are based on greed. I think the traditional Ainu way is a good one.

After the wonderful food and stories told long into the night, and the relaxation of the hotspring-fed *ofuro* (bath), we left Teshikaga to meet our next interviewee.

It's not just the Japanese who can learn a more balanced relationship with the Earth from Ainu tradition. Many Ainu themselves, having been assimilated (some would say forcibly brainwashed) into Japanese society, are returning to their cultural roots. Like many First Nations people in North America, who were brought up with the negative and often self-fulfilling images in "cowboys and Indians" movies and the popular notion of "drunken Indians" on reserves or skid row but have now returned to their roots, many Ainu are finding strength and purpose in the wisdom of their elders.

On our trip to eastern Hokkaido, we stopped in Nemuro, the most eastern city of Japan, to meet such a person. Mieko Chikkup is an embroidery artist and human-rights activist whose facial features — a strong aquiline nose and big round eyes — immediately informed us she was not Japanese.

Chikkup had travelled from her home in Sapporo to accompany us in our quest to see the *shima-fukuro* (Blakiston's fish owl), one of the most important Ainu gods and guardian of the *kotan* (community). We were led into the forest by owl expert Sumio Yamamoto.

It was a beautiful evening: snow was on the ground and the sky was clear. The moon shone through the intertwining branches of the trees. After a long walk, Yamamoto signalled to us that he had seen an owl. We approached quietly and slowly. Then suddenly he gestured that there were two. These birds are close to extinction, and we were thrilled to see them. They sat erect and dignified as if proud of their bearing.

We stopped and looked through binoculars, then we noticed that Chikkup kept slowly moving closer. When she got very close to the owls, it was almost as if they were having a discussion. We were enthralled by the sight of these beautiful birds, but for Chikkup, it was a spiritual experience, another step in her discovery and connection with the gods and culture of her people.

Later Chikkup told us how she became an activist. She was born in Kushiro, a fishing port in Hokkaido with a population of about 200,000. There were Ainu in the city, but no *kotan* where they were concentrated. Many of the fishermen eked out a living growing *kombu*, a seaweed prized for flavouring soups.

A book called *Ethnography of Ainu*[3] was published, and in it there was a picture of me playing a mouth harp when I was young. There was another picture in the book showing a person's back to show how hairy Ainu were. My picture and one of Mr. Kayano were used without our permission. It was at once clear to me that the attitude in the book was one of contempt, depicting Ainu as a disappearing race. I knew Ainu culture was not officially recognized, but for me it was a real thing. I grew up with proud people. If this book was allowed to pass, I'd have to deny my whole background. I became angry. I thought of my daughter and the younger Ainu. I wondered, "What do they mean by disappearing race when I'm worried about the next generation?" But it was the attitude of the book's producers that angered me the most. They didn't even think about asking our permission, but they would never do that to Japanese people.

Since the book was produced by the top intellectuals of Hokkaido, no one felt there was a problem. A Hokkaido historian, Genzo Sarashina, was one of those involved, so I approached him. He said, "Ainu have nothing left. What is the problem?" He was the one who freely gave out pictures. He told me, "I'm a good neighbour of the Ainu," and that I was the first person to object.

The Japanese are not a litigious people by nature. There are more lawyers in the city of Toronto than there are in all of Japan. Even when suits occur, judges prefer to have both parties settle out of court, with acknowledgment that there may have been blame on both sides. Chikkup first went to see the publishers of the book, but when her concerns were shrugged off, she decided to take the extraordinary step of suing them. It would change the course of her life. "As the court case started," she told us, "I had to begin studying my own past intensively. I was over thirty when I first read my mother's journals, which I had kept for many years."

When Chikkup was a child, her father was a ne'er-do-well, an alcoholic who became violent and beat her mother. Her mother was artistic and loved song, dance, and crafts. Even though she was poor with little formal education, she wrote extensively, recording her feelings in detail in her daily journal.

From the journals, I learned that during the war, my father and my mother's brother, Tasuke Yamamoto, who later became a great Ainu leader, were soldiers. They had been told by Japanese that "Ainu, too, are children of the emperor and by going to war, you can prove it." So they joined up only to learn that in the army, Ainu continued to be discriminated against as they always had been. My uncle realized that it was all an assimilationist policy by the government and it made him resist. But my father was different. He succumbed to the prejudice and was beaten by it. He vented his rage on my mother.

Her mother died when Mieko Chikkup was eighteen, and it was only years later that the journals revealed her mother's deepest thoughts. "When I was a kid," Chikkup said, "I asked her why she wrote so much. She told me, 'This is for you so you won't forget where your people come from.'"

Even though Chikkup lived as the Japanese did and went to school with them, she learned traditional embroidery and Ainu culture from her mother. Her uncle Tasuke was a major influence on the way she saw the world. She listened to his conversations with his friends, and she recorded the Ainu stories and legends he dictated. In primary school the children taunted the Ainu, calling them "dirty," "hairy," "smelly." They used a play on words — *A inu*, meaning "Ah, a dog." All four of her brothers quit school early, and Chikkup barely made it through junior high.

When she was about seventeen, NHK did a program about the Ainu, and she was in it. That's when she met Shigeru Kayano, now the major force of the Ainu people since his election to the National Diet.

> He was in his mid-thirties. For the first time I found an Ainu man very attractive, not in a physical sense, but he was stately and lively and able to explain about Ainu to Japanese. He had pride and he showed it. He was like my uncle and gave me a sense of pride.

After the death of her mother, Chikkup visited her brother, who was working as a carver in the Ainu *kotan* of Akan. There she met a visiting Japanese student. They fell in love, got married and moved to Tokyo, where he got a job with a big company. Chikkup had one child, a daughter (nineteen years old at the time of our interview). When she was married, Chikkup thought nothing of moving to Tokyo and leaving Ainu culture behind. She was young and in love. Only much later did she realize there was an emptiness; she was lonely and missed Hokkaido. She continued the embroidery she had learned from her mother and started to teach it, as well. She stayed involved in Ainu matters in Tokyo through a group of Ainu women who would meet to sing and dance. There were fifteen or sixteen of them, all married to Japanese men; most of them later ended up divorced. Chikkup was only one of two who was still married. Since her husband had a good job and she worked part-time, she was better off financially than most and she had spare time. She therefore became a central figure in the group. If someone got sick or needed help or there was work to do, she could do it. When one member of the group heard about an act of discrimination, she'd try to do something about it.

Ethnography of Ainu, which changed Chikkup's life, was published on the one hundredth anniversary of the beginning of colonization of Hokkaido by Japanese. To the Ainu, that marked a devastating period of invasion, humiliation, and oppression, hardly a time to celebrate.

The trial in which Chikkup sued the publisher was held in Tokyo, but at one point was moved to Hokkaido. There, Ainu elders and supporters testified in support of Chikkup's suit. The defendants also had their own experts, one of whom actually said that the Ainu were gone, having been successfully assimilated into Japanese society. He also said that their habit of piercing ears was a sign of how barbaric they were. When Chikkup's lawyer asked what that said about all the young Japanese girls who were piercing their ears, the whole courtroom burst out laughing. Chikkup told us:

> My main objection was the attitude in the book. It was the way "experts" could dig up the bones of our ancestors, take them to the university and measure them, all without any respect for what we felt. I had a hard time deciding what I wanted. I was angry with experts who might say, "I'm sorry," but then kept on doing the same things. Since they put so much value on written things, I demanded a written apology. Money was secondary, so the lawyers set the amount lower.

As Chikkup became more involved, she began to meet people from different minority communities.

> I never imagined my case would become such a major case and cause célèbre for minority groups. At one point my lawyers took me to a meeting. When we got there, there were a lot of people lounging around looking sour and upset. Then I learned they were journalists there to cover the court case, and they were annoyed because I was an hour late. When I sat down, I was intrigued by all the microphones

until I realized they were all there to record me! There were all kinds of lights and cameras focused on me.

The case and her subsequent victory, a negotiated settlement that included both a sum of money and a written apology, transformed her life. It catapulted her into the public spotlight and further strained her already troubled marriage.

As a result of the case, I was invited to a woman's conference in Nairobi. It was my first trip overseas. Since at that time I had been thinking of leaving my husband, it was an important personal trip. It had become clear that my husband didn't support my Ainu interests and activities. He wanted me to limit them to embroidery and stay at home like a traditional wife. But I wanted to do more. I wanted to live as an Ainu. I was becoming very busy and no longer fulfilled the Japanese image of a wife. I wanted to be free. When I told him I was going to leave him, he was surprised and upset. He became violent and threatened me. Even after we separated, he would call and harass me. But since I had been asked by people in Hokkaido to become more involved with them, it was a good time to flee my marriage and get closer to my roots. So I moved to Sapporo.

"I work within traditional patterns, but I use richer colours and variation that corresponds to what we see. Colour is a reflection of natur

MIEKO CHIKKUP,
EMBROIDERY ARTIST AND
HUMAN-RIGHTS ACTIVIST

Since then, Chikkup's political activities have been intense, organizing and participating in conferences, travelling extensively to give lectures and writing. But her priority remains Ainu embroidery.

When I was a child, it was fun just drawing and making patterns for embroidery. Since I always liked art, at twenty-five I decided to make it my life's work and I quit oil painting. I began to study seriously, read books, went to museums with my daughter. I practised over and over for five years but then hit a block and just couldn't do any more. One day I was looking at some traditional Ainu work in a glass case when I felt the embroidery begin to talk to me. The message it gave me was, "This practice is not a mechanical thing, it came from nature." I had forgotten nature. The voice was telling me to look with more of a natural frame of mind as a free person. I realized it was true. I had forgotten nature. After that, my lines became freer, more gentle. Of course, I work within traditional patterns, but I use richer colours and variation that corresponds to what we see. Colour is a reflection of nature, although materials are very limited compared to the natural world. It became fun and I began to enjoy the depths of this practice.

To me, it's a way to tell our history, a history of racism and persecution, a history as told by women. This tradition was kept going by Ainu women. Each movement of the needle has a prayer. Arabesque and thorn patterns on the sleeves, collar, and hem are a protection against disease. By the needlework women were praying that their beloved would be protected. The power you see in Ainu embroidery comes from women's prayers.

Chikkup hadn't thought of the issues she was involved with as women's issues but rather as Ainu issues. Mostly, the minority groups she had met were through her Ainu women's group in Tokyo.

On the plane to Nairobi were some Japanese women who were into women's liberation. I couldn't get over how naïve they were. They were interested in only specific issues of concern to middle-class women, issues like the gap in salaries between men and women. They had no idea about whole groups who were suppressed, men and women. When I would say that there was no way aboriginal groups could stand at the same level as the women's liberationists, they would only get angry and retort, "It's not our fault. We didn't know about the Ainu." I gave up. I didn't have time for them.

It's not that I'm not interested in women's issues, but I resent the hollowness of words like "solidarity" without an understanding of racism and oppression. When I met Third World women, it was completely different. Although we were severely restricted by language, we could understand each other and talk about the philosophy of nature, which we have in common.

The aboriginals of other countries Chikkup met overseas invariably told her about Mother Earth. Each time she was struck by the concept's beauty and strength. It was as if she found a bridge to connect herself back to Ainu Moshir (Ainu term for Hokkaido).

We reminded her of the time we had gone out into the bush with Sumio Yamamoto to find a wild owl. She replied:

That was the first time I had seen an owl. Until then, the owl was in my uncle Tasuke Yamamoto's world, not mine. I thought I had no experience of living in a community in which the gods watched over us. But seeing that owl, I began to understand that this god is protecting our community. Old stories, *yukar*, came back to me.

Chikkup is an Ainu word meaning bird. She adopted it, while keeping her Japanese first name, Mieko.

When I changed my name, I was thinking about *kamui chikkup* [sacred bird]. I wanted to be a bird, but I didn't have the right to the sacred. Chikkup was part of the songs of lament sung by women who were forcibly moved — "If I had wings like a bird, I'd fly back to my home." Through the generations, women taught their daughters songs that say, "When you grow up and fall in love, you'll wish you are a bird to fly to the man you love." They'd sing this while embroidering.

I wanted to share that with aboriginal people overseas. So I went to the Earth Summit in Rio. They welcomed me warmly, but were shocked to meet an aboriginal person from a highly developed country like Japan. I was wearing clothes similar to everyone else, but the South American Indians were wearing body paint and very little clothes as was appropriate for the climate. They looked at me strangely and made me nervous. They seemed to question whether I was an aboriginal person. I felt there was a lot of pressure on me. But thanks to that, I felt more responsible, more determined about being an indigenous person.

We asked her how her life has changed since her return to the ways of the Ainu.

My thoughts have become deeper since the court case and my travels abroad. Learning from others is learning about myself. In Rio I heard directly from aboriginal people about their philosophy, and my uncle's thoughts began to come back. I can now remember him saying human beings are just one part of nature. Since Rio, all the elements are coming back together.

To most visitors from abroad, the Ainu and Uilta would appear to be part of a uniform people, the Japanese. To us (Keibo and David), some of the Ainu do appear physically distinct, but what quickly reveals the vast differences between Ainu and the dominant Yamato people is their conversation. After fourteen hundred years of oppression and racism, the Ainu people and culture still exist, and now there is a growing pride in being Ainu among the young people. To a dominant Japanese society that is hell-bent on consumption and material comfort, the Ainu represent an opportunity to see themselves through very different lenses and perhaps to realize that there are other values related to our connection with the Earth.

CHAPTER 6

SHARED BLOOD,
DIFFERENT FUTURES

"I want a society in which we live

together but one in

which we respect differences."

AKEHIKO ASAI

WE'VE all heard the saying "Blood is thicker than water," a folkloric recognition that genetic bonds matter. And certainly in Japan, birth or longtime residence in the country, fluency in the language, or acceptance of the culture is not sufficient to ensure citizenship, as Koreans born in Japan can attest. Genetic origin would appear to be the defining factor. If racial similarity is the precondition for full Japanesehood, that might explain the difficulties encountered by Koreans, Chinese, and children of Japanese mothers and American soldiers.

But that is contradicted by generations of genetically pure Japanese born in other countries who encounter hostility or prejudice in Japan. These Nikkei (Japanese born in other countries) often have only a limited level of speaking ability in Japanese, and this immense barrier to communication precludes their acceptance by Japanese society. But it's more than just linguistic and cultural.

What qualifies a person as Japanese is not just heredity but cultural purity. As an island nation, Japan has been protected from ready invasion, although now, with a global economy, even Japan cannot keep out foreign ideas, money, products, and people. But Japan has a long tradition of concern about "contamination" or "pollution" by foreign ideas and activity. The Japanese company man who is posted abroad with his family for several years finds upon returning to Japan that his children are at a disadvantage compared to other youngsters. They are seen as having been contaminated by their foreign ideas, education, experience, and friends.

We travelled to Kawasaki, an industrial city south of Tokyo, to meet Luis Kaneshiro and Ayako Noborikawa, both Japanese-Peruvian Nikkei. As we came through the automatic wicket, we entered a huge concourse filled with people rushing about. Kawasaki is known as the city of the working class and has a high concentration of foreign workers. Kaneshiro and Noborikawa were waiting for us in the crowded concourse. Without exchanging information about our physical features and clothing, we wouldn't have been able to find each other. Kaneshiro is a stocky man with thick glasses and a serious demeanour. Noborikawa seemed nervous and shy.

They took us to a South American restaurant called Arco Iris (rainbow), a hangout for Brazilian, Peruvian, and Argentinean Japanese "returnees" — those who have come back to the land of their ancestors. On the walls were pictures from Latin America; the music was South American as was the video station on the TV. The people who filled the restaurant were physically Japanese in appearance, and yet we instantly knew they were somehow different. It took us a minute to realize that the difference lay in their body language. They spoke loudly and with animation accompanied by a lot of laughter and exaggerated gestures. They were Latin Americans!

We sat down and chatted with the Nikkei. Initially we encountered some language difficulties since Kaneshiro spoke only Japanese and Spanish, while Noborikawa spoke English, Japanese, and Spanish. But with our mix of languages, everybody was soon interpreting for one another. Eventually Kaneshiro and Noborikawa relaxed, discarding their shy and serious facades.

Kaneshiro's grandparents had emigrated from Okinawa to Peru before the Second World War. The prewar Japanese government, with its problems of overpopulation and poverty in farming communities, had encouraged farmers, especially those who were not in a position to inherit a family farm, to emigrate. As a result, Brazil has more than one million Japanese. Peru has 80,000 Japanese families, including that of the president of the country who was a *nisei* (the name given to the first generation *born* in the new country). One demographic characteristic of the Japanese-Peruvians was that about half of them are Okinawan descendants.

Kaneshiro told us there were at least 30,000 returnees, and the rate of migration had picked up since 1990. They were returning because the wages were better in Japan and because of terrorism and other unstable social and economic factors in their country. But recently, with the recession in Japan, fewer jobs, and less overtime, a lot of those who came just to make money were returning to South America.

Kaneshiro told us that he was staying in Japan because he'd become accustomed to it here. "After five years, I went back to Peru, but I couldn't adjust there, so I came back again. But I still encounter lots of discrimination here."

Noborikawa, also a migrant worker, told us of her experiences. "We Japanese-Peruvians had an image of Japanese as kind and nice. We come here and are shocked. Japanese are cold. After coming here I started to hate to be Japanese. I cried when we left Peru."

Kaneshiro was president of the Peru Nikkei Association, established in 1987.

> Our people are moving all the time. It's theoretically possible to become a Japanese citizen, but most immigrants are not interested because they will one day return to South America. I'm not so sure

what I'll do myself. I've been here fifteen years and renew my visa every three years, which I don't find that inconvenient.

Nikkei in any country are identified by the number of generations they are removed from Japan. Thus, the generation that emigrates is called *issei*, the first. Their children, born in the new country, are *nisei*, the second. *Sansei*, *yonsei*, and *gosei* are the third, fourth, and fifth. "Japanese policy makes it easier for *nisei* to get in than *sansei* or interracial people," Kaneshiro explained. "*Yonsei* may not get in at all. The Japanese rationale is that it's for *their* benefit."

The rationale for the Japanese immigration policy smacks of the same justification the U.S. and Canada used for incarcerating people of Japanese descent during the Second World War. According to that reasoning, the governments couldn't guarantee the safety of Japanese, so incarceration was for *their* protection. Japanese immigration policy makes more sense if we interpret it as a concern over contamination, which becomes greater with each generation away from Japan.

"I was shocked at first when I came here," Noborikawa said, "but I can't change them, so I accept it. I find it hard to make friends with Japanese because they always treat me like a *gaijin* [foreigner]."

From her attitude and way of speaking we could see why she had trouble with everyday Japanese people. She was vivacious and laughed out loud without covering her mouth as so many Japanese women do. She gestured extravagantly and talked frankly and fast.

"What's in it for me to become a citizen?" Kaneshiro responded. "What will change? Because I work with Japanese, I feel like I'm one, but then I realize that I'm not, I'm a Peruvian."

Noborikawa leapt in again.

Most Japanese in Peru go to Japanese schools. Those who do go to Peruvian schools come out at the top. Peruvians say it is because we are Japanese, but we're just sons and daughters of immigrants. They say there's a *community* of Japanese in Peru, but it's not true, it's just a group of immigrants and their children. In Japan my co-workers tell me, "You are not Japanese. You are an immigrant."

In both countries, their differences set them apart, isolate them.

Sitting in the Arco Iris, eating South American food, talking to Kaneshiro, Noborikawa, and their friends, we found ourselves wondering what creates a sense of identity. As we looked around the restaurant, we couldn't help being puzzled. Who were these people? But then we looked at each other and wondered who *we* were.

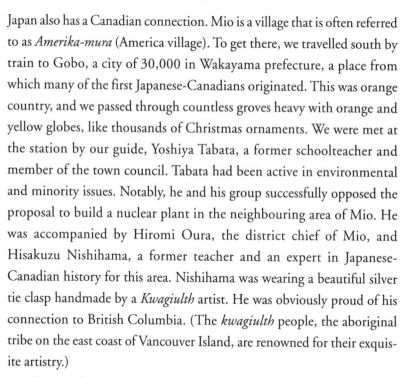

Japan also has a Canadian connection. Mio is a village that is often referred to as *Amerika-mura* (America village). To get there, we travelled south by train to Gobo, a city of 30,000 in Wakayama prefecture, a place from which many of the first Japanese-Canadians originated. This was orange country, and we passed through countless groves heavy with orange and yellow globes, like thousands of Christmas ornaments. We were met at the station by our guide, Yoshiya Tabata, a former schoolteacher and member of the town council. Tabata had been active in environmental and minority issues. Notably, he and his group successfully opposed the proposal to build a nuclear plant in the neighbouring area of Mio. He was accompanied by Hiromi Oura, the district chief of Mio, and Hisakuzu Nishihama, a former teacher and an expert in Japanese-Canadian history for this area. Nishihama was wearing a beautiful silver tie clasp handmade by a *Kwagiulth* artist. He was obviously proud of his connection to British Columbia. (The *kwagiulth* people, the aboriginal tribe on the east coast of Vancouver Island, are renowned for their exquisite artistry.)

From Gobo we drove along the coastline to Mio. It had a population of nine hundred, which for years had remained stable. Any growth in the number of people was absorbed by emigration to North America, specifically to Canada.

The inn Tabata arranged for us to stay in was located on the top of a hill at the end of a point called Hinomisaki. From there we had a panoramic view of the Pacific Ocean; we could almost feel the roundness of the Earth. Looking down, we could also see the entire bay, with the tiny village of Mio on its shore, surrounded by mountains. Mio's beauty was breathtaking. Little land was available for the villagers to cultivate, and there was no room for the village population to grow. Farther along the coast we could see the city of Gobo, covered by a thin cloud of smog and, even farther, the ominous structure of a thermoelectric power plant.

It was a beautiful sunny day, and we were taken to a wall along the beach with a plaque to Gihe, a man who went to Canada from this village in 1888. He was the pioneer — one of the first Japanese to set foot on Canada — and he encouraged other fishermen from Mio to go there to fish for salmon. Many went and settled in Steveston, a fishing town at the mouth of the Fraser River just south of Vancouver. This was the beginning of the history of Japanese in Canada.

Steveston blossomed as the flow of Japanese increased. Soon Japanese boats were a vital part of the British Columbia fishing fleet. The immigrants' skills, as well as their strange customs and language, aroused envy and considerable resentment. It was possible for Japanese to live in Steveston without learning to speak English, because there were Canadian-born children who spoke the language, as well as bilingual entrepreneurs who mediated between Japanese and Canadians. The Japanese were a major presence in Steveston, but after Pearl Harbor and the evacuation that took place in 1942, there were blocks of empty houses. Many people returned to Mio after the end of the war.

Not many Japanese or Canadians paid attention to this tiny village in Japan until the Japanese-Canadian redress settlement in 1988. Following the formal settlement, the Canadian government sent a team to Japan to make sure all those who were eligible for the monetary compensation applied. The team came to Mio. Until then, the majority of the villagers didn't know anything about the redress issue either. It came as a surprise, and for those who were eligible, it turned out to be a pleasant one. And it became an opportunity for them to reflect on those days during the war.

From the beach we were guided to the Hozen-ji, a recently renovated Buddhist temple. At the entrance, small wooden plaques listed the donors, many of whom were from Vancouver and Toronto, revealing the strong ties that remained between the two communities separated by the ocean. We then visited a lovely shrine called Ryuo Jinja on the point of land from Mio. As at the temple, many Canadian donors were listed here. Before citizens of Mio left for Canada, they came here to pray for a safe trip. When they returned, they came here to give thanks.

As we walked through the town, we saw the Canadian influence everywhere. The roofs were made of familiar Japanese tile, but many of the houses were painted on the outside, something Japanese do not do. That unusual combination made the homes look charming and distinctive. Japanese signs were often accompanied by English words such as Post or Fire Hydrant. We also saw Canadian-style clapboard construction and, inside the houses, beds and sofas, which are rare in remote Japanese fishing villages.

After the tour, Tabata, our guide, arranged for us to meet with and listen to people's stories at our inn. Hisakuzu Nishihama, the former teacher and local historian, was one of the first to speak. His older brothers were born in Canada, and he and his other brothers and sisters had been born in Japan. For many years the family was split between Canada and Japan. He remembers when his older brother arrived, along with the four hundred Japanese-Canadians after the war.

> There was no work, there was little to buy. Of course, everyone had a hard time. It was a time of tremendous inflation, and money couldn't be taken out of savings because of regulations. So to buy rice, we had to sell things like kimonos. But soon we began to get presents from Canada, which we sold for money. In one case, saccharine came in and was sold for enough money to build a house.
>
> The several years that my older brother from Canada spent with us were dark. He was depressed and morose; first of all, he was bitter about what Canada did to him and the fact that he had to lose

everything that he had built before the war. During the war, he was separated from his wife and family, who were stuck in Japan. He was arrested as one of the pro-Japan elements who resisted the Canadian authorities by refusing to obey the government order to move to the areas where Japanese were gathered prior to evacuation. So he was interned as a resister at Angler POW camp in Ontario. And what he found when he came back to Mio was starvation and poverty. I can't blame him for having been so bitter. In five or six years, we found that most of the returnees were going back to Canada.

Yoshiya Tabata, our guide, was born in Steveston, British Columbia, in 1923. Three brothers were also born there, and they were all sent to Japan in 1929. When Yoshiya returned to Steveston many years after the war, he didn't recognize the place.

It was partly perception — he'd been only a small child when he left — but Steveston had indeed changed radically from the collection of huts and ramshackle homes to a typical modern suburb. He remembered the canneries and the row upon row of Japanese houses, but now there were shops and large homes.

The uprooting and incarceration of Japanese–North Americans had been justified on the basis of the threat they represented. In Canada, many *nisei* had been registered by their parents as Japanese nationals, even though the children had never been to Japan. This is not unusual. Often English or American parents will register their Canadian-born children in England or the United States, respectively. But in a time of war this practice became suspect. There were many Japanese social, cultural, and martial-arts organizations to which people belonged, but that only enhanced the perceived differences and isolation of the Japanese community, rendering them vulnerable to suspicion and rumour.

Ironically, Tabata told us, in Mio the very same suspicions were brought against the Japanese who had spent time or been born in Canada! There was a rumour that because Mio was an *Amerika-mura*, there were spies there; people reported that lights were seen signalling the enemy offshore. In Canada similar claims were made against Japanese-Canadians. Exhaustive studies have uncovered no case of Nikkei espionage or treachery on behalf of Japan. Nevertheless, the rumours persist.

As we bade farewell to our newfound friends and settled on the train back to Tokyo, we couldn't help but muse on this little enclave of connection with North America. It took great courage (and desperation) to venture to such a faraway and alien place as Canada, where anti-Asian bigotry has been a constant. As relatives and friends were persuaded to seek their fortunes in Canada, children born in Canada but living in Japan and children born in Canada but moved to Japan tied Mio inextricably to Steveston. The Second World War exposed the racism in both countries, with Canadians rounding up all people of Japanese origin, immigrant and Canadian-born, as potential enemies, and Japanese in Japan suspecting all Japanese who had worked in Canada of having been contaminated. Happily, the ex-Mio inhabitants who were still in Canada at war's end were able to help their war-ravaged relatives with boxes of invaluable gifts.

It's one thing to be suspicious of people who may have been polluted by experiences outside Japan, but quite another to suspect those who have never left. The irrationality and arbitrariness of Japanese bigotry was revealed when we examined the treatment of a group of people who have always resided in the country and remain genetically, culturally, and linguistically Japanese. Today they are referred to as *burakumin* (which means, literally, people of the hamlet) and their often segregated community as *buraku* (hamlet).

Like many cultures, Japanese society has always had an abhorrence of certain associations with death. Death is the ultimate source of pollution. Those who disposed of dead people and animals were regarded as doing unclean or dirty work. Ever since it was imported to Japan in the sixth century, Buddhism reinforced the prejudice against those who dealt with dead animals, because of its condemnation of butchering and the eating of meat. The prejudice even extended to people like tanners and leather workers who dealt with things derived from dead animals. These people were called *eta* (heavily polluted) or *hinin* (nonhuman). Makers of military equipment, who used leather in their work, cobblers, sweepers, certain entertainers, beggars, vagrants, and those afflicted with diseases like leprosy also came to be classed as *eta* or *hinin*. Originally a person could work his or her way out of this level, but in the early seventeenth century, Tokugawa rulers froze the social order. By that arbitrary edict, the group of Japanese distinguished by their social status was declared *untouchable*. From that point on, the status of the *burakumin* was fixed. It was soon to become a birthright.

The original of the *buraku* can be found before the Tokugawa feudal era (1603–1867) that defined the class system. Even after the feudal system was abolished, discrimination against the *burakumin* persisted. Thus, some have argued that the nature of the *buraku* is closely linked to the continuation of the emperor system.

Restrictions were placed on where *burakumin* could live, the quality of their housing, their mobility in and out of their villages, their clothing, hairstyles, and even their footwear. They were prohibited from buying land, were not allowed to pawn things or enter peasant homes, and were ordered to walk on the edge of the street. A curfew was also set that prohibited them from entering the city after eight at night. They were thought of as dirty, vulgar, smelly, untrustworthy, dangerous, treacherous, subhuman creatures.

During the Meiji Period, *taiko* drum-making remained an important *burakumin* activity, but as westernization changed people's lifestyles, many found new work as shoemakers. They worked in slaughterhouses and with leather. They took menial jobs repairing and shining shoes.

In 1871 legal discrimination against the *burakumin* was stopped by a government decree. For decades, however, government, citizens, and authorities continued to discriminate and insist that the *burakumin* were a lower class of people. Some *burakumin* tried to pass themselves off as everyday Japanese as they do not have any distinctive racial features. But even today, because of the law that one has to be registered in the place of his or her birth, the identity of *burakumin* is revealed by their address.

On March 3, 1922, the founding convention of the National Levellers Association met and drafted a declaration:

Fellow *burakumin* throughout the country, unite!
Brothers and sisters who have for a long time been persecuted:
    In the past half century, various reform efforts undertaken on our behalf by many people have not yielded any appreciable results. This failure should be regarded as punishment for permitting others as well as ourselves to debase our human dignity.

    Previous movements, though seemingly motivated by compassion and humanity, have actually ruined many of our brothers and sisters.

    Thus, it is now imperative for us to initiate within ourselves a collective movement by which we shall liberate ourselves through our respect for humanity.

    Brothers and sisters, our ancestors were pursuers of freedom and equality and executors of these principles.

    They were the victims of contemptible caste policies, and courageous martyrs of their occupations.

    In recompense for skinning animals, they were skinned of the respect due humans.

    For tearing out the hearts of animals, their human hearts were torn apart and despicable ridicule was spat upon them.

    Yet all through these cursed nights of nightmares, human dignity ran deep in their blood.

    Indeed, we, who were born of this blood, are now living in an era when humans are willing to take over the gods.

    The time has come for the oppressed to throw off their stigma. The time has come for the martyrs to receive the blessing for their crown of thorns.

    The time has come when we can take pride in being *eta*. We must never shame our ancestors nor profane humanity by demeaning words or cowardly deeds.

    We know very well how cold the coldness of human society can be, and how warm it is when one cares for another.

We therefore from the bottom of our heart revere and pursue the warmth and light of human life.

Thus born is the Levellers Association.

Let there be warmth in society, let there be light in humanity.

Today the city of Osaka has ten *buraku* districts with a total of perhaps 500,000 people. The biggest is Naniwa district — also the biggest in Japan — with about 200,000 *burakumin*. There are fifty-two *buraku* areas in all of Osaka prefecture. The government says there are about 4,600 communities in Japan and just over one million *burakumin*. However, the Buraku Liberation League (BLL) suggests there are more than 1,000 communities that aren't listed. According to the government, before the Second World War there were 5,300 communities and two million *burakumin*. The BLL thinks there must be at least three million *burakumin* living in Japan today.

We visited a hall in Osaka where a *taiko* drum group, made up exclusively of young *burakumin*, were about to start their weekly rehearsal. The small gymnasium was filled with *taiko* drums of all sizes. The smallest was about the size of a snare drum, the largest about the size of a compact car. The Japanese drum group Kodo have made this type of drum well known in the West. As the pounding rhythm began, we noted the intense concentration etched on the faces of the young drummers, yet at the same time their performance had almost a serene quality. Their prime motivation didn't seem to be to entertain their audience but to purge themselves of something we may never understand. One particularly striking teenage girl had an expression on her face like a Buddhist statue. While her small hands firmly grasped the large drumsticks and pounded the stretched skins, her features remained impassive, even meditative. The leader had a scarf wrapped around his head, and with expressions and gestures, he egged on and inspired the other players. They drummed as if they were waiting for something to well up from deep inside their souls. As the rhythm built, getting louder and faster but always remaining controlled, the sounds spoke of struggle against social obstacles and prejudice. The sound cried out as a victorious rhythm against their oppressors. We felt the drums and the rhythms reverberating throughout our bodies, and at the end of the performance we were left breathless.

Kiyoji Ota, relaxed in blue jeans and a T-shirt, joined us. The drum group's leader, Akehiko Asai, wearing a suit and smoking a cigarette, leaned against a back wall during the performance, tapping his foot to the rhythms and beaming with pride at his *burakumin taiko* drum group. A few years ago the mere idea of putting a group like this together was so audacious that most people thought Asai had taken leave of his senses, and few believed he could pull it off. Asai told us that the name of the group is Ikari (Anger). "When we get invited to perform as a *taiko* drum group," he said, "there's interest that we're *burakumin* as well."

After the performance, Asai and Ota took us to a *taiko* drum shop where these beautiful instruments are made. As we walked into the small store, we noticed the smell of animal skins and glue, and recalled the slur once widespread among Japanese: the *burakumin* "stink like animals." There were drums of all shapes and sizes, and a craftsman in the back was stretching a large cow hide. He explained to us that if the skin was in perfect condition, with no stains or scars, he could make a large drum out of it. But that was very rare. As he pointed out a defect in the hide, he chuckled and said it looked as if he'd be making a smaller drum with this particular skin.

"Taiko-making is the most important industry of our community and taiko makers are the backbone, yet they lived as if they were in hiding."

(Photo: Ikari [anger], a Taiko drum group, Osaka)

The manager of the store told us that a hundred percent of Japanese traditional drums were made in *buraku* communities. This community of Naniwa was known historically as one of the major centres of *taiko* production. As we snapped pictures, Asai pointed out that until recently *taiko* makers were made to feel inferior and would have felt uncomfortable having their pictures taken.

"*Taiko*-making," he said, "is the most important industry of our community and *taiko* makers are the backbone, yet they lived as if they were in hiding." That is what his drum group is trying to correct.

A drum is a powerful instrument in many societies. North American aboriginals refer to the drum's rhythms as the heartbeat of the people. The *taiko* drum is a sacred instrument, which is played as an offering in the Shinto festivals. One of the craftsmen told us the drums are not so much musical instruments as a battle between the player and the drum. The drum is played not so much for the ear as to be felt by the body. We wondered at the cruelty of the rulers who dictated that the *burakumin*, who were the sole producers of *taiko*, were discouraged from playing it. In certain districts, there were even laws forbidding it. Asai explained:

> About seven years ago, a *taiko* drum group from Yomitan village in Okinawa came here to Osaka to buy drums. I was guiding them around. They said, "This is a town of *taiko*, so there must be some great drummers. Please introduce them to us." But I had to tell him there were none. That started me wondering why. Then I remembered a friend whose dad was a maker of the *shamisen*, a traditional three-stringed instrument. A television program had been made on the *shamisen*. The program showed the process of making and playing the instrument, but the part his dad played at the very beginning of the instrument's life was left out! That's when I realized that *burakumin* were being purposely excluded. This was discrimination.

So he decided, in 1985 to start a *taiko* drum group, reasoning that if they could achieve some kind of fame, it would also bring recognition to the drum-makers and improve their social and economic conditions. When asked where they were from, they would be able to answer proudly that their home is the centre for making *taiko* drums and that it was a *burakumin* activity.

> People thought I was nuts. But now we're getting better-known and getting more support. One of our best players has just made a TV commercial. Workers from a drum factory came and said, "We make

the drums, but we never knew how they were played. We were ashamed of what we did. But we saw it on TV. Now our kids ask us, 'Dad, did you make that?' And I say yes, and I'm proud."

Asai's group learned to play the drums by looking at videos of the top players. They also visited the drummers from Yomitan village, who have been helping them out.

Now we're improvising our own routines. The group you saw is aged sixteen to twenty-six. There's also a group of middle-aged women and a group in grades three to nine. All kinds of people are now playing. We've got a real spirit. We are producers of drums. How can we be inferior? I think we're up to a semipro level.

As we left the *taiko* shop, Asai looked around.

You can't eliminate history. I want a society in which we live together but one in which we respect differences. It's important that my children acknowledge they are *burakumin*. It's no good if you have to hide your background and who you are.

Asai and Ota offered to take us for something to eat. We walked to the Ashiwarabashi station, which is surrounded by little crowded streets, jammed with small stores and restaurants. Ota and Asai chuckled as they anticipated the meal we were about to have, and we wondered what we'd got ourselves into. From the outside the restaurant looked tiny, but once inside we could see it had a number of rooms and was actually much bigger than it appeared. We were guided into a back room and seated ourselves on *tatami* mats. Ota explained that they'd brought us to this place to eat *burakumin* food, which most Japanese have never tried. Ota and Asai joked that to them the food is so good they hope the rest of Japanese society never finds out about it.

Asai described his childhood. His expressions were often comical, even when talking about tragedy.

My parents never told me I was *burakumin*. I was in grade seven and we were learning about *burakumin* in class. As I heard how discriminated against they were, I thought, "Those poor guys." A teacher went on to say there were even *burakumin* people in this school, and I wondered, "Who are they?" Then the teacher described the part of town where they lived and I realized, "That's where *I* live! I went home crying and bawled out my mother, "Why did you give birth to me?" My mother just hung her head and didn't say anything. My first reaction was to run away.

We asked Asai how he overcame his initial distress at discovering he was *burakumin*.

A classmate was telling us about a well-known singer. He told me that the singer's family owned a butcher shop and whenever he had to pass it, he ran by as fast as he could. I asked him why and the boy held up four fingers, signalling *yotsu*, the four legs of an animal, and whispered, "*Eta*." I slugged the boy. When he cried, "Why did you hit me?" I pointed to my chest and said, "I'm one too!"

Discrimination in Japan was in law. During the Edo Period [1603–1867], we weren't allowed to intermarry. So it is only within the last hundred and some years that it hasn't been illegal to intermarry. We also lived in ghettos. We have a system of law that requires registration in the villages of our origin (*honseki*). Only in the last thirty years have borough offices stopped using special seals to stamp our records. One of my friends tried to change his *honseki*. But he was found out by detectives who do a search when you apply to get married. My wife is non*burakumin*, but she became classed as *burakumin* because she married me and moved into my *honseki*.

Ota explained the basis for the prejudice:

Discrimination against the *burakumin* was based on the sense of pollution, because anything to do with animals was considered polluted. Footwear is close to the earth, so those who made them were considered dirty. *Burakumin* were cleaners of temples and streets. Pollution had to be cleansed by the polluted. After executions,

SHARED BLOOD, DIFFERENT FUTURES

burakumin would take the body away. All polluted occupations were done by *eta* who were born to the class.

The *burakumin* took part in festivals, but they were excluded from the important parts because they were considered polluted. So the sacred object was made exclusively by such polluted people, but the drum could only be played by unpolluted people! At the time of a festival, a *burakumin* person might actually lead the parade, but his role was to cleanse the ground in front of the parade. Once the parade reached its destination, then the *burakumin* had to eat and drink in a segregated part of the grounds.

It is not hard to imagine that many *burakumin* attempted to escape their poverty and oppression during the wave of emigration from Japan to the Americas in the late 1800s and early 1900s. Often they were unable to escape the stigma of being *buraku* because their fellow Japanese immigrants carried the bigotry with them to their new countries.

Ota told us about a Brazilian-Japanese who emigrated to Japan as a teacher. He began to work in the *buraku* and ten years later discovered that he himself was a *burakumin*. By emigrating to Brazil, his parents had successfully hidden his *burakumin* origins from him.

The food began to arrive — definitely not your normal Japanese food! There was a jellied tendon mix that looked like headcheese. We also had smoked horse meat, fried intestine with noodles, and a Korean-influenced spicy cabbage mix. *Burakumin* dealt with butchering animals but could rarely afford the meat. So they ate the leftovers (*horumon*: a pun on a Kansai dialect meaning "discarded things" and hormone, suggesting something nutritious). Asai explained that for centuries the *burakumin* were called all kinds of names because they ate foods the rest of society considered inedible. "But," he added, laughing delightedly, "they have no idea what they're missing, and I won't tell them about this either."

Ota nodded his head in agreement. The situation reminded us of how proud African-Americans often are of their delicious chitlins, wings, oxtails: their soul food.

Asai also told us a funny story about his youth. At school *burakumin* children were so afraid their Japanese classmates would look in their lunch boxes and see *burakumin* food that they would hide their food while they were eating. Then one day Asai looked around and saw that the Korean kids in his class were hiding their food too. From that point on Asai would go up to the Koreans, look at what they were eating, and ask if they wanted to trade. Ota told us that because *burakumin* and Koreans were both discriminated against and often lived in the same disadvantaged areas, they now share a lot of different foods and other cultural characteristics.

> But today we all love our mother's *horumon* dishes and every so often I have to eat my mother's cooking. Whenever I eat this food I feel good, and I think it's because I'm involved in the liberation movement.

Although Ota is not *burakumin*, he works full-time with the Buraku Liberation League. "My wife is from a *buraku*. I've been working here with the BLL since 1974. I was born in a tiny village with forty families. I never knew anything about *burakumin*."

After he graduated from university in 1971, he moved to the United States, where he first experienced bigotry. During the two years he worked there, illegally, his boss would tell him, "Japanese are intelligent. But whites are the best and you are second." Ota's boss warned him not to befriend blacks, then threatened if he did hang around with them, he would have to tell the authorities he was working illegally. Ota later moved to New York, where he found it more comfortable to hang around with Koreans and Chinese, who educated him about prejudice in America.

> When I returned to Japan, I ran into a professor of mine and told him about my experiences with prejudice. He told me about the *burakumin*. I then learned about the Edo Period and the class system and encountered the words *eta* and *hinin*. So I went to the office of

the Buraku Liberation League to learn more about *burakumin*. It was my shame that I didn't know. They talked to me about it and invited me to join. That's when I began to visit *buraku* communities and found that their experiences were very similar to mine in the United States.

Ota fell in love with a woman who was also working at the BLL. When he took her home to meet his parents, his father accepted her. "My mother didn't say anything, but at one point, she said, 'You're going to marry an *eta*.'"

Once they decided to get married, Ota went to see her family, but her father objected to the union. He continued to object for two years because he was concerned about discrimination and thought the marriage wouldn't work. When they were finally married, Ota's mother and father, his brother and his brother's wife were the only people from his family who attended the wedding. In his village, everyone was like family. People were very nervous meeting his wife, but when he spoke out about being married to a *burakumin* woman, they simply nodded and said nothing. Ota and his wife have now been married for fifteen years. He told us:

> We live in the *buraku* area, which is right next to a non-*buraku* area. There has never been a marriage of a *burakumin* with a non*burakumin* from the adjacent area even though they attended the same schools. When my children were born, my parents wanted me to register them in the village where I was born so they wouldn't have to have a *buraku honseki*. A few years ago we found out that there was a book put out by a company that listed all the *buraku* areas and typical *burakumin* names, as well as the handicapped and Koreans. The book was sold as a reference for companies. So you can see what having a *buraku honseki* still means.

Naniwa, the biggest *buraku* in Japan, has a long history. During the Edo Period, Naniwa was a segregated village called Watanabe Mura with its own chief. The villagers made *taiko* drums and sandals, and had no rights to move out or to intermarry. They were classed as *eta*. Words like *do eta*, *eta*, and *yotsu* have acquired derogatory connotations as offensive as "nigger." Often these very poor people were made to change locations. Ota told us:

> Since the sixteenth century, this *burakumin* community was forced to move six times. Originally they were made to live near the river, which flooded periodically. But as the river became important for commerce and transportation, *burakumin* were moved away again.

This story of forced upheaval and movement is reminiscent of the way aboriginal people have been treated in North America. When arrangements were made to provide land for different tribal groups, the reserves were usually in the areas deemed to have the least value for the white settlers. But as the years passed, reserve lands, once thought to be worthless, were often found to have things of great value — water, minerals, oil and gas, trees. Many times aboriginal people, already restricted to tiny areas in comparison to their past territory, have been forced to move repeatedly to make way for dams or other development projects.

We asked Ota about the *burakumin* sense of community and culture.

> *Burakumin* are not an ethnic culture. But the sense of community and cooperation are very strong. When I started working here, people said, "We have no culture to be proud of." My reaction was there must be a culture. Every group of human beings who share something and live together must have what could be called a culture. And a group suffering from discrimination must have its own culture based on their experience. This drumming comes out of what is part of the *burakumin* experience and is part of its culture.

The *burakumin* have a long way to go to reach educational and professional parity with other Japanese. Neither Asai nor Ota know of any *burakumin* lawyers, and only one *burakumin* doctor and another about to graduate. The government does have grants for *burakumin* students, but their proportion in universities is less than half what their numbers should produce. *Burakumin* performance in school is much lower than that of other Japanese students. It is these kinds of performance statistics that have fuelled the race-IQ controversy in the United States. As geneticists well know, as long as there is discrimination based merely on skin colour, it can never be demonstrated scientifically that the difference in performance between blacks and whites reflects genetic differences. In the case of *burakumin*, who are genetically Japanese, the performance deficits clearly reflect the terrible price of bigotry.

Asai told us that a good education for children is now a major priority for the members of the *burakumin* community. They raised the money to build a primary school by asking people to voluntarily tithe one-eightieth of their income for three years. To pay for the school's operation, people gathered, packaged, and sold human excrement as fertilizer.

We asked whether the goal was to remove all discrimination and barriers so that the *burakumin* would disappear through assimilation. Asai answered that while it was hard to say, he would like to retain the community's values. Ota replied:

> The *taiko* movement is very important. *Taiko* drum-makers are easy to identify because one hundred percent of *taiko* are made in the buraku shops. Being a *taiko*-maker carries a stigma. We want to revise the negative image and say, "Listen to the beautiful sound. Who produced this?" It's the same with bamboo craft, baseball gloves, spikes. Of course, it's a way to make a living, but it's not just a job. We are contributing. We are playing an important role. One day we'd like to reach a point where we can say, "I'm *burakumin*," and other people will look at us with respect.

We suggested another contribution *burakumin* could make. As victims of discrimination, they had an opportunity to humanize the rest of the Japanese by reminding them of the pain and irrationality of bigotry. How have *burakumin* responded to the prejudice?

"I've lived with the *burakumin* because it's comfortable," Ota answered. "The warmth that has resulted from prejudice we experienced, that is nice."

And Asai added, "We have been discriminated against. That doesn't give us the right to discriminate against others."

As the meal ended, Asai and Ota asked us how we enjoyed our first *burakumin* dining experience. We had to agree that we might have to visit Asai again to get some of his mother's home cooking.

The Fukuoka prefecture, the northern part of the island of Kyushu, is one of the oldest settled areas of Japan. In feudal times, the region had strong feudal lords who enjoyed an unusual amount of autonomy and frequently traded with Asia. It lost much of its importance as an economic and cultural crossroads when the centralized Meiji Japan (1868–1912) started to look towards Europe, neglecting Asia. (*Datsua-nyuo* — forget Asia, enter Europe.) With westernization and modernization, the area thrived because of its rich coal deposits that fuelled industry. It is said that Fukuoka city was one of the targets originally considered for the second atomic bomb, but it was dropped on Nagasaki because of the weather. The city was, however, extensively bombed during the war and in the past fifty years has been rebuilt. It's now a modern city of 1.2 million people.

After twenty minutes by train from Fukuoka city, we arrived in Tsukushino city, where our guide, Megumi Matsumoto, was waiting for us. Matsumoto had a boyish haircut and big bright eyes. From the first moment of our meeting she seemed free of the stifling Japanese formalities. Instead, she was open and down-to-earth, her speech was direct and to the point. Matsumoto split her time between living in a *buraku* community in Fukuoka and in Tokyo with her family.

She first took us to Kyomachi, a *buraku* community of about 130 households. Unlike many other *buraku* communities, it didn't have a specific *buraku* industry to call its own. But as in Naniwa, *taiko* drum groups were started among elementary schoolchildren; the names of the groups were Warmth, Light, and Fire. One important program that characterized this community was its literacy project. Matsumoto took us to the Kyomachi Community Centre to meet two women who were the main organizers of a program to teach adult *burakumin* to read and write.

"The sunset is beautiful since I learned to write." These are the words of a *burakumin* woman in Kochi prefecture. She learned to write in a special literacy class as she approached her seventieth year. In the *buraku* communities there were many like her, people deprived of opportunities to go to school because of discrimination and poverty.

The literacy movement became a symbol of the struggle of the *buraku* community. Matsumoto introduced us to seventy-nine-year-old Takeyo Abe, who is known widely in the community as one of the founders of the literacy movement, and forty-four-year-old Takako Nakajima, a leader representing a younger generation. Although Abe was the president of the community centre and a leader in the community, she had an open, warm, and humble attitude. Nakajima at first seemed shy, but when she spoke she betrayed the passion behind her convictions. It was the beginning of an enjoyable stay in which we experienced, with warmth and a sense of nostalgia, a feeling we tend to forget — community.

The two women led us into a large empty auditorium at the edge of which were a couch and some seats. When we had made ourselves comfortable, Abe began to tell us about her life:

> I was born in a *buraku* but I didn't know that was why I was discriminated against. I thought it was because we were poor. At school they called me *eta hinin*, but I didn't know what it meant. Parents taught their children to say such things about the *burakumin*, but in our families we weren't told because they wanted to protect us and spare us the pain of knowing who we were.
>
> I went to school, but I was bullied and called names. I left school in grade two and stayed home but hated it because we were so poor. I was the eldest of six, so I did the housework and took care of the other

kids until I was fourteen. I never learned to read or write. My father was drunk every day. He was a peasant who also worked as a shoe shiner. My mother had a hard time. She made slippers and sold junk, but my father would take the extra money she earned and spend it.

Abe took a job as a maid for a banker when she was fourteen. Then her grandfather, who had moved to China, invited her to join him there. He sent her the money for passage and asked a friend on the ship to watch out for her because she couldn't read. In Tsingtao, a large port city on the east coast of China, there was a large Japanese population. She moved in with her grandmother, who made and sold *manju* (cakes filled with sweet bean paste), and her grandfather, a masseur. Abe didn't have to go to school or work too hard, so she had a great time, but she worried so much about her mother she eventually returned to Japan.

She went back to Tsingtao in 1931, after the Manchurian Incident in which mid-level Japanese officers deliberately blew up a section of tracks belonging to the South Manchurian Railway, which was owned by Japan. Claiming sabotage, Japan used the pretext to overrun all of Manchuria in what was the beginning of fifteen years of war, which culminated in the Pacific war against the Allies. Lots of Japanese soldiers were stationed in China, and Abe worked in a restaurant. The owner of the restaurant, a man from Osaka, told her that people would indicate four fingers in his direction. She said she didn't know what "four" signified, so he told her it meant *eta hinin*.

> I was asked to join the Fukuoka Association in Tsingtao, but didn't dare because people would find out my address and know from the location that I was *burakumin*. Soldiers would ask if I wanted them to take anything to my family in Fukuoka, but I was too ashamed.

Abe met a Japanese man from Manchuria who was a customer at the restaurant and married him. At first she didn't tell him she was from a *buraku*, but when they went back to Japan, she admitted it. Her husband told her he had worked for a rich *buraku* man when he was going to college and had no problem accepting it.

We returned to Japan after the war in 1945. In 1955 I applied for a job in the postwar employment program. We were sent out to work as a road crew, and I soon realized that even for a job like that, we needed to read. We had to write monthly reports and took turns at it.

There was a newsletter published by the employment program, and we would get together to read and discuss it. But *burakumin* didn't go to school and so couldn't do the reports. I first learned to write my name and address. I could do it at home, but when I had to do it in front of officials, I forgot how. In 1962 about thirty people in the employment program got together and started to learn to write.

According to Abe, illiteracy could mean many things. If illiterate people took a bus or train, they wouldn't know whether to get off, so even though they couldn't afford it, they would take a taxi. Then people would accuse *buraku* of being wasteful or living luxuriously.

"I was born in a buraku *but I didn't know that was why I wa[s] discriminated against. I thoug[ht] it was because we were poor."*

TAKEYO ABE (RIGHT), WITH TAKAKO NAKAJIMA, LITERACY ACTIVISTS

The literacy movement led to the realization of our background and why we couldn't go to school. I came to realize we have to raise children who will fight racism. We had a passion to send our children to school to educate them. Of course they went through a lot of hardships, but many went up to middle school [grade seven to nine].

A *gaijin* (foreigner) who can't read the Japanese language would know very well how helpless one can be if unable to read street signs or instructions on an elevator.

We have developed our own teaching methods. The words are written out in columns with a space beside them so that the student can copy them. The information written out also serves as a newspaper. Because I was illiterate, I learned to see and hear what was being said. I remember things, a lot of detail. That's how I compensated. I was already in my late forties when I first learned to read. When I learned letters, I began to realize my history. I realized why my father drank. I had hated him and even wanted to kill him, but now I understood the pain and unhappiness that caused him to behave as he had.

Takako Nakajima interjected with the story of how she got into the literacy program, first as a student teaching assistant and then as a teacher.

Until I was twenty-four, I didn't know I was a *burakumin* and was even afraid of *burakumin* and quite prejudiced against them. I was employed at city hall as a part-time worker. One of the city officials took me to the *burakumin* community centre, and I found out that I had come to where I was born! I went home and wondered about how to kill myself. I went to my room and lay on my bed, not caring about anything anymore. My mother was quite worried and came in to ask what was wrong. I said, "I found out what I am. But why does that have to be?" I didn't know it, but my mother was going to writing class herself.

It puzzled us that so many *burakumin* apparently neglected to tell their children about how being *burakumin* would affect them in later life. We could see from the hurt in Nakajima's eyes and passion in her voice that she was still deeply affected by her experiences.

My mother was working so hard she didn't have time to teach us. She was practising writing at home all the time. I felt ashamed of her attempts. I was so ignorant. By the time I began to learn why she had tried so hard, she had already died and I never made it up to her. It hurts me for what I did to her. That's what keeps me going, to try to make it up to her.

By learning to read and write and taking some pride in their culture and history, the elders of the community are gaining some of what they never had. Nakajima spoke of the elders:

> Looking at them, I'm very moved. I'm very proud of them. The way they live is wonderful. I started to work for the program about sixteen years ago. Everyone was older and they had to first learn how to hold the pencil. They had no experience of writing letters. It took a year for them to learn how to write one card and two hours to write that one card.

Being freed from the shackles of illiteracy is an amazingly liberating experience, Abe told us.

> When we learned to read, we were free to go out. I could stop and read and enjoy it. I began to see how society is made. I recognized how ignorant we'd been kept. I realized we are the ones who have to correct this. The literacy movement did a lot of things.

We asked Abe and Nakajima whether there was a growing sense of militancy within the *burakumin* community. Abe replied:

> My parents' attitude was to keep quiet and let the storm pass. That attitude still exists, but if we keep things from our children, outsiders will teach them our tradition in a distorted way.

Nakajima added:

> My children still encounter nasty graffiti and other incidents. But since discrimination is made by human beings, it can be corrected by human beings. The children are learning that just blaming the discriminators is not enough. We have to grow ourselves by being good people.

At this point David interjected a personal anecdote:

> Because many relatively well-educated immigrants had come to British Columbia from England to take positions in the civil service, my father blamed "the English" for the Japanese-Canadian evacuation. When I was a teenager, he had told me that an English

girl was not acceptable as a potential wife. When I married Tara, who is English, he would often reduce her to tears by saying, "your people" did this or that. It ended only when I confronted him with the fact that victims of bigotry do not have some kind of right to be bigots themselves. When I called him a bigot, he broke down and wept.

Abe vigorously agreed with the need to overcome those feelings.

It's been only ten years that we could say, "Yes, I'm *burakumin*." We always tried to hide it. I changed when I saw the physically handicapped. They couldn't hide their impediment, so they expressed themselves. We thought we could hide. I learned from the handicapped people we were wrong. Like them, we didn't choose to be born what we are, *burakumin*. So there's nothing to hide. Today, wherever I go, I can openly say, "I'm *burakumin*."

Nakajima added:

When we apply for a job, they ask where we live and we tell them the area. They immediately ask which side, and from the side of the river, they know immediately that we are *burakumin*. Before, I couldn't even tell them where I was born. I told you how I hated my mother, but I wouldn't want my child to feel that way towards me. Now they are proud of where they come from. I've been raising my children that way and I have nothing to hide. It makes no sense to hide where we're from. Unfortunately some people still hide because discrimination remains severe in jobs and marriage.

The pressure against intermarriage is a vital concern. Recently a *burakumin* girl got engaged and her fiancé was under great pressure from the family to call it off. When he finally gave in and broke the engagement, the girl killed herself.

Abe told us that this initial fear and prejudice could be overcome:

Lots of times in marriages between *burakumin* and non-*burakumin*, the parents won't even visit to see their grandchildren. But when they learn of the warmth, they change. When human beings encounter and feel one another's human warmth, they will overcome their prejudices.

Nakajima, too, had marriage troubles. "My husband is not a *burakumin*," she said. "His family objected to me. But he is a teacher and he convinced them by logic. Now everything is fine. They were so misinformed."

Nakajima thinks pride is at the root of it. "A person like myself who hated to be *burakumin*," she said, "is now happy and proud to be one. Since I can feel other people's pain, I could never discriminate."

Abe added:

Here we're learning about our history. We're very happy and positive. Our aim is not to blame the others. We have to grow so we don't look down on others or discriminate. We are learning compassion and tolerance. When these kids apply for jobs, they might be tempted to hide it, but they will remember what they learned here.

Nakajima nodded and said:

We learn that we hate racism and discrimination, not that we hate human beings. In a way we feel sorry for those who are so misinformed and ignorant that they discriminate. We ask them if what they are doing is making them richer, happier, or more human. This movement is not just for ourselves, it's also for everyone outside. We hope to learn and grow together. One quality of the *burakumin* life is trust. They have been deceived and betrayed so many times, yet somehow they've been able to keep that trust and the ability to believe. They believe in the humanity of hateful people, who would, in the end, understand one another.

David then told them that as a teenager growing up in Canada after the war, he was ashamed of his slanted eyes and had yearned to have an operation on them. Abe responded:

I understand what you said about your eyes. But changing them would make matters *worse*. Stay as you are and get people to accept you as you are. Changing yourself on the outside won't change anything.

In the Kyomachi day-care centre were thirty youngsters ranging from newborns to six-year-olds and a working staff of twenty. A big sign over the doorway, done in beautiful Japanese calligraphy, said, "Let there be warmth in society, let there be light in humanity." The rooms were bright and clean, and the teachers were friendly and told us how much they enjoyed working there. They were proud of the centre, which is on a par with or better than most Japanese day-care centres.

The Korean anthropologist Byung-ho Chung has done an extensive study on day-care centres in Japan.[1] According to Chung, the most innovative and progressive day-care facilities are run by and for *burakumin* and Korean residents, and do not cater to mainstream Japanese. One of the reasons the teacher-student ratio is so low at the Kyomachi centre was that although non-*burakumin* are allowed to enrol, most don't. Even the neighbours send their children to other centres farther away.

Almost immediately after we entered, a small, obviously mentally handicapped child began to follow us, hoping to touch, hug, and kiss us. The director explained that children who have difficulties in other institutions are often sent to Kyomachi.

The next day Megumi Matsumoto took us around to three other *buraku* communities. As a guide she had been efficient and practical, but we knew little about her. At the end of the tour we finally got a chance to sit with her in a coffee shop near Tsukushino station. It was a small shop and we sat near the window watching the trains shoot by every few minutes. There she told us about her involvement with the *burakumin*.

For more than twenty years *buraku* people have been Matsumoto's consuming passion. While talking to us, she never referred to herself as a feminist or discussed the oppression of women, but her story revealed a focused human being determined to follow her own course.

Matsumoto was born in 1948 and lived in Tokyo until she was twenty-four. She married a journalist for one of the major newspapers, *Asahi Shinbun*, who specialized in foreign affairs in Africa and the Middle East. Like many of her era, she had been an activist in the student movement. She was a nonsectarian and remembered attending a rally in support of Kazuo Ishikawa, a *burakumin* who was accused of murder. But it was just one of many issues she was concerned with at the time. After her two children were born, her husband was transferred to Kyushu, the south-west island of Japan. Matsumoto didn't want to go. For her, Kyushu was like a foreign country.

> By chance, we moved to a *buraku* neighbourhood. I wanted to work, so I looked for a day-care where I could send my children. I found a play school that was under construction, so I went to the municipal hall to apply for a place for my children. I was told I couldn't place my children there because it was for the *burakumin*. I didn't understand, so I went to the Buraku Liberation League office where they explained the objectives of the school. I said if that's what they would do, then I want my children there, in fact, I would love it. So I negotiated between city hall and the BLL, and they decided to allow my children to register. The policy at first was not to take non-*burakumin* children and then over the years gradually accept non-*burakumin*.

At first her husband didn't want to send the children to a day-care centre, but Matsumoto convinced him that she needed to work. Once the children were in the school, Matsumoto became involved with creating a curriculum called "liberation education." She had a full-time job in publishing but, through the school, found herself being drawn deeper into the *burakumin* community. She discovered a deep sense of communication especially with the elders, and she was receptive to what they told her.

> My husband had to move every three years. I didn't want to move, so I told him to go and I'd commute. I quit working for the publisher and was hired as research director of *buraku* history for the city. I

continue with that job today. I talk to old people and record
interviews with them.

When her children were eight and ten years old, her husband was
assigned to Nairobi.

He insisted I come or our relationship might end. He demanded I
make a choice between him and the movement, but I remained
silent, which not so eloquently expressed the choice I'd made. I went
to see my friends in the *buraku* community, crying, and told them
about the choice my husband had demanded. They said, "Of course,
we'd be glad if you stayed with us, but you have to think, what is the
movement if you have to hurt your own children and husband? If
you continue like that, pushing yourself, there'll come a time when
you can't go any further."

It made sense to me. They added, "You're not *burakumin*. You're
here by choice. We have no choice. If you sacrifice your family, you
would suffer more than we would." So I was pushing myself to be
able to share their joys and feelings, but I couldn't because I wasn't
burakumin. I tried tracing my lineage to see if there was a *burakumin*
in it, but found it was wrong. How could I be myself and remain part
of the movement? Africa was the answer.

What finally made me decide to go was the children. They had
grown up without a father. But they had a right to live with him. I was
so absorbed with the BLL I was becoming too narrowly focused. I
would attend meeting after meeting about research and was a slave to
the demands on me. So I thought if the movement is about liberation,
I would have to liberate myself. So I decided to take a break.

She promised her husband she would go for two years. After he'd
been in Nairobi for six months, she and the children joined him. She
didn't speak the language and Kenya was a far cry from Japan in terms of
customs, lifestyle, and just about everything else, yet after three days she
felt quite at home and happy. She ended up spending four years there.

When I returned I applied the African lifestyle: keep busy but not frantic. They have an expression — "*pore pore*," meaning slowly, slowly. In my mind, I've slowed down — everyone says I've changed. I had felt that, without me, the movement wouldn't exist, but I'm different now. I don't have masks to put on.

Matsumoto had come to understand that much of her frantic involvement with the *burakumin* community had been an ego trip; she had wanted to be indispensable.

She and her husband returned to Japan in 1987, and ever since she has commuted between their apartments in Tokyo and Fukuoka. In 1988, when the International Movement Against Any Form of Racism and Discrimination was formed, Matsumoto took on the job of overseeing the section on Africa and women. "What keeps your commitment and dedication?" we asked.

Growing up in Tokyo, we didn't know warmth in the community. There's an acceptance here. I feel cold in other places. My children are very warm and kind to people, and I think it's because they experienced that from the elders, the *burakumin*. If I had no money, I know even though the *burakumin* are not rich, they would help me. Abe-san is like a mother to me, and Nakajima-san a sister.

It is that sense of community that is so central to Matsumoto's needs and is clearly fulfilled by her place with the *burakumin*.

Visiting *buraku* communities reminded us of the song "Human," in which the African-American singer Dionne Farris states, "Before I am black, I am a human. / Because I am black, I am human." In a *buraku*, one might say, "Before I'm *burakumin*, I am human, but it is also true *because* I am *burakumin*, I am human."

The proud yet compassionate faces of Asai, Ota, Nakajima, Abe, Matsumoto, and others we met in *burakumin* communities seemed to exemplify the subtle balance they kept between the "because I am" and the "before I am."

To many the goal for minorities and the dispossessed is to become assimilated into the flow of mainstream society. Visiting *burakumin* communities and meeting older and younger *burakumin*, as well as non-*burakumin* who identify themselves with the *burakumin*, showed us viable possibilities for the future.

The concept that everyone is equal before the law is a magnificent achievement. But the biological reality is that all of us are different. As biologists have found, diversity at the genetic, ecological, and cultural levels is a critical element in any population. *Diversity* is the property that confers adaptability and resilience when change occurs.

Humanity needs ways to appreciate and celebrate the differences while simultaneously supporting the society's commonality of culture, beliefs, and values. Ironically, it is often the victims of discrimination who have a gift for their oppressors — a greater sense of humanity, generosity, and kindness, which are so often the consequence of suffering.

CHAPTER 7

tHe KoReaN
mIRROR

"The problem is the Koreans. Outwardly, they appear

to be submissive, but inwardly, they resist. . . .

We should adopt the same kind of policy Hitler has

used against the Jews. All the lawless Koreans

should be banished to an island and castrated. . . .

In the West, the German and Italian races, and

in the East, the Yamato race are destined to rule over

other races. This is Heaven's will."

HEISUKE YANAGAWA, JAPAN'S JUSTICE MINISTER,

AT A PRESS CONFERENCE IN 1941

●

JAPAN continues to try to keep its racial diversity to a minimum, but the influx accelerates. In recent years the Japanese have begun to encounter many unfamiliar faces and hear unfamiliar sounds. Workers brought in as cheap labour from Iran, Bangladesh, and the Philippines are a fact in today's Japan, but resistance to their inclusion into Japanese culture and society is still strong. After the Vietnam War, poignant images of boat people attempting to escape the horrors in their country prompted an immediate acceptance of 50,000 Vietnamese immigrants by Canada in one year alone. In the same year Japan reluctantly accepted fewer than a hundred. One member of the Diet justified this pitiful number as a generous impulse to protect the Vietnamese from the difficulties they'd encounter in Japan!

Throughout human existence, people have handled encounters with different tribal groups in a number of ways, ranging from peaceful coexistence to expulsion, elimination or absorption. That process continues to the present, as battles in Ireland, Palestine, Bosnia, and Rwanda remind us how difficult it is to avoid hatred and bloodshed between people who see themselves as different.

Modern communication and transportation have shrunk the physical distances separating people. We can watch events in remote parts of the world as they actually take place, while jet planes can whisk us over vast distances in hours. Global economics is a major force in the opening of borders, not only to goods and resources but to people.

Ever since the Europeans discovered North America, successive waves of immigrants have arrived in search of wealth, adventure, or freedom from persecution. Canada and the United States have dealt with the increasing ethnic diversity within their borders differently. In the U.S. the concept of the "melting pot" encourages the integration of newcomers into the dominant society and their absorption of its mores and values. Canada, in contrast, has adopted the model of an "ethnic mosaic," which encourages the maintenance of cultural and linguistic diversity within the Canadian context. In both countries, newcomers from all parts of the world are welcomed as part of this young experiment in mixing.

To North Americans, Japan seems radically different, an island nation that is overwhelmingly homogeneous, held together by a common history, culture, and language. Both the Japanese and others perceive the social cohesion that results from this uniformity to be Japan's strength. This notion of their homogeneity is, in fact, an illusion: there is a great deal of diversity within the country. The hierarchical social structure, deference to authority, and a rigid version of history tend to repress an awareness of the diversity and attendant discrimination within the nation. Until very recently, these invisible elements within the country kept quiet, preferring to avoid public disputes and more humiliation. That attitude is changing as Japanese people are beginning to learn about the diversity within, while minority groups are becoming more vocal and proud of their differences.

For many Japanese, finding out about these minority groups within their midst has been a revelation.

To most Caucasians, Koreans appear so similar to Japanese physically that it is difficult to distinguish between them on that basis alone. Their appearance reflects their close genetic similarity, which in turn suggests a shared not-so-distant past. Nevertheless, in modern times, Japanese military aggression into Korea, annexation of the peninsula as a Japanese colony, atrocities and forced labour have created hatreds and prejudice that live on. In Japan itself, a large Korean minority with a past comparable to African-Americans' is becoming far more visible.

●

Kawasaki city is southwest of Tokyo. We visited the part of Kawasaki known for its heavy industry, air pollution, and "Korean ghetto." We went there to meet Inha Lee, a Christian minister whose congregation is about fifty percent Korean. The rest are Filipinos and Japanese. Lee has experienced the racism against Koreans and represents one part of the Korean community's response to it.

Lee met us on the steps of his church. A tall man with white hair, tanned features, and a congenial smile, he showed us through the modest chapel with obvious pride. He pointed out three stained-glass windows that symbolize the church's commitments. The first shows Noah and a rainbow; Noah signifies a rebirth, and the rainbow represents a coalition of different peoples. The second illustrates Jesus washing Peter's feet, signifying the church serving the community. And the third window depicts the Resurrection, with Jesus breaking bread with two disciples, that foretold of the coming kingdom and Jesus' position as the mediator.

Besides speaking fluent Korean and Japanese, Lee speaks excellent English, having spent two years in Canada.

When I arrived here in 1960, there was a clash between Koreans and Japanese. There was a summer festival that was deeply rooted in Shinto [Japan's national religion]. People came to collect money for the festival and I refused, remembering that the wartime Japanese government had used the festival to promote emperor worship and the war effort in occupied Korea. My Japanese neighbours were very angry. They came to the church grounds with a shrine on poles and entered the yard and smashed the flower garden.

Japanese oppression and violence against Koreans was institutionalized during the Meiji Era (1867–1912). To strengthen itself internally and as a leading player in Asia, Japan developed a two-pronged plan. Internally the policy was called Fukoku Kyohei (building a rich country and strong army). But externally they called for the liberation of Asia from western influence, which meant the subjugation of Taiwan and Korea.

In 1905, as a result of growing Japanese influence on the Korean peninsula, Tokyo assumed control over Korean foreign affairs. In a special treaty with Japan, Korea acknowledged that it was a "backward" country and that Japan could help "develop" it. In 1910 Korea was annexed by Japan, which imposed Japanese nationality on Koreans and began a process of forced ethnic conversion. Into this colonized country, Lee was born in 1925.

At the end of the Meiji Era, prisoner labour was banned. So labourers had to be brought to Hokkaido from Honshu, the main island of Japan, and put up in huge dorms. The labourers were from the dispossessed and unemployed masses, who were often deceived by promises of money. Like the Japanese who moved to North and South America, the people brought to Hokkaido were motivated by crushing poverty.

Many people recruited to come to Hokkaido believed they would farm, but the government had a different agenda. It was thinking about future defence against an invasion by Russia. Those men who had come to be farmers were forced into military training, and it was often women, children, and old people who ended up doing the work in the fields. The recruited labourers were forbidden from leaving Hokkaido, so they were just like prisoners.

The Japanese also demanded that land holdings be registered. Koreans didn't have a system of land registration since they knew who the land belonged to, so most ignored the registration order. The non-registrants were simply not recognized, and the Japanese took over their land. The disenfranchised were forced to leave, some going to China and many others to Japan. The Japanese eventually occupied sixty percent of the cultivated land in Korea.

In the meantime the Japanese developed policies to suppress Korean identity and eliminate Korean culture. The use of Korean names was forbidden, and the Korean language was not allowed to be spoken in public, including in schools, and Koreans were forced to worship at nationalistic Shinto shrines. As European colonizers to Africa, the Americas, and Australia have found, an effective way to weaken an occupied people is to ban their language, traditions, and rituals. But such actions also create a committed opposition.

Towards the end of the 1930s, as Japan's war effort in Asia escalated, Japanese began to conscript Koreans and force them to go to Japan to work. The Korean labourers helped to build dams for hydroelectric projects and worked in coal mines and steel mills. They were treated like slaves and often beaten and killed with little regard or thought. Kawasaki, with its steel mills, was one of the many centres in which Korean labourers were concentrated. Lee told us:

My background is very different from that of the great majority of resident Koreans in Japan. My mother was from South Korea; my father worked in North Korea. I was going to a private high school on the peninsula. My school was closed by the Japanese because it didn't meet the "assimilation policies" of raising the Japanese flag, praying towards Japan, and pledging allegiance. Some Japanese people felt guilty about doing this, so the governor promised to send fifty of the best students to Japan. I was one of them.

This was in 1941. Later that year Japan attacked Pearl Harbor.

The Japanese Lee had learned in Korea was different from that spoken in Japan. As a result, he was cruelly taunted by the Japanese kids. "I remember the history teacher saying in class that 'certain people in Asia have to fade away.' It was just like the Nazis and Jews."

During the Pacific war of 1941–1945, Japan forced Chinese and Korean conscripts to Japan. Many were kidnapped, thrown onto trains like baggage, and sent to Hokkaido where they were forced to work, mainly in the mines.

Japanese colonization of Korea lasted until 1945. To Japan, the end of the Second World War meant surrender and a miserable defeat. But to Koreans it was emancipation. Although most of the two million Koreans in Japan opted to return home, many were prevented from returning by turbulent social and political conditions in Korea.

> The end of the war came when I was a college student mobilized to work in a munitions factory as forced labour. I clearly remember the day. We all stood at attention as Emperor Hirohito's announcement of the defeat came over the radio. As I listened, I heard the sound of sobbing from the Japanese students. But at that moment I didn't feel anything. My mind was blank. Then a Japanese student from Osaka University called out to me, "Congratulations! The Korean people are finally liberated." I was stunned by his words.

Lee was part of an *assimilated* generation. He had been so thoroughly absorbed into the Japanese way of life that he was forced to consider what being "liberated" really meant. Eventually he was happy, but at the same time he was seized with a feeling of anxiety. With freedom came a whole new world of responsibility. Until that time he had been part of the system that had enslaved him. Now he was supposedly free.

As Lee contemplated his future, he recalled an incident that occurred during the war. One day he had returned to his room in Kyoto and found that he had been visited by the Japanese special police, who had gone through his things and read his diaries. One of his teachers, Tadashi Wada, stood up for the students who had been violated.

He defended us, took our fate as his responsibility. He suffered greatly from the police. He was a Christian and that influenced me. In the scripture, there is no distinction between Jews or Greeks. Those invited into the Kingdom of God are first the oppressed. Those in power first have to be brought down. So I became a Christian.

Like the Koreans, the Chinese suffered brutally at the hands of the Japanese. After the war, Wada went to China as a self-appointed missionary to rectify the injustices of Japan. "At least I can die as a Japanese for one Chinese life," he said. His determination to redress the past wrongs still inspires Lee.

As we sat on *tatami* mats in a church meeting room, Lee continued with his story.

I wanted to return home, but after independence, Korea was in such a state of turmoil that I prolonged my stay here. In the meantime I fell in love with a Japanese woman whom I had met in the church. For marrying me, my wife had to lose her Japanese citizenship, but couldn't get Korean citizenship either. So she became stateless.

On April 28, 1952, the San Francisco Peace Treaty went into effect, ending seven years of U.S. military occupation and restoring Japanese sovereignty.[1] On that day the Japanese government stripped Korean and Taiwanese residents of their limited rights as Japanese nationals. They now fell under the new Alien Registration Law (ARL), which took effect simultaneously. Japanese nationality once imposed on Koreans and Taiwanese without their consent was now taken away, again without their consent, as if nothing had ever occurred. The ARL required fingerprinting and the possession at all times of an alien passbook bearing print, photo, and personal data; violators faced stiff criminal penalties. In 1987 the African-American social activist Jesse Jackson wrote to Japan's Justice Minister:

> The Alien Registration Law . . . is reminiscent of the pass laws in South Africa. The eyes of the world are on Japan today. As an economic giant, there is much to be respected, but no nation should have an economic surplus and a moral deficit. Fingerprinting aliens is offensive to many people as it treats law-abiding non-citizens as second-class human beings, singled out like criminals.[2]

In 1987, after intense protests, the ARL was revised but only with minor changes, the passbook being replaced by a computerized fingerprint card. Lee has been a passionate opponent of the ARL for many years. According to him, the object of the ARL was to exclude those who were from former colonies — Korea and Taiwan — from the basic human-rights provisions in the new Japanese Constitution. Lee told us how the ARL affected his own son.

> When my son was fourteen, we forgot to renew his registration. He was charged and fined, a child of fourteen, and was given a criminal record. When I protested that as his father I should be charged, I was told that "the law is the law."

Lee shook his head at the injustice of it all. This legal discrimination mirrored the social discrimination that Korean residents had been experiencing in their daily lives for many years. As a pastor, Lee had had to go to the police station many times to secure the release of those apprehended while not carrying their alien registration card. Lee was convinced that the ARL was against the spirit of the Japanese Constitution.

There are one million Koreans in Japan if the roughly 300,000 who have naturalized since 1952 are added to the 680,000 registered as Korean nationals. Most were forced, or are the descendants of those who were forced, to leave their homeland as displaced farmers or conscripted labourers to fuel Japan's military and industrial expansion during its thirty-five-year colonization of Korea, which began in 1910.

There were typically two reactions among Japanese to the Korean "problem." One was to say, "If you have so many complaints, why don't you go back to Korea?" The other is, "You are just like us, speaking Japanese, living like Japanese, so why don't you just become Japanese?" But, Lee believes, the matter is not that simple. Lee, who had spoken with many younger Korean residents, knew that few of them had ever visited their homeland and did not know its language or customs, making it difficult for them to live there. What's more, the "Korean problem" is not something Koreans created. It is, in reality, a Japanese problem. Lee also believes its solution has ramifications elsewhere for how the world solves the increasingly complex but significant problems of ethnic conflict and conciliation.

"When my son was fourteen, we forgot to renew his registration He was charged and fined, a child of fourteen, and was given a criminal record."

INHA LEE, KOREAN-BORN
CHRISTIAN MINISTER

Many resident Koreans feel that changing nationality and becoming Japanese would be like a surrender to the Japanese demand to deny their ethnic origins and cultural background, and "forget" what happened to them in the past. In 1987 Manabu Hatakeyama, a justice ministry official, wrote:

> The longer Koreans remain in Japan, the more they identify with Japan and Japanese society, and the more the historical circumstances that brought them to Japan — the colonization of Korea — fade from their memory. There is no longer any need to create a special legal status for Koreans in Japan.[3]

In 1988 the National Council for Combatting Discrimination Against Ethnic People in Japan (*Min-To-Ren*) determined that resident Koreans who had been injured in military service should get compensation.[4] Since 1952 more than ¥37-trillion have been given for war compensation and pensions to Japanese families for death and injuries in military service. About 240,000 Koreans and 210,000 Taiwanese fought for Japan, 22,000 Koreans and 30,000 Taiwanese were killed and many more wounded, yet no money has been spent on them. The Japanese government has been denying any responsibility.

Every year on August 15 the government organizes a ceremony in the presence of the emperor and his wife. The announcement for the event reads, "Tomorrow, August 15, is the day to remember those who died in the war and pray for peace. Our condolences are for the more than three million people who died inside and outside of Japan during the last world war." Three million people is the official number of deaths of Japanese *nationals*. Completely forgotten are those who were victims of war but were not Japanese.

Lee showed us an article on "comfort women" — non-Japanese women, including many Koreans, who were forced to serve soldiers as sex slaves in the brothels established by the military.[5] For decades, such women had been mute, hiding their physical and psychic scars behind a wall of shame and silence. But more recently the surviving women have begun to speak out and demand restitution. And like a festering boil that has been lanced, the stories have burst forth. The article Lee showed us said that on August 22, 1994, citizens' groups in support of foreign victims of Japanese wartime aggression criticized government plans to set up a ¥10-billion fund from private-sector donations to help women whom the Japanese Imperial Army forced to be sex slaves. The government's official position was not to compensate individual victims. It would therefore pay only for the administrative costs of a nonprofit foundation to be set up to distribute money to the claimants. The money was to be handled as "gift money," a mere token of sympathy, rather than financial compensation. But, the victims argued, they were not looking for an expression of sympathy; they wanted the Japanese government to admit its culpability in these atrocities. They demanded an apology and individual compensation to symbolize the society's will to redress.

Since the Second World War, German governments have apologized to Jews, have erected monuments to past victims, and have paid massive reparations and vigilantly denounced racism as a reminder of Germany's complicity in wartime atrocities. It is only through this expiation of its past that Germany can develop a future with Israel and other countries.

In Japan the need to acknowledge the existence of victims of the Japanese military has gone unanswered, as has the victims' right to be recognized and receive redress. This is not dredging up an ancient past but a recent history within memory of most of Japan's citizens. Often the crucial task of remembering falls on the shoulders of disenfranchised minorities, whose collective memories are an invaluable reminder to society of our capacity for inhumanity and cruelty.

As well, in other countries history is remembered very differently. For example, as recently as 1995, former foreign minister Michio Watanabe stated that Korea had been under no military pressure from Japan when it signed the 1919 treaty that handed over its sovereignty to Japan. Throughout Asia there were calls of protest. They saw the 1910 annexation as the symbol of Japanese aggression in Asia, which culminated in the Pacific war. By justifying the annexation, they thought Watanabe and other conservative politicians were trying to justify the militaristic government of Japan's entire war effort. South Korean Prime Minister Lee Hong Koo reacted strongly:

> Our government and all the people of our nation cannot help showing shock and concern. . . . The remarks outside the bounds of common knowledge by a person in a leading position in Japan poses a big problem not only to the future relations between [South] Korea and Japan but also to our future-oriented efforts to build an Asia-Pacific community.[6]

The next day, June 6, 1995, students in South Korea attacked the Japanese Cultural Centre in Seoul. The enraged Koreans threw gasoline bombs, broke windows, and set the building on fire. Under pressure, Watanabe apologized, saying:

> The 1910 Korean annexation treaty was concluded amid the historical circumstances of international relations and other factors at the time. Earlier, I said the treaty was "formed peacefully." I now retract this "peacefully" and apologize.[7]

China's Foreign Ministry criticized Watanabe and called on the parliament to overcome their differences in drafting the resolution. Ministry spokesperson Shen Guofang said:

> The war of aggression that Japan launched against many Asian nations and its past colonial rule of the Korean peninsula brought untold suffering to the peoples of all these countries. This is an undeniable historical fact. We hope the Japanese government will take a very serious approach to this matter."[8]

The conservative block within the LDP (Liberal Democratic Party), the former governing party, opposed using the words "colonial rule" or "aggression" in the resolution until the last moment. They insisted that the legislature does not have a mandate to make judgements on history. After many months of negotiations, the original text has been diluted to the extent that the "determination to forever renounce war" has been replaced by a vague expression of "determination to open a future of peaceful coexistence for humankind."

When we got off the subway at Tsuruhashi station in Osaka, we found ourselves in the middle of Osaka's Korean district, which people refer to as "the ghetto." There we met Paggie Cho, a Korean singer and teacher, who wheeled up on his bike. He was an imposing figure, his long black hair pulled back in a ponytail. Clad in a thigh-length leather jacket, he had the demeanour of a gentle black bear. He wore wraparound sunglasses, partly to hide a bad eye. He smiled easily and earnestly and answered questions in good English.

Cho took us on a tour of his home turf in the Ikuno borough of Osaka. Ikuno is home to one of the highest concentrations of Koreans in Japan. Approximately 280,000 Koreans live in Osaka prefecture; of the 140,000 located in Osaka city, 40,000 live in Ikuno.

There are two Korean markets in this area. One is attached to Tsuruhashi station, and the other, known as the "international market," is located in the community of Ikaino. Both are warrens of small shops selling everything from Korean traditional costumes to religious paraphernalia, pig's ears, and spicy *kimchi* pickles.

Cho's parents are both from Korea, but his mother came to Japan at the end of the war when she was still a child. Cho was born in 1956 and grew up in Nishinari borough, an "international" district of Osaka. (The label "international" means its residents are a mixture of many Korean, *burakumin*, and Okinawans.) When he was going to elementary school, his class had about ten Koreans, ten Okinawans, and twenty *burakumin*. Although the *burakumin* are ethnically Japanese, many Japanese parents told their children that they were not, insinuating they had come from somewhere else. In its concern over the de facto segregation of *burakumin* schoolchildren by non-*burakumin* parents, school officials had instituted a program of "education for liberation." Designed to reduce fears and mistrust born of ignorance, the program sought to portray different groups in a positive way. As a result of this attempt to improve education for *burakumin*, the school system in Osaka gradually improved for all of the "internationals."

As a Korean, Cho recalled being overwhelmed with a sense of inferiority. Until he was in high school, he tried to deny being Korean and to be Japanese. If he had revealed that he was Korean, he would have been harassed. He felt ashamed of what he was — a Korean in Japan. But, Cho told us, in university he started to change.

As we walked, an elevated train rumbled overhead. The sound, sights, and smells varied from enchanting to overwhelming. The stores were tiny, for the most part consisting of three walls where the merchandise is displayed and the fourth open onto the covered walkway. One can take in the entire contents of a shop at a glance. Customers usually sat on the floor in the middle of the shop with their backs to the walkway. The salesperson took whatever a buyer pointed to down from the shelves. It was obviously a social meeting place, as well as a market. Cho talked as we walked.

For most of my early life, I was known by my Japanese surname, Nishiyama. I thought my Korean name would bring me bad luck.

Then I was accepted into university and I realized that, all of a sudden, I was among the elite and I must act responsibly. I started studying the Korean language and met some Korean *sempai* [seniors] who used their Korean names.

Names are an explosive subject to Koreans. During Japan's occupation of Korea, the Japanese forced Koreans to change their names. This practice ended in 1945, and in Korea, names were changed back from Japanese to Korean. But for the resident Koreans in Japan, names continued to be a problem. Until recently those who were naturalized as Japanese citizens were required to change their names to Japanese. Those who retained Korean nationality usually had a legal Korean name but also a Japanese name for daily use. Which name was used often indicated that person's attitude to his or her identity. Cho related his own experience to us:

> I told my teacher that I, too, wanted to start using my Korean name. He said he always knew that I would and congratulated me. My teacher helped me by taking thirty minutes at the beginning of one of his classes to explain to the other students why I was changing my name.
>
> My mother was delighted when I started using my Korean name. She had a modern type of Korean pride. My father, an illiterate welder, was different. He had never gone to school and had nothing good to say about Koreans, especially Communists. In spite of his experience as a target of discrimination, he despised the *burakumin* and the Okinawans, even though we share some of the same foods, like pig's feet and intestines, which the Japanese won't eat. He couldn't help me deal with my identity problems. He just taught me, "Get rich." When I changed my name, he simply acknowledged it. I don't know what he really thought.
>
> My father's attitude was confusing. Sometimes he said it was okay to be Japanese because Koreans are inferior. He had a negative self-image. But sometimes he was angry at the Japanese for their prejudice.

Eldridge Cleaver, in *Soul on Ice*, talks about how black men lust for blond white women because the majority population imposes on black people its image of what is beautiful and desirable. By accepting the standards set by others, one becomes ashamed of who one is. Like Cho's father, many victims of discrimination eventually believe the attitudes of the majority and end up loathing themselves.

Although there are now more and more Korean doctors and lawyers, most Korean businesses are *pachinko* parlours (the attraction of these popular pinball-type machines mystifies many westerners), restaurants, money-lending, and garbage collection. A disproportionately high percentage of Korean descendants have achieved fame in the world of professional sports, entertainment, and letters, although quite a few still use Japanese names and remain reticent about revealing their Korean backgrounds.

From the market we walked to Hirano Canal. Built by Korean labourers, it serves as the symbolic monument of the Ikaino Korean community. Historians say the "ghetto" of Ikaino was formed originally by the labourers who built the canal. On the bridge spanning the canal, an older woman was selling imported Korean carrots (ginseng), a symbol of strength and longevity. Cho was quite well known in Osaka and the Kansai area. As we walked, people waved to him and he greeted them in Japanese and Korean.

I am the rector of a prep school. I teach English, though I have never visited an English-speaking country. I am also a musician. Some of my songs are about Korea, though I have never been there either. My wife is a Korean whose parents were brought to Japan to build this Hirano Canal. Thousands of Koreans were shipped in to build this canal. Countless numbers of them died during construction. Her birth mother was Japanese. Her parents already had two daughters and wanted a son, so the father went to a geisha and paid her to have his child. But she gave birth to another girl. Her father's wife raised her like her own daughter. That sort of "double marriage" is illegal now, but in the old days, rich Koreans were proud of how many mistresses they had.

My wife, like me, is a *zainichi* [resident Korean in Japan]. She was in Seoul for two years to learn singing and dancing. She went to a Korean school in Japan. Her parents spoke Korean at home. She was brought up in Ikaino. So her cultural background as a Korean is much more solid than mine. Our daughter can already sing a few Korean songs.

Cho took us to a small Korean restaurant for lunch. Because we arrived later in the day, the lunch crowd had come and gone, and we were the only customers. As we ate the Korean barbecue, Cho told us of his ethnic identity:

I always want something from Korea. I long for its culture and history. But that doesn't mean I can identify with the politics of either North or South Korea. My friends still have romantic ideas of their homeland of Korea. But I don't have such a sense. I'm from Osaka, I live in Ikaino: that's how I identify myself.

Before and during the war, Koreans had to be 120 percent Japanese. Now we are foreigners. But the majority of resident Koreans, especially those cut off from large Korean communities, are still trying to pass themselves off as Japanese. Many want to be naturalized as Japanese citizens. But I don't want to become naturalized. For me naturalization means surrender on their terms. I must submit to interviews and background checks and then only after a few years will I learn if they have decided to accept me. *They* get to decide. If it were a human right, I'd apply tomorrow. But unless the minister of justice allows, I can't get Japanese citizenship. It should be *my* right to choose.

To Cho, becoming Japanese means assimilation into the dominant Japanese society and forgetting his Korean roots. As a result he, like many others, has chosen not to become Japanese.

Being naturalized would not solve the real problems because the system of discrimination remains untouched. Strictly speaking, naturalization doesn't mean getting just Japanese nationality. We must make up *honseki* [family records of our birthplace.] It means getting a new family record, then getting Japanese nationality. It is understandable that some Korean groups are asking for easier forms of naturalization and new laws.

Yet like Japanese-Canadians and Japanese-Americans, Koreans in Japan have begun to climb the socioeconomic ladder, and education is the essential element to achieve economic and social security. In Japan, Cho said, eighty-three percent of Korean marriages involved intermarriage with a Japanese. In North America now most *sansei* and *yonsei* are marrying non-Japanese partners. Yet in spite of the high degree of assimilation into the dominant society, both groups feel a difference in behaviour or values that sets them apart from the dominant members of society.

Like many ethnic communities, the Koreans in Japan have been torn and divided. Basically there are three groups defined by generation and the degree of assimilation and how they identify themselves. The other division is based on political allegiance, reflecting the political division of the Korean peninsula — South is the Republic of Korea, and North is the Democratic Peoples' Republic of Korea. Cho explained:

Until the mid-1960s, most Koreans in Japan supported North Korea. In 1965 the South Korea–Japan Treaty was ratified and the Japanese government started giving favours only to those who identified with the South. A split occurred within the community.

Those who sympathized with the South joined an organization called *Min-Dan*, while those who supported the North became members of *So-Ren*.

This division has had many ramifications. Until the 1970s, Japanese banks and schools refused to deal with Koreans. The community therefore set up a parallel system that inevitably became politicized. Because of the divisions, the community now has banks and schools run exclusively by and for members of *So-Ren*, and banks and schools run exclusively by and for members of *Min-Dan*.

The division often tore apart families and friendships.

I was in a pro-North student group, though my family was pro-South. I had many friends in both. Political and ideological conflicts were intense, but the divisions between North and South are usually not what they seem. Many times they are allegiances based on expediency. For example, in order to travel abroad, it's more convenient with a South Korean passport.

For young people in the 1970s, the North-South problem started to seem irrelevant.

These days, the community is less and less interested in politics. Fewer and fewer students attend Korean school, and many of those who do aren't interested in the pro-North or -South propaganda. Many schools have shifted their emphasis from politics to culture and run after-hours, nonpolitical, "ethnic education" programs.

Cho considers himself a member of an ethnic minority and is keenly interested in other minority groups, such as Ainu, Okinawans, and *burakumin*.

The pro-North *So-Ren* people still argue that resident Koreans in Japan are part of the Korean state; therefore they are *not* an ethnic minority in Japan. They regard themselves as foreign citizens. I cannot subscribe to this. Many people say that the problems that resident Koreans have here must be dealt with between the states of Korea and Japan. From that standpoint, the past has already been dealt with. But not for me. I think of myself as a minority member. Being a minority has to mean reflecting back to colonial times and trying to redress past wrongs. I'm like a thorn in the side of the *So-Ren* people, and it's threatening to many of them.

Old timers used to tell us to identify ourselves with our beloved country, Korea. The problem is, first, it has been bitterly divided, and second, I am not crazy about either of the sides. Until quite recently, both have been run by dictatorships. But both *So-Ren* and *Min-Dan* groups are becoming smaller because younger Koreans are not joining. Their priorities are no longer the conflict between North and South. It's understandable for young Koreans to want to become Japanese in order to escape discrimination.

Before, I was a militant and was always angry and impatient. But I have changed. Now I tell the young generation, "Please learn in detail our history and situation. After that, you make up your mind." Before, I didn't know my history and hated myself. In my student days, I went around demanding that people change. I wanted them to do the same as I did. As you can imagine, it was not too successful. Now I just want to tell young people, "Define yourself. Don't let them define you."

As an activist working for civil rights of Koreans, Cho recognizes that the fate of other minority groups in Japan is tied up with his. He is therefore a member of the Kansai University Research Group on Human Rights, which has interests far beyond the borders of his own community and encompassing the causes of all minorities in Japan.

He is especially interested in Ainu issues and became so close to them that he even got married in the Ainu village of Nibutani. In Nibutani the local inn is run by an Ainu. In this remote village, one can still be treated to excellent *kimchi*. The reason these spicy Korean pickles are available in Hokkaido is that the inn owner got them from his friend — Paggie Cho.

Cho is also very active in the music scene. His band, "Garnet Rage," has released two CDs. He sang in Japanese, English, and Korean, and mixed a variety of music ranging from traditional Korean to heavy metal. His music is an extension of his political and human-rights commitment, and an expression of his grassroots multiculturalism.

Keibo recalls the time when he found out about his background:

When I finally found out that my father was originally from North

Korea, I felt, on the one hand, a strong sense of happiness and delight but, on the other, an immense void. For thirty years I had thought I was Japanese. It was with these conflicting emotions that I took the Bullet Train to Osaka. I went directly to the Korean "ghetto," and for hours I walked around in the markets, struck by the exotic atmosphere of the Koreans. Down the side streets were small factories with machines that produced cheap sandals, shoes, plastics, rubber, vinyl products, and bags. This was the bottom rung of the notorious subcontract system.

Then I walked through the narrow alleys of Ikaino. The houses were tiny and stuck together in row upon row surrounded by potted plants and bonsai trees. I looked at each of the nameplates on the houses and felt good when I found Korean names.

It was on that trip that I walked into a bookstore and for the first time saw a book of poetry, entitled *Poems of Ikaino*, by a *zainichi* author, Shijong Kim.

Shijong Kim was born in 1925 in Wonsan, Korea, but moved to Cheju Island, south of the peninsula, where his mother came from. After the war, he moved to Japan and became an activist in *Min-Sen* (Zainichi Korean United Democratic Front), but because of his literary activities, he was gradually alienated from politics. After working in numerous jobs, he became a Korean teacher in a high school.

Today, he is a well-respected poet in both the Korean and Japanese communities in Japan. He had recently published two large volumes of poems and essays in Japanese. He is also known as the spokesperson for the emotionally and politically loaded concept of *zainichi*.

We met Shijong Kim at Tsuruhashi station in Osaka. From his poems and life story we expected Kim to be a big, tough-looking character. But the person we met was handsome, slight of build, almost delicate in his manner, and spoke Japanese with a slight accent. As people around us rushed to catch their trains, Kim suggested we go to the coffee shop on the second floor of the station. There we found a dingy little place full of people. We were able to grab a table, but the waitress was tired and bored, and the coffee was bad. But the atmosphere didn't matter; our focus was on learning more about this most fascinating man.

It was obvious Kim was well prepared for our meeting. He had read David's book *Inventing the Future* in Japanese and, probably for that reason, elected to tell us a story about an ecological miracle that happened in Wakayama prefecture, near Mio (*Amerika-mura*).

A nuclear plant was going to be built there. Some members of a literary club I'm involved with asked me to help fight against it. *Ayu*, the little trout that are a delicacy in Japan, hadn't spawned in the area for five years. The fishermen had considered the ocean dead and so had been recruited to support the nuclear plant in the hopes of getting a few jobs. Two days before the final decision was to be made, a huge run of *ayu* came in to spawn. Upon seeing the *ayu* return, the village executives, who were fishermen and had been for the plant, suddenly changed their minds. They realized the ocean was still alive.

"That's amazing," we interjected. "It was like it was a divine intervention."

"Yes, it was," Kim said. "I have this feeling that things that are wished for strongly by people have to come true." He then began to explain the term "*zainichi.*"

Zainichi is the basis of my existence. When you take the broadest sense of the word, which literally means "being in Japan," even the Japanese are *zainichi*. But they take it for granted that they live in Japan. So *zainichi* is a word that has no meaning to them. This makes them Japanese.

Between those like us who have to be conscious of the fact that they are living in Japan and those who take it for granted, there is a huge gap. We are children of those who were forced to be apart from their native land. This is why *zainichi* is important for us.

There are five million Koreans living outside Korea — two million in the United States, 1.8 million in China, and the rest in Japan, the former Soviet Union, Europe, Canada, and Australia. But according to

Kim, *zainichi* existence in Japan is a distinctive phenomenon because they aren't here by choice, but were forced to live here.

For me, a Korean poet having to write in Japanese, to write about myself meant to write about my relationship with Japan. I had to question why I was here in Japan.

Koreans in Japan don't have to be politicized, because from the beginning we have been political. Our existence itself is political. For *zainichi* writers to write under real names or not, that's already a political act.

Hihyo — criticism. It means a frame of mind that cannot allow itself to be in harmony with the status quo. It's constant questioning, not to indulge in or be spoiled by the status quo. If Koreans in Japan have this, we are automatically dismissed by Japanese poets. It's called dangerous.

Japanese critics have reviewed my work and they often say that it is a mirror on Japanese society. Using the mirror metaphor, I may say the writing of Koreans in Japan is a mirror to see ourselves and the Japanese. We don't force Japanese to look at themselves. If we are digging into the Japanese-Korean psyche, we automatically see ourselves.

The Korean War was fought by the United States against North Korea, using Japan as the base. All planes used in the Korean War flew from Japanese bases. All the bombs dropped in Korea came from Japan. One of the bombs, a fragmentation weapon called "parent-child" bomb was manufactured by Japanese corporations. The Korean War, and later the Vietnam War, gave the post–Second World War Japanese economy a boost. Like many resident Koreans, however, Kim was active in the anti-war movement during the Korean War.

In those days, Korean organizations were illegal. An organization called Min-Sen [Zainichi Korean United Democratic Front] had ninety percent of resident Koreans behind it. Trains were loaded with bombs. If they could be stopped for ten minutes, it would save 10,000 lives in Korea. So we'd lie on tracks or break signals so they were fixed on Stop. People died by being electrocuted or falling off the poles.

The Japanese government, with help from the CIA, did all they could to crush us. The tragic thing was that other Koreans in Japan worked to make bombs. Koreans desperately needed work and would take any job offered to them. Huge corporations would place orders with small factories to make parts — nuts and bolts. Since there were lots of small businesses, no one knew they were working on bombs when they were only making nuts and bolts.

That was real darkness, the Korean War. Resident Koreans were mobilized to kill their compatriots. But can we blame them when they were making nuts and bolts? Then, can we allow bombs to be made? So our movement against the war would go around and destroy the small factories.

Imagine how helpless the small factories were. Koreans in the Ikaino community were bidding against each other, bringing prices down. Japanese wouldn't take the contracts at such low prices. Koreans would put the whole family to work, competing with each other, while the big corporations took advantage and made a lot of money. I can still see it vividly. At the time, the Hirano Canal was full of iron dust from the waste dumped in the canal by many small factories making nuts and bolts. People would scoop up the mud for the iron dust to make a bit of money.

The reason I talk at such great length is the big word *zainichi*, which is ourselves. I don't want to draw a nice picture about ourselves. This muddy, desperate situation is our place called Ikaino.

But, on the other hand, Ikaino was a haven for us Zainichi. When someone was chased by the police, if they could get to Ikaino, they were safe. Up to the 1960s, Japanese police couldn't come into Ikaino safely. Of course, Koreans were fighting each other, but any Korean in this area was protected by everyone from the Japanese enemy. So we called Ikaino a liberated quarter.

Ikaino represented our struggle, conflicts, confusion, and chaos, yet we always maintained this communal feeling rooted in our common struggle to survive. All of these elements merged into one. When I write about indigenousness and nativeness in my poems, I am talking about the inevitability of fighting and hating each other, yet having to live together. We are the people who from the beginning of existence were devoid of social, civil, and legal rights. We are abandoned people. We are people without strong roots, yet somehow on hard work, we survived by extending small rootlets. Even if we hate each other, we have to live together and even learn to love each other by entangling our roots. And Ikaino is the symbol of such existence.

In fact the name Ikaino (whose Chinese characters mean "the field where hogs are raised") doesn't exist on the map anymore. When Osaka decided to erase this name to incorporate the town into a larger area, many residents were opposed. They felt that the Japanese were trying to destroy their identity by erasing the name that served as a symbol of the Korean minority in Japan. Kim wrote a poem about Ikaino, called "The Invisible Town":

The town which is there yet not there
The town which disappears while being there
The town which even trains detour
But they make sure the crematorium is right there
Everybody knows it
But the town's not on the map
Because it's not on the map, it's not Japan
Because it's not Japan, it's okay if it disappears
Because it doesn't matter, we feel free

There everybody talks loudly
Accents are spoken proudly
Even the plates have an appetite
People's stomachs are so strong
That they consume from the tip of the nose
To the bottom of the heel

They arrogantly claim

They are responsible for Japan's nutrition. [9]

Kim continued with his explanation of the term *zainichi*:

> Such is the nature of *zainichi*. It is in this entangled coexistence that I
> see a big potential for the future of Korean people, including those in
> North and South Korea. We are experimenting in Japan for the
> future of North and South Korea. Maybe here we can find the
> possibility of our future unification: living
> together in spite of disagreements. In other
> words, our existence itself points to the future of
> our people.
>
> What made this kind of existence and what
> made it so strong is our elders and their
> nativeness. They still keep customs and
> traditions forgotten in Korea. They can be
> mocked as old-fashioned, but they are stubborn.
> Korean *issei* in Japan [the immigrant generation]
> are almost gone, *nisei* are up to seventy years old.
> Even today at funerals, there are fights among
> *nisei* over the order of offerings. For example,
> which direction is the head of the fish to point?
> Does it matter? It seems laughable in the modern
> age, but I find it precious in the context of our
> history. I cherish it. I feel frustrated at not being
> able to convey this to the younger generation.

"Koreans in Japan don't have to be politicized, because from the beginning we have been political. Our existence itself is political."

SHIJONG KIM, KOREAN-BORN POET

The poet, however, had no romantic illusions
about his own people.

> I'm against discrimination. But I can't subscribe to those who feel
> that being discriminated against means automatically they are on the
> side of justice. I hate that attitude. I see egotism not just on the side
> of the bigot, but on the side of the victim, and that can be even more
> of a danger.

I want to end my prolonged talk with an ancient parable. A parrot was looking at a copper mirror. While looking, it pecked at the mirror until it destroyed its own beak. What I'm doing is just like that: looking at the mirror and looking at myself pecking at my own image. If something shocks me, that would be my own bloody bill, face and flesh.

Back in Sakuramoto, in the Korean district in Kawasaki city, we once again joined Inha Lee. On that day, he was at the cross-cultural day-care centre he set up and operates. We walked among a group of three- and four-year-olds busily playing in the front yard. Lee explained to us that after he began working at the church in 1959, he felt it was imperative to get closer to the community and to bridge the gap between the Japanese and Korean communities. "So I decided to open my sanctuary for children," he said simply.

Like the *burakumin* day-care centre we had visited with Megumi Matsumoto, Lee's centre brought Korean and Japanese children together under one roof. They learned about Korean language and culture, and they developed an attitude of understanding and respect. The day-care also had children with Latin American and Filipino backgrounds. Lee told us:

> In the beginning when parents found their children were assigned to a nursery where the head was a Korean, they tried to pull their children out. Sometimes they'd lie and say they had been transferred to another place. But the children love it here and don't want to leave. Parents are always defeated by their children because they love them. After a while, Japanese parents confess, "We inherited our prejudice against Koreans." When they say that, Korean women clap and say, "Now we can become real friends."

Lee's passion for helping Koreans establish themselves in the community includes a drive to improve Japanese society as well. He has always urged young Koreans to become a creative, useful force within society, not just to merge into the majority.

Minority groups have suffered pain. If we inflict it on others, we are not mature. We must each overcome this as individuals. By raising our own demands and issues, we make the majority face themselves. The Japanese confess that Koreans are a mirror for themselves.

Although Lee has suffered a lifetime of persecution, he has taken a conciliatory position.

It makes me angry the way Koreans have been treated by the Japanese, but I also feel sorry for racist Japanese. They are just victims of the Imperial system and an education system that fosters hatred and ignorance.

Lee has a positive attitude towards the people and country he had adopted as his own. "Although I hate what they did to us, I cannot hate the Japanese."

Lee's concerns and activities are concentrated in one particular locality, the Sakuramoto district in Kawasaki, yet his philosophy has no place for narrow-minded nationalism and regionalism. As he showed us around Sakuramoto, he bubbled over with energy and enthusiasm, and his passion never seemed fanatical or overbearing. His ideas were radical and progressive, yet in his radicalism there was something gentle and cheerful. Even when he talked of the atrocities his people have had to endure, we didn't see any anger or bitterness. He said, "I enjoy being a minority person," and even, "I enjoy living in Japan."

We asked him, "What makes being a minority person enjoyable for you?"

"It is perhaps because I am in a position to deal and associate with a wider range of humanity," he replied. "When you have a broader and deeper question, the answer will be likewise wider and deeper."

Being the victim of discrimination and persecution is hard, but living with such abuse can have positive effects, as it forces the minority to ask difficult questions about human nature. In trying to answer those questions, minority members can experience growth, which humanizes them. Lee told us:

Korean boys in the neighbourhood are very popular among young Japanese girls. Knowing the daily behaviour of these youngsters fairly well, I sometimes have to discourage Japanese girls from getting involved with Korean boys, but most girls are persistent and say, "Korean boys are more attractive."

What does this all mean? According to Lee, girls probably find a quality, a sense of purpose, in Korean boys that Japanese boys don't seem to have. Being with someone who is suffering from discrimination and fighting to overcome it perhaps gives the girls a sense of personal growth.

In our conversation, Lee often said, "There's no absolute in culture." He explained that culture is constantly changing. "It is constantly mixing and becoming something else. In that sense, acculturation is an inevitable and even natural process."

We asked him if we could call him an assimilationist, then. He replied that, in fact, he is often called an assimilationist by other *zainichi* from various political camps. Yet he was most adamantly opposed to an assimilation in which one's self is submerged. Lee proposed that we be tolerant with both what one felt he or she was today and what one might feel in the future. Again there is no absolute in culture and one's identity in the historical process, and it is when we are free from cultural absolutism that a constructive dialogue becomes possible between ethnicities and cultures.

Unlike *burakumin*, who have yet to achieve university education and to expand into professions and business, Koreans have attained considerable success in Japanese society. Like their Nikkei counterparts in North America, these Koreans have endured a history of exploitation and abuse, which they are only now openly discussing among themselves and with Japanese. Like other minority groups, they confront the Japanese with the reality that Japan is not homogenous and that the diversity is a gift to the Japanese. As Koreans in Japan reflect on their differences and what their heritage is, they provide a mirror for Japanese to see themselves.

CHAPTER 8

voices from
the belly

"The orthodox tradition of male domination has

been expressed in Japan since the mid-1800s.

But there has been a hidden tradition. This is

represented within the household, by women.

However much Japanese soldiers worshipped the

emperor outwardly, when the war ship

Musashi *sank, young sailors who lay dying on the*

deck cried out for their mothers, not the emperor."

SHUNSUKE TSURUMI

LIKE those in most countries in the world, Japan's political and business spheres are dominated by men. And the popular western image of a Japanese woman is of one who is submissive, obedient, and attentive to men's every whim — even walking a few paces behind. But today Japanese women are better educated, freed from much of the drudgery of household work, and domiciled away from the extended family. They have greater opportunities for leisure, recreation, and reflection, although the heavy demands of most men's long workdays and weeks mean that wives and mothers spend much of their time alone or with young children. Long before the changes in Japanese modern women's education and way of life, there was a hidden tradition of women at the fore. These women in mythology and folklore can be bawdy, aggressive, and funny.

In Kyoto, we met Shunsuke Tsurumi (see Chapter 3), a leading philosopher who has written extensively about the history of thought. Among the many subjects he had dealt with, he chose to tell us a remarkable story from his book, *Amenouzume-den*.[1] It goes as follows:

Sayo Kitamura was born in 1900 and died in 1967. She was a farming woman in Yamaguchi prefecture. On May 4, 1944, she got up early for her ritual prayer at the Shinto altar. But when she walked by her still-sleeping husband, she kicked the pillow and a voice came out of her throat that seemed to come from someone else: "Hey! Listen, Sayanoshin! The heartfelt prayers that Sayo has been offering in the middle of morning and afternoon, even on the coldest winter days, have certainly reached my ears. In contrast with her, you, another of my children, do away with such prayers and indulge in sleep. Get up and pray at once!"

Until that moment, Kitamura had been a hardworking peasant's wife who had accepted her lot as her husband's sixth wife and who bore the heavy burden of a domineering mother-in-law. She was a dutiful citizen, never questioning the emperor and the military. But on that fateful morning, she was transformed by a god who entered her belly and used her as his mouthpiece. She would suddenly scream, often in crude language, berating people. Initially she supported the war effort and urged people to sacrifice for Japan's victory, but by the fall of 1944 the god in Kitamura was criticizing the imperial family, something breathtakingly audacious for a citizen. On September 28 Kitamura had a conversation with the god in her belly, and the god warned that this criticism could lead to persecution of her family. Her son in the military would have to commit *seppuku* (ritual suicide), her husband could go insane, and they could lose all their property. When Kitamura asked whether the god was a good or bad one, the god replied that he was benevolent but needed someone willing to make sacrifices for the sake of the nation. Kitamura responded, "All right! If by sacrificing my life, the lives of my family members and our petty property, I can save our nation, then fine, go ahead and continue to use me!" Immediately her body floated in the air a couple of feet above the ground.

The loss of the war left people all across Japan in a state of shock, cities were flattened, the land pocked with bomb craters, and the citizens bereft of leadership. Into that psychic vacuum, Sayo Kitamura and the god in her belly offered something to cling to. On August 16, after Japan's surrender, Kitamura declared in a half song, half chant, "Wake up, maggots! Wake up, traitors! Wake up, all you scavengers and beggars! Now the heavenly door of rocks has opened to a new world." Songs, chants, and speeches spewed out of her mouth, and people around found that often in spite of themselves, they would end up joining her as if the sounds were coming from their own bellies. Then Kitamura would often dance, and this, in turn, stimulated people to leap into a frenzy of dancing. This group ecstasy became known as the "dancing religion." When Kitamura visited Tokyo, her train was surrounded by dancing people. Word spread that dancing was healing. In this turbulent period, when all seemed so hopeless and life was a constant struggle to survive, there was little infrastructure to serve the physical and psychic needs of a defeated nation. Kitamura offered relief from the relentless stress of postwar Japan.

Somehow, although there was nothing in her early life that would have hinted at Kitamura's extraordinary transformation, she had tapped into the healing powers of music and dance. For the nation, monumental decisions were being made as the Allies moved in to set Japan on a new course of democracy. Not surprisingly, Kitamura was treated derisively by the media as an ignorant, superstitious woman who was irrelevant in a country that was rejecting its militaristic, imperial tradition for western democracy and capitalism. But in a time of desperate need and pain, the god in Kitamura's belly offered people respite and relief from their suffering. According to Tsurumi, Kitamura was only one of the contemporary examples of women offering a different perspective. This tradition of unorthodox women goes far back in Japanese history.

We left Tsurumi to travel to the manufacturing city of Osaka. It struck us as a huge, cluttered, dirty city, and Minami, its commercial centre, was frenetically active. To get to our goal — the office of activist Yumi Horikoshi — we passed through the narrow streets behind the Nikko Hotel to an unprepossessing door. At the top of a long, narrow staircase were two tiny rooms filled with boxes overflowing with paper, two huge photocopy and fax machines, and walls plastered with posters, memos, and little gifts left by the constant flow of visitors. This cluttered warren was the heart and nerve centre of Yumi Horikoshi's remarkable network. She greeted us and explained:

> Unlike other activists, I am not interested in justice. I am not motivated by the fury of wrongs that need righting. Anger never got me anywhere. If I am angry I will immediately shout or yell and get rid of it. I am motivated by my feelings about life. I feel the spirits guide me to the role I must play and all I do is peacefully accept. I am lucky.

Horikoshi manoeuvred gracefully around her compact office, pulling out files, making tea, and chain-smoking Marlboros. Against the wall behind her desk were neat, orderly files marked "Sacred Run '93," "Japan-Ainu Foundation," "Dennis Banks," and many more. They represent the practical part of her world, the place where information was received, stored, and then retrieved. Pinned to the wall facing her desk was an impressive collection of jewellery given to her by friends or bought on trips. In the corner, to the left behind her desk, was an eclectic shrine incorporating a figure of the Buddha, Native American art, and other objects that have meaning to her. Sage burned in the incense holder.

The warm serenity of her office was shattered only by the thunderous ringing of the telephone (because of a childhood vaccine gone wrong, her inner ears were damaged and she has difficulty hearing) and the constant chatter of incoming faxes.

Horikoshi was born on February 9, 1949, in a family deeply rooted in a Japan of the past.

My family was part of a unique world of refined leisure activities. My grandfather, a very talented man, was a traditional puppet player. Had he lived longer he would have become a national treasure of Japan. He came to train in Kyoto and met my grandmother, who was a *geisha*. People often have a completely wrong impression of *geisha*. Some have made the word mean "prostitute" when really it has nothing to do with that. *Geisha* are highly paid, extremely well-trained entertainers. My grandmother had undergone very severe training. She married my grandfather and they opened a *geisha* house. It was an inn, a social club, a restaurant, but very refined, very high class. You don't see that sort of place anymore. It was a special, different kind of world: a world of convention and form.

Her grandparents were childless, and as was quite common at the time, they adopted two girls from relatives — Horikoshi's mother and aunt. The aunt was trained in bookkeeping to take over the accounting for the *geisha* house, and Horikoshi's mother, who had artistic talents, was taught the flute, drumming, *shamisen* (three-stringed instrument), the tea ceremony, and dancing.

My mother became a *geisha*, a highly refined professional entertainer. To be entertained by a *geisha* of this calibre was very expensive. But my mother fell in love with a client and became his mistress. The man had a family, so they could never really be together.

Horikoshi grew up without a father. As a teenager, she heard his name, but it made no impression on her. She simply accepted life without a father. He wasn't even listed in the official birth records.

In a nation in which appearance and harmony are so important, even as a child, Horikoshi stood out in her directness and honesty. "I was different from other children of my age," she said. "I was very honest about my tastes. Once I liked doing something, I would continue to do it all day. I was very active, like a boy."

She was often told, "You left your penis in your mother's womb." Her mother's background meant Horikoshi had to learn the traditional arts even as she was yearning to do more modern things.

I went to art high school and there I met a teacher who interested me in design and modern art. I had nothing to do with the student movements or antiwar protests that were so prevalent at the time. I was into modern art and fashion. When I was nineteen, I established myself as an independent designer. I was asked to design children's clothes for a very big department store, and my business became quite successful.

Horikoshi's unusual attitudes were revealed as she recounted the story of her marriage and the birth of her child.

I was twenty-seven when I met my husband. He was already involved with a woman, but I took him from her. When I became pregnant, I was not at all interested in my unborn child. I felt victimized and tried to deny what was about to happen by working until three days before I gave birth. I almost miscarried. When my son, Dai-jiro, was born, I felt no special recognition or bond. It was a fact that he had come from me through my body, but that was not what I felt. He came from somewhere else. For him, my body was just a vehicle. It took about a month to put everything together after his birth. My emotional development always seems to be one step behind what is going on in my life.

Her marriage lasted only three years.

It turned out my husband was good only for seed. That was the last time I chose a man over my work. But I learned a valuable lesson: don't take a person away from someone else. When I got divorced, I seriously considered giving my ex-husband custody of Dai. I thought he was the better parent. Then one day I was in the park with Dai and suddenly I began crying. I realized that the only hope for both mother and son was for us to stay together.

When we met Horikoshi, her son was a teenager who towered over his mother and wore his hair in a long ponytail. He was treated like an adult by his mother who obviously adored him without suffocating him. He frequently travelled and stayed with his mother's many contacts in different parts of the world.

But at the same time I learned from my son that life was shining in him. My son is indescribably precious. What was important was not just him but the environment in which he could be precious. So I began to study everything that surrounded this life. The human body, medicine, food, air, water, the sun, all the things necessary for life to survive. My way was to try anything. I have no background in academics. At the same time people began to come to my place with all kinds of questions. But whenever I received a question, I had to learn in order to answer it. I was never a teacher, I was more like a *connector*. Someone needed information and I could find out where an answer was available, connecting those who need help and those who can help. But still, in order to determine what the real problem was, I had to keep learning.

She eventually opened a centre called Yumi's Laboratory of Living Studies and put out a newsletter on topics ranging from nutrition to health care, human relationships to spirituality. Sometimes she put out special issues on topics she was digging into, such as new forms of birth control. She also ran a successful shop called Making Lives of Mothers and Children More Enjoyable, which became an information centre. People with problems or questions about child-rearing, health, and life crises would call or drop in.

When Horikoshi was still a baby, her mother had saved enough to leave the *geisha* house and open her own high-class tempura restaurant, her dream since childhood. Horikoshi still owned it when we met her, but it was run with her aunt as an ordinary lunch restaurant.

When Horikoshi was thirty-nine, her mother was diagnosed with a rare brain cancer.

> My mother and I were always fighting because we were so similar. We fought about anything. But she loved me so much. During her last three months, she and I became real mother and child. I took care of her totally. During the last two weeks, she was unconscious but I kept talking to her, letting her know that I would be there when she died. I was determined to be present right until the end. When her heart stopped, everyone panicked. I was calm. I said thank-you to the doctor. I put makeup on the body.

Horikoshi gave permission for an autopsy on the condition that she be present.

> I was there when they cut her chest open. It didn't bleed, it just fell open. You could see white fat. I was surprised. When you are alive, a pinprick will make you bleed. So this was death.

> As a person, as a human being, as a whole, I greatly respect my mother's way of doing things and of feeling. I know that at the end of my life, I won't be superior to her.

> As I learned all kinds of things, I realized living and dying are the same thing. I realized in this society, to be born naturally and to die naturally are becoming very difficult. But what really matters is to know how to die, which is in the end the same thing as knowing how to live. How to die is something I often contemplate. I have been learning that dying is something not to be afraid of. Dying means living happily and fully, being a full person. Then I look around and see how the environment is deteriorating so rapidly and badly. To live as a person is becoming increasingly difficult.

Horikoshi herself has seamlessly combined spirituality, organization, and laughter. As a representative in Japan for Dennis Banks, one of the leaders of the American Indian Movement, she coordinated the Sacred Run, an event Banks founded. She also managed her restaurant, has organized events for the Ainu and other minorities, talked and — more importantly — listened to countless people who have passed through her office seeking advice and friendship. A stream of people have climbed that steep staircase with minds to be healed and descended with fulfilled hearts. Her place is a hangout for young people who come and go as freely as if they were in their own homes. In addition, she has written books and pamphlets. She is a mother, a teacher, an artist; she has cranked out newsletters, acted as a clearing house of information of all sorts, and been consulted by citizens groups and anthropologists alike. All of these roles have been accomplished in an atmosphere of calm. She told us that she did not seek to be a leader, but she believes this is where the spirits have led her, so she must accept their call.

Horikoshi represents a completely new type of politics based on individual action, womanhood, and community building, yet her originality is deeply rooted in Japanese tradition. Her family is very traditional. She has never lived abroad. She is an important part of her community.

"Simply, the Earth is the mother and all things in it are children."

YUMI HORIKOSHI,
RESTAURATEUR,
ACTIVIST

Following the Meiji Era [1868–1912], the Japanese became artificially rigid in their movements. It was a part of modernization and industrialization. Those in my mother's world retained some aspects of that old culture in the Edo Period (1603–1867) and the premodern physicality and sense of body movement. There was a culture based on feeling, rather than a culture based heavily on words. I am very responsive to that kind of tradition.

That Horikoshi has broken out of conventional strictures of Japanese tradition was clear the minute we entered her office. The posters on the walls were mostly of North American Indians, and the shelves overflowed with eagle feathers and aboriginal jewellery. She has a deep attachment to North American aboriginal people, and her description of how she got involved with them had an almost mystical air about it.

I'm now connected with all kinds of people and issues. One person, Kiyoshi Miyata, was a filmmaker who had done a film about Hopi Indians, called *Hopi Prophecy*. Just before he contacted me, I was in bed with a strange disease. Since childhood I've always had a special sensitivity. I don't know what it is, whether it is physical or mental. I just knew spiritually it was a prophecy that something very important would come to me. I was in bed when Miyata called about something called Hoppy or Poppy, which didn't mean a thing to me. He was talking about Hiroshima and I thought, "Who cares?" So I resisted. But he insisted and finally talked me into going to see the film. The opening scene was the bombing of Hiroshima and Nagasaki, and I thought, "Oh, this is going to be depressing." But eventually I was in tears. It wasn't surprise or sadness but recognition. I knew exactly what the Indians were trying to say about the Earth being the mother and all living things her children. I had been thinking about and living the mother-child relationship for years. By the end, when the Hopi Declaration of Peace came on, I felt everything I had been doing was expressed so clearly. I knew this was an extremely important film.

When we visited, the Hopi Declaration hung on the inside of the toilet door. It reads:

The traditional Hopi people preserve the sacred knowledge about the way of the Earth because the true Hopi People know that the Earth is a living, growing person. And all things on it are her children.

Horikoshi continued:

It wasn't that I cared about Indians, but I wanted the message to be taken to the Japanese. I offered to help by selling tickets to the film, but they talked me into organizing the whole event. They said they needed a woman to play that role. So I said, "Only once." For the

Osaka opening, we booked a place with six hundred seats. We had only nineteen days to the opening. The day before the opening, only fifty tickets had been sold. Next day, the line went around the block! The film had an explosive impact. It spread through Japan. I found myself in the thick of it. I felt the blood boiling in me whenever I saw the film. It was *en*, a special connection between me and the film; me and the Indians.

The word *en* is a Buddhist notion that means destiny and the invisible network that interconnects people, things, and events.

For many young Japanese activists who have taken up environmental causes, the Ainu people are often an avenue for new insights. Horikoshi is one of these activists. From aboriginal people, she believes, Japanese could learn a new relationship with the Earth.

I think native people have the key to open the future of every living form on the Earth. Their way of living teaches us how all forms of life are supposed to live. They taught me why I had been concerned with mothers and children. What I've been doing and the way they are made a circle. Simply, the Earth is the mother and all things in it are children. The anthropocentric view has no place in this. We have to be humble and go back to a humble way of being. What I'm doing is not for native people. I'm not doing things for them. I have no desire to become an Indian. As an outsider, I'm willing to help when they need it. But I'm not doing things just for them. I work for the seventh generation [she was referring to the aboriginal notion that before any major decision is made, one should reflect back on seven generations of our ancestors and ahead to the seventh generation of our children before acting]. That means for myself. My work is about how I live and die.

I do feel American Indians and Japanese are closely related. I feel the same about the Ainu. It's as if we used to live in the same village. I see Japanese who get the message and apply that to their own way of living. Quite a few people absorb it and incorporate it. It's a process of questioning and asking oneself, "How can I live on this land?" My friends got enlightened by contacting natives, but all went back to their own identity. It's painful to live in a city like Osaka. More and more young people are looking for a new human way to live, realizing how crazy this is. It may be hard to put it in practice, but they're questioning and seeking. Of course, they're still a minority, but they are an important group.

In Japan as in North America, modernity has accelerated the pace of life and opened professional opportunities for women. But in the process, society has been spun apart by the swirl of change.

Extended families, communities, neighbourhoods are pretty much gone. Before the war, it would have been impossible for a mother with a young child to have been left on her own. Now mothers don't know what to do, how to raise their kids. Individuals are so lonely and isolated. People have no one to talk to. Many precious things have been lost. People talk to me because I am a rare example of a frank person.

Horikoshi had a keen interest in the ways that men and women are different. She believes that men and women both have masculine and feminine qualities, and that the way women are is men's fault and the way men are is women's fault.

Man's point of view is society's point of view. Men themselves have internalized it. To escape from that is the meaning of growth. Most men haven't grown as they should. We have many stunted men. Often I ask, "How long can they remain so childish?" and then I just sigh. Women grow, but most men don't, and neither knows about the other. A relationship that is *sukoyaka* [healthy] is very rare.

Horikoshi believes duty is frequently the glue that holds families together.

Often the same day the youngest child gets married and the mother considers her family duties finished, she serves her husband with divorce papers. Usually the husbands are completely shocked. These divorced men are so dependent on their wives that they either collapse and shrink into something else or barely survive. Some don't even know where their underwear is. Some of these newly divorced women schemed to get money out of their husbands. Others are so eager to be free that they don't care what happens next. In my case, I just wanted to be free, to be rid of him. After that I began to try to figure out how to survive.

We suggested that her lack of ego gave her power and asked if this was part of her womanhood.

My distinction between men and women is not biological. It's a way of thinking and feeling. It's a style of sensitivity that many of my male friends have. We can say there is a feminine way of thinking, but it doesn't mean men can't think that way.

Look at modern materialistic civilization and all its consumer products. It is obviously based on what I call male thinking — a greed for honour, and a desire to take and possess. I know I have male in me at the depths of my existence. I don't know whether I am a feminist. If I am, my feminism doesn't mean confrontation with men. I don't like that.

Men have the desire to get credit — "I created this, I did that." When people want credit, I say, "Go ahead." I don't care. I have no interest in those kinds of thoughts. I have no background in academics, no knowledge or ability, but if you can find some use for me, please use me, without giving me credit. That's my attitude. To certain people in Japan, my existence is intolerable because I don't fit in with their worldview. The pyramid structure created by men will collapse completely. I'm not denying the importance of men, but the structure will have to go. The Hopi elder Thomas Banyacya at the United Nations said that when women start to move, that will be the final time.

Her words were deceptively simple. They revealed someone who had experienced a great deal, thought about it, and worked out a philosophy that cut through the artifice and barriers. Watching her constantly responding to demands while making it seem effortless, we were struck by her calm. She had achieved a kind of inner peace that let her bear constant pressure and demands without caving in.

Throughout our stay in the Kansai area, Horikoshi kindly volunteered to act as our guide. She was with us when we visited many of the different communities, including the *burakumin*, Korean, and Japanese-Canadian. She connected us to many incredible people.

Toward the end of our stay she invited us to a formal tempura dinner in the special upstairs room of her restaurant. The restaurant was originally built to reflect the refined and traditional world of the *geisha*. It had beautifully polished hardwood floors and trim and many separate rooms, each designed for a special purpose. The ceilings were partly formed by handmade paper made by an artist friend of Horikoshi's. As we entered the room she greeted us by sitting on the floor and bowing deeply in a traditional manner. The woman we had met in jeans and an embroidered Indian jacket with her hair tied in a ponytail was completely transformed. It was as if she had become another person. She was wearing a beautiful kimono, had carefully applied makeup, and all her movements seemed carefully choreographed. We sat in front of a low counter on the other side of which Horikoshi prepared a four-course meal while entertaining us. It was a beautiful meal: artistic and gastronomic at the same time. We were amazed at this refined woman who could assume such a traditional demeanour for this evening but has evolved a uniquely modern, yet Japanese role for herself.

Iriomote, an island on the southwestern edge of the Okinawan chain, is rugged, remote, and beautifully lush. Most of the island is designated as a national park. The verdant park and its mangrove-rimmed rivers team with wildlife, including a rare, primitive species of wild cat (*yamaneko*). It is the second-last island before Taiwan.

We had to travel this far, to the very edge of Japan, to find unspoiled nature. Twenty minutes from the harbour, we reached the village of Sonai, one of the oldest settlements, at the far end of the island.

We had come to visit Akiko Ishigaki (see also Chapter 4), whose way of life was different from Yumi Horikoshi's, yet both shared a grounding in place and the feminine. Ishigaki is a small, elegant woman who could have stepped out of a painting by Gauguin. The clothes she wore that day were from Bali, Indonesia, a place she adored and loved to visit. Akiko brought the craft of weaving to Iriomote from her home island of Taketomi, a neighbouring island especially renowned for its weaving. Since moving to Iriomote, Ishigaki has played an important role in reactivating traditional weaving, which she also taught to others.

> My work is a craft. Of course it's artistic, but it's also practical. Any locality and the environment around it naturally produce crafts. It's a natural spontaneous urge that brings out craft. To me, *rootedness* is very important.

Ishigaki's deep interest in local history and tradition shows in her weaving. She took us on a tour of her stunningly beautiful studio, a lovely open shedlike structure surrounded by the gardens in which she grows the plants she uses to make dyes. She is almost completely self-sufficient. Her way of working is time-consuming and utterly cost-ineffective in a world of mass production. But here, it is clearly the only true way of doing things.

> All materials used are natural. You grow the plant, make threads, and you dye them. The dyes are made from leaves, insects, and seeds, using up to one hundred different kinds of plants. It's the original way.

Ishigaki uses traditional weaving techniques that were popular in the sixteenth and seventeenth centuries. The areas of Yaiyama and Miyako were especially famous for their weaving, called *jofu*, or high-class clothes. The designs themselves were standardized by the lords of the royal castle in the capital, Shuri. If the new work wasn't a perfect match with the standard, the weavers were punished. The women had to work hard, eight to ten hours a day. A single piece of clothing could take up to two months. From Shuri, clothing was sent to the mainland of Japan and distributed all over the rest of the nation. At one time, all women wove, but today almost no one does because it is such hard work and there is such a low return. Ishigaki told us:

> Scientifically produced things are used anywhere by anybody.
> Okinawa designs were used for tools for everyday use, and the
> patterns came from nature — wind, bird, water, cloud, butterfly,
> flowers. The patterns symbolized things and were transmitted as
> traditions from Okinawa. The patterns bear the names of their
> inventors. Symbols can be combined in many different patterns. A
> cloth-making craft that began in Okinawa flowed north and
> influenced centres in Japan.

Today, with the expansion of machines and chemicals, there are ways
to mass-produce materials and new synthetic dyes and fibres. We asked
Ishigaki how her work fit in with this trend, if at all.

> I'm going against the trend now, but maybe later we'll be part of a
> different movement. We have to compromise. We can't cut ourselves
> off completely from commercialization, but at the same time, we
> can't lose our sense of balance. I must maintain a sense of balance or
> I'm lost. We can mass-produce things that most ordinary people
> cannot tell from my kind of work. But a few people know and can tell
> the difference. People who were once part of that mass-production
> world have cut their links and come here to reconnect.

Ishigaki's work became more widely recognized since the famous
Japanese designer Issei Miyake discovered her. But her success hasn't gone
to her head.

Ishigaki's search for cultural independence from Japan and from
material needs from outside is a form of parochialism or local chauvin-
ism. Yet she still feels connected to cities and urban life. Her son from her
first marriage lives in Tokyo, and from time to time, she visits him there.
She also places her work in exhibitions in Tokyo a few times a year.

> We shouldn't be completely separated from what goes on in the
> cities. We get a lot of information from the city. We have to learn to
> select what is important. I understand that. Communication between
> urban dwellers and us is becoming more and more important. We

should learn what is important in their lives, like their increased desire for natural products, and respond to that. We need to know what kind of person is wearing the kimono we are making.

Today people aren't interested in production. Consumption is everything. The silk, linen, textile industry are all dead. We don't produce things to eat. We destroy the environment to make things to consume. This trend must be reversed.

Another connection Sonai has with tradition are its festivities. Twice a year, the normally sleepy village erupts into a pageant of colour and song, festivals to reassert the community and, more importantly, to ask the gods for a good harvest in the following year.

This area is rich in rituals and festivals. A festival is an offering to gods, spirits, and ancestors. There is a saying that you should offer the gods two flowers. The flower of the hands (weaving) and the flower of the body (dance). So, handicraft and rituals are inseparable. Women play the central role in both handicrafts and festivals. What is most important in life is what you can't see — for example, the weaving that makes the clothes. The same is true of the festival. The centre of the festival is not the men's drinking or spectacular dance, but the women's cooking and praying. From ancient times, women were central in religious rituals. The main island of Okinawa is losing that tradition, but here in Iriomote it's still alive.

For Ishigaki, what has been important is connecting herself with the traditional knowledge passed down by the elders, then handing it down accurately to the next generation. It is very important for her to ensure that everything is accurate. Her motto for weaving is, quite simply, quality not quantity.

Even university graduates don't know the difference between silk and plant material. It's strange, but even craftspeople don't know the source of their material. The craftspeople are like the flowers of society, but many don't know their roots.

Nature and weaving are a common environment for Okinawans;

they are part of life, not something separate. I tell the people who come here to weave that they should come when it feels right. Some people are married, some work. They should just find three hours. As long as people are comfortable, they'll come when they can.

According to Ishigaki, nature, women, and the art of weaving are inseparably intertwined. She told us how the cycles and rhythms of nature affect her work.

It's hot in the summer and we don't have air-conditioning or fans, so weavers complain about the heat. Our materials depend on the seasons and the plants that are available, so we're very aware of the cycles. When you work with natural materials, you know that they are sensitive to heat, season, humidity, time of day.

I use banana-leaf fibre only when it's wet or raining. The material is so sensitive to humidity. It can't be worked in air-conditioning. I can't work on it when the sun is out. On the other hand, dyes like mangrove or indigo work well when the sun is out.

Synthetic material doesn't depend on natural conditions. It can imitate material but is never real. That's why it can be mass-produced. Natural colours and synthetic colours, when done, look exactly the same. But as they age, they change. Natural colour becomes more beautiful, artificial becomes ugly. There is a sense of time and the way material is used in products. Natural things become more beautiful as they're used.

Ishigaki also believes that weaving is primarily women's art.

I would like to see weaving as part of the daily life of women. Weavers are invariably women, and it may be that they're more sensitive to natural cycles and connections with food.

Of course, men can become very good weavers like women. But in daily life, women take it more naturally. It's peaceful and is part of a natural rhythm. Women have a natural menstrual cycle and are used to the slowness of time and pay attention to detail. These fit with women. It's calm work, not aggressive.

When I work, I entrust my existence to nature and time. To make a piece of cloth forty centimetres wide, I need 1,200 threads, which have to be threaded one by one. It's the way we deal with time.

Ishigaki herself came from an even smaller island. We asked her about the younger generation, many of whom have been tempted to leave the island. Where will the future of the island culture come from?

I was raised in this environment, but young people now go to school and learn about things in a formal book way. I, too, wanted to go to Tokyo and become a designer and never return. At first it seemed very convenient living in Tokyo, with its public transportation and technology, but then it became clear that urban life was very inconvenient. When I began to work in the artistic world, I realized something else: if there was material I wanted for my work, it was impossible to find sand, soil, plants, anything. But here I can always get what I need.

"When I work,

I entrust my existence

to nature and time."

AKIKE ISHIGAKI,

WEAVER

One day in a museum, I saw a display case full of material from my home place, things my grandmother had made and we had used. I realized how precious our crafts were.

There is no high school on Iriomote, so the children must now leave the island. Trying to force them to stay is futile. We must let them go, but at the same time we must work hard to create an environment to which young people would love to return.

Many people take it as fate that youths do not return. It's true there is a lack of jobs here. But the most important thing is that people have lost pride and cannot teach their children. People tend to forget that living from the Earth must be the basis of our pride.

Ishigaki wants to remind people of how much island culture had to offer young women from the big cities in Japan. She saw many who, when they came to Iriomote Island, were under stress, their skin covered in a rash. After a few weeks, their skin cleared up and they left glowing. It was hardly surprising. We found the air over the island to be clean. And while there was evidence of building (the highway was under construction), there was no urban congestion with all of its attendant pressures. For city folk, coming to work in her studios was like coming to Paradise. There, young weavers could learn about nature and its connection to them as women.

As males raised in families in which male dominance was taken for granted, we have direct personal experience of the way our sisters were brought up since childhood to serve us. Most North American women today would not tolerate the expectations and demands once assumed. Yet Japanese women who have become activists for women's rights and equality often admit that even as enlightened people, their early conditioning often leads them to perform services for men as an automatic response to a situation. Indeed, they say that when they were teenagers, they can recall thinking that boys who offered to help with the dishes, opened doors, or did the shopping were spineless wimps.

Nevertheless, traditional Japanese lore is populated with goddesses who are lustful, exuberant, and joyful. Tsurumi told us of the myth of the "stripper goddess," who shed her clothes in a seductive dance for the sheer joy of it. Sayo Kitamura was a recent case in a long line of women who achieved a following by breaking out of the traditional woman's role.

Throughout this book, we introduce ordinary women doing extraordinary things in their local communities: Toshi Maruki with a lifelong commitment to using her art to deplore the horrors of war and oppression (Chapter 1); Meiko Chikkup, an Ainu woman who sued a publisher to protect her dignity and now communicates with a network of aboriginal people around the world (Chapter 5); Setsuko Yamazato who found her roots in the Okinawan village of Shiraho and has waged a successful battle to stop an airstrip that would have destroyed a life-giving reef (Chapter 10); Toshiko Toriyama, a teacher who has brought urban children into an understanding of their biological roots (Chapter 12). These and many others have played prominent roles in the peace, human-rights, and environmental movements in Japan. The women in this chapter continue to lead lives that are deeply embedded in tradition. But in retaining their attachment to their community and customs, they have not allowed their personalities and individualism to be subsumed.

part three

nature and environmentalism

CHAPTER 9

POISONeD

wateRs

"Shozo shares the life of all natural things. If they die,

so will he. When he fell ill, it was because the

rivers and forests of Ashio and Ashikaga are dying

and Japan herself too. . . . If those who come to

ask after him hope for his recovery, let them first

restore the ravaged hills and rivers and forests,

and then Shozo will be well again."

SHOZO TANAKA

tHE love of nature was once an important part of Japanese culture and religion. Nature worship is integral to Shinto, Japan's shamanistic religious tradition with its ancestor worship. However, Shinto has been in disrepute since the end of the war because the worship of the emperor was part of the justification for Japan's military expansion. After the war, cities exploded in size and vigour, pulling people from villages and farms. Now most Japanese live in crowded conditions in concrete structures. They have become profoundly disconnected from nature, a state that makes it easier for them to tolerate the assault their lifestyles wreak on the environment.

For many North American environmental activists, Japan symbolizes all that is wrong with the economic paradigm that now encompasses the world. In the pursuit of profit and short-term benefits, industries have little incentive or responsibility for long-term sustainability of communities or ecosystems. Japan's use of driftnets that each night spread more than fifty thousand kilometres across the oceans like destructive curtains of death was a chilling example of environmental shortsightedness. Japan continues to be the greatest predator of tropical hardwood, as well as a major contributor to the denuding of the boreal forests of Canada and Siberia. Japan presses for a quota for harvesting of whales while camouflaging its continued whale "harvests" as "scientific research."

In Japan there is, however, a growing grassroots awareness of environmental concerns. And while it is deeply rooted to place and is a truly indigenous movement, its participants are aware of their interconnections with the rest of the world.

We investigated the roots of the modern environmental movement in Japan by travelling to the mountainous area north of Tokyo where Shozo Tanaka spent the last decades of his life fighting the source of poison in this valley. Our journey took us through a spectacular valley to the headwaters of the Watarase River, where a rich copper deposit had been mined in the last century. At the Ashio copper mine, the intimate connection between environmental health and human welfare was crystal clear. Rusting buildings clung to the side of the steep riverbanks, and a large pipe hung over the river. We wondered whether this pipe was the conduit of the poisons out of the copper mine that had such a devastating impact on the plains kilometres below.

Our first stop was the local museum in Sano city. As we entered the courtyard, the first thing we saw was an imposing statue of Shozo Tanaka, a man who died more than eighty years ago and who has since become one of the strongest influences on the environmental movement in Japan today. At the turn of the century, when Japan was rushing towards westernization and modernization, Tanaka was a lone voice advocating environmental and humanist principles.

The two men who had agreed to be our guides, Satoru Fukawa and Taichi Akiyama, walked down the front steps of the museum to greet us. Together they run the Shozo Tanaka College, and they believe they carry on Tanaka's struggle. Fukawa, the preeminent expert on local history, concentrates his research on Shozo Tanaka. Akiyama, a carpenter from Sano city, is involved with Dennis Banks's Sacred Run and has run on many continents.

On entering the museum, we passed into the Tanaka Room, which was dominated by another large statue of the great man; Tanaka would surely never have dreamed he would become a tourist attraction! A glass case held a cloth bag, three small stones, the Bible, a book of St. Matthew, the Imperial Constitution of 1889, a diary, and what looked like a very old manuscript. Fukawa told us that these were the only possessions that Tanaka had on him when he died. Then we moved to a large map in the middle of which was that tall statue of Tanaka dressed in his travelling peasant clothes, a straw coat draped over his shoulders

"The people of Yanaka have no learning, no money, no food, no houses; but they are God."

SHOZO TANAKA, FATHER O

JAPAN'S ENVIRONMENTAL

MOVEMENT

and a walking stick in one hand. Pointing to the map, Fukawa began to explain the history.

> This is the Ashio copper mine that Tanaka spent his life fighting. This is the Watarase River on which people lived for centuries. The copper mine poisoned the river, and when it flooded, the whole area was inundated.

Shozo Tanaka was born in 1841, the son of the head of the Konaka village in Tochigi prefecture, close to the northern edge of the Kanto plain, about seventy kilometres north of Tokyo. One of the reasons that Tokyo, formerly called Edo, was chosen as the nation's capital was that it was surrounded by the fertile and productive land of the Kanto plain. In his biography of Shozo Tanaka, Kenneth Strong writes:

> Thanks to the purity of the mountain water and its suitability for dyeing processes, a silk weaving and dyeing industry had flourished on the banks of the Watarase for over a thousand years. And that was not all. The river abounded in fish; a catch of a hundred pounds' weight in one man's net in a single night was nothing uncommon, so that a good living could be made in this way if a man had no land to grow his rice. In the mid-nineteenth century nearly 4,000 fishermen worked the Watarase and its tributaries."[1]

Tanaka grew up in the turmoil of the end of the feudalistic society and the birth of modern Japan, and he aspired to a political career. His philosophy was a hybrid of traditional localism and western democracy. After years as a local politician, he successfully ran in the first election for the national Diet in 1890. By then Japan was embarked on a course of rapid modernization.

In 1877 Ichibei Furukawa, founder of the Furukawa Corporation, one of the giants in the financial combine called the *zaibatsu*, opened a new refinery at the Ashio copper mine. In seven years the Ashio mine became the largest in all of Japan. In 1885 the first report was recorded of thousands of fish dying mysteriously in the Watarase River.

Just after Tanaka was elected, the Watarase River flooded over a large area of land. Once the water had receded, it was found that the land had been poisoned. Crops wouldn't grow, and farmers immediately began to demand the shutdown of the copper mine. Tanaka didn't hesitate; he took this cause up as his fight. It was the beginning of what would be a lifetime battle.

The flood of 1896 caused the poisoning of 46,723 hectares of land. By then, the hills of Ashio were barren due to many years of clear-cutting and air pollution (mainly sulphurous and acid gas), which amplified the effects of erosion. It was reported that sedimentation of soil in the middle stretch of Watarase reached five feet in height at one point.

In 1897 the farmers whose land had been devastated by the Ashio copper mine pollution organized their first protest march. In 1900, when they started their fourth protest march towards Tokyo, they were stopped in Kawamata and beaten by police. More than a hundred people were arrested. The following year, Tanaka resigned from his seat in the Diet and, as a last resort, wrote a letter to the emperor. It was considered a near treasonous act and there was a huge uproar.

Around this time, Tanaka wrote a wry self-portrait in his diary:

Beaten, buffeted
By the rain and the wind,
An ox drags his load
Past, and is gone —
Leaving only
Wheeltracks in mud
And the sadness of things.[2]

At the age of sixty, Tanaka, without any political or social status, made the fight of the farmers whose fields had been poisoned his passion and focus. By 1904 Tanaka had moved into the nearby village of Yanaka, which was scheduled to be evacuated and flooded.

The next stop on our tour was the copper mine itself. In Ashio, the air was blue with pollution. Akiyama told us that it blew in from Tokyo and was trapped there by the mountains. We drove through a steep canyon surrounded by hills. There, the air was perceptibly clearer. The mountains had been clear-cut and then planted with rows of pine. Fukawa told us that the clear-cutting was one of the major causes of the repeated flooding the area had suffered. The water in the river was a milky green, a result of many years of copper pollution.

Next we visited a local ghost town. Once, Akiyama told us, this was a boom area where company employees earned a good living. There was a theatre, and the food was always the freshest. Fresh sushi was even brought in from the coast. When the mine was shut down in 1973, workers were laid off en masse and the young people left. The old timers who still hung on were living in poverty.

At the rusting refinery, we found the pipes that once dumped effluent straight into the river still hanging out over the chasm. The head of the valley looked like a lunar landscape — stark, desolate, almost devoid of plants.

A massive chimney dominated the refinery. At one time, the owners proposed to build it much higher to send the pollution farther away. It was stopped only because that would have polluted Nikko, with its beautiful national park, resort, and historic monuments from the Edo Period on the other side of the mountain. The line that the emissions once followed was marked by environmental destruction. The refinery and the surrounding area were a sad monument to the lives of people and other creatures that had been devastated.

At a lookout, a recorded female voice informed us, "Sometimes technology has harmful effects, so we have to be more careful. But now look around — we are restoring nature. The challenge is to show that science and technology can manage the land better." We had seen one of the government's attempts to regreen the mountains earlier. A single helicopter carrying a bucket underneath had shuttled back and forth in the valley. Akiyama had explained that after mining and logging, so little soil was left on the rock that the government was actually trying to replace it! After ten years of work, there was still little evidence of success.

A busload of children scrambled about the lookout posing for pictures and sightseeing. What did the youngsters see, we wondered, as they looked down the length of the valley? Did they see progress and the wonder of development, or destruction and the horror of development gone mad?

Our guides next took us to a huge marsh. We walked along a small path surrounded by reeds and came to a slightly raised area, the former site of Yanaka village, which had been Tanaka's stronghold from which to fight the government and the company. Fukawa told us:

> When Tanaka quit the Diet, he planned to organize a movement that
> was better than politics. He wanted to get away from the pursuit of

votes. Belonging to another party would not do any good either. So he quit. In his diary near the end, he said that having nothing was better; it liberated him. Politics was going in the opposite direction. Human rights of the individual were sacrificed for the emperor or the state. Respect for ordinary people's rights and happiness and small villages like Yanaka were not a part of the agenda.

Tanaka spent the last part of his life in Yanaka, and his message became simpler and stronger: "To kill the people is to kill the nation. To destroy a village means to destroy the country."[3]

On June 29, 1907, the forced destruction of Yanaka village finally began. More than two hundred police with dozens of construction workers came to the village to demolish it. They spent seven days pulling down all the houses and buildings. While protesting vehemently, Tanaka convinced the people to remain calm. Tanaka declared to the head of the police that, henceforth, he would live as a beggar. The villagers set up temporary shelters in their determination to remain. Unfortunately it was in the middle of the rainy season, and a big flood swept the shelters away, forcing the villagers to move to higher ground. According to our guides, after the village was flooded, Tanaka's fight became more and more focused, and he evolved into an environmental philosopher.

We walked up to a small rise that was spared at the time of the flood. The village head man's house used to stand on this spot. As we moved into the shade of a large tree, we had a pleasant surprise. There stood a mulberry tree, heavy with ripe berries. In this devastated valley, this one tree at least was thriving and healthy.

In his final years, Tanaka became increasingly religious. He said:

In their work the young men of Yanaka must respect what their elders say and value the advice of the fine spirits that you have among you. If you worship the God of Heaven, he is there in your homes. But there are gods among men, too. For Yanaka folk, to revere the noble ones among you is the same as to revere the gods and Buddhas whose shrines you keep in your homes. The people of Yanaka are God. Though Japan is bent on destroying herself, the spirit of the people of Yanaka will not die.

. . . The people of Yanaka have no learning, no money, no food, no houses; but they are God."[4]

We next visited Konaka, the village of Tanaka's birth. The house where he was born and grew up has been largely preserved. Our guide, Tatsuo Sakahara, the director of the Shozo Tanaka College, told us that the college had been started in this old house.

We have regular classes and fieldwork. His house is the centre from which we create a network. The central issue is the environment. But we also focus on cultural groups and education. We see him as a pioneer in human rights and local autonomy.

Sakahara was also born in the town.

When I had a critical crisis in my life, I discovered Tanaka. I left my town to go to college in Tokyo, but after learning about Tanaka I came back. Tanaka gave me pride as someone who was born and grew up in this region.

Fukawa added:

What's important is not that he died poor. You have to see him in the context of growing Japanese imperialism and modernization. His ideal from the start was to recognize each individual's right to live with dignity.

Sakahara replied:

From birth to death, he raised many questions: he kicked out bad administrators, he was part of the movement leading to the first Imperial parliament established in 1890 and the constitution of 1889, helping put democracy into practice, and he fought the Ashio-copper pollution. We learn from these three aspects and ask how we can apply them today.

Tanaka died in 1913, but until the end he fought pollution. For a long time he had stopped caring about his appearance. He spent much of his time walking like a madman along the river and across the valley. Seeing him in his shabby peasant clothes and carrying a walking stick, many people thought he'd gone completely mad. But he was actually studying the catchment of the river system to show its complexity in his search for ecological understanding and protection of the environment. At his death, his hair and beard were long and unkempt, and his possessions few. In contrast to this abject physical state, his philosophies and views on nature were getting clearer and more profound every day. In his last days he wrote in his diary:

> I often see people washing and rinsing their hands. Not their minds. They wash their faces, their bodies, their mouths, eyes, noses. But these are only the branches, not the root. So with rivers. If a man thinks clearing a river's passage and helping it flow is conservation, that's because he knows only the branches and not the root; the root of river-care lies at the source, in the mountains, lakes and forests.[5]

Referring to himself in the third person, Tanaka also wrote about his illness and the people who came to comfort him.

> Shozo shares the life of all natural things. If they die, so will he. When he fell ill, it was because the rivers and forests of Ashio and Ashikaga are dying and Japan herself too.... If those who come to ask after him hope for his recovery, let them first restore the ravaged hills and rivers and forests, and then Shozo will be well again.[6]

Fukawa commented to us that, unlike Jesus Christ or Buddha, Tanaka at his death was surrounded by lots of sympathizers but few disciples who would carry on his fight. From his deathbed Tanaka called an assistant who was in charge of visitors.

> There seem to be a lot of them outside, but they're no comfort to me. They sympathize with Shozo, but not a single one of them believes in his work. Go outside and tell them so![7]

Before we left the region, we wanted to visit Isoyama Shinto Shrine, a local memorial on the hill overlooking the village. It was known for its worship of snakes, which symbolize the flowing water of a river. At the foot of the hill was a sacred fountain. Akiyama told us that because the mountain was made of limestone, the water was the purest in the world.

Akiyama remarked that in his grandparents' day people respected the sacredness of nature. But once that respect was gone, there seemed no point resisting development.

Whenever I come here, I feel revived. There are special places where you go and feel good; I think it's because we're animals. There used to be such places all over, but now there are hardly any. Instead, we have *pachinko* parlours and electronic-game centres. Tanaka said the force of destruction resides in us. If the conflict is between us and corporations or government, that's simple. But within every individual is the force of destruction. Therefore, the struggle is to change ourselves and the system at the same time. We have to restore a good relationship with the land and also the sacred things in ourselves.

We looked down on what was once a lovely valley surrounded by picturesque mountains; now houses and roads take up at least three-quarters of the land, while farms occupy the rest. Akiyama added pointedly, "Another thing Tanaka taught me was not to look at progress in terms of technology. Now I look from the standpoint of Mother Earth and assess science and technology that way."

Tanaka's legacy has not died. People are taking up the cause and are willing to suffer the consequences. We visited one such man in Okinawa.

When Professor Jun Ui and his wife, Noriko, arrived at the resort hotel in Okinawa, we were waiting in the large lobby. Ui, one of the leading minds of Japan's environmental movement today, had spent twenty-one years as an assistant researcher at Tokyo University, but had never been promoted. When we met him, he was a professor at a small private university in Naha, Okinawa. For mainstream Japanese academics this job would have been considered a great career downfall, but Ui told us that coming to

Okinawa had brought him closer to Asia and the Third World. Ui's career was held back because of his activism in environmental issues, the most notorious being the case of mercury poisoning at Minamata. While he admitted this was a factor, he added that the bureaucracy of a large university had also contributed to his problems. Like many academic departments, the one where Ui had been valued theoretical work over the practical.

When we asked Ui's wife, Noriko, if she knew he had a nonconformist streak, she replied that when they married, she had expected he would go through the normal steps of promotion up the academic ladder. Thinking about it more, she recalled that while he was courting her ("It was a standard arranged marriage," he interjected), he wrote a column under a pseudonym attacking the establishment.

Ui graduated from the undergraduate school at Tokyo University in 1956 and took a job with a plastics company producing PVC (polyvinyl chloride) used to make a wide variety of products from pipes to shopping bags. The chemical process required mercury catalysts, and he occasionally discarded the spent catalysts into the river — but only at night under the cover of darkness.

> I had never intended to stay working with one company for the rest of my life, so after four years, I went back to Tokyo University to study synthetic polymers. Then I heard the news about Minamata and the terrible diseases in which mercury was suspected. I worried that perhaps it might be *my* mercury. I began to investigate the known effects but encountered strong pressure against my investigation. The university supported the suspected polluting company and tried to suppress the truth.

Minamata disease is caused by an accumulation of methyl mercury in the body's internal systems, mainly the central nervous system and peripheral nerves. Its symptoms include sensory disturbances, lack of coordination, dysphasia, impaired vision, loss of hearing, and tremors. It is a devastating, debilitating, and ultimately lethal condition. If loss of mental function and debilitation isn't bad enough, it is made worse by the terribly contorted limbs and face that accompany the tightening muscles.

Ui searched for another department where he could study pollution. He chose civil engineering and earned a PhD.

In 1959 the Chisso Company, a large chemical company in Minamata prefecture, already knew from experiments being performed by its own scientists, led by Dr. Hajime Hosokawa of the company hospital, that mercury caused Minamata-like disease in cats. The experiments were soon stopped. Ui explained:

> In 1962 I identified crystals of methyl mercury in wastewater, and in 1963, I discovered the company paper that proved that methyl mercury causes Minamata-like disease in cats. I went to the factory hospital to talk to Dr. Hosokawa but discovered he had retired. A young man came out and said he had worked on some of the experiments with Dr. Hosokawa. While he was talking, a secretary took him away for a phone call. When he left, I shuffled through the papers on his desk and found the article and photographed it. When the man came back, he told me he had given me all the information there was. I said, "Yes you have," thanked him and left. But I was too afraid to publish the article.

Ui then confronted Dr. Hosokawa with the results in the paper and asked him if they were true. Hosokawa admitted they were but asked Ui not to release the findings because he was afraid of what might happen to him. Then, a few years later, there was news of a Minamata-like disease in Niigata prefecture on the west coast of Honshu.

> I asked Dr. Hosokawa to come with me and examine the patient. He agreed and confirmed that it was indeed Minamata disease. With this case, I decided to release everything. It was 1965, just a month after I had secured a position at Tokyo University.

When Ui realized he would have to release the information on mercury poisoning that would implicate the Chisso Company and their coverup attempts, he consulted his wife, offering her the opportunity to leave and avoid the controversy. Noriko Ui stayed, although it was not easy. She received threatening notes and calls, and she was warned to keep her child inside or she would be hurt. She worried about the location of a window in a new house they were building and had it reinforced with mesh wiring.

In 1968 the company finally admitted causing the disease in people and officially apologized. More than 10,000 people applied for compensation, but only 2,400 were accepted. Of those, by 1995 about 1,000 were dead and about 1,400 still survived.

In 1990 the United Nations Environmental Program announced that Ui had been elected to the prestigious Global 500 list, which includes leading individuals and organizations that are working on environmental issues. Many Japanese newspapers picked up the story, and it was printed without confirmation from Ui. When finally contacted by a newspaper, Ui was incredulous and said he didn't think he would receive the award "because the government wouldn't allow it." Incredible as it seems, he was right. He never received formal word from UNEP! Apparently the Japanese government was able to thwart the award. Thanks to the persistence of his nominators, however, Ui finally received the award a year later.

My generation was taught that the world was reasonable in a scientific way. There was no room for spirits, no sense of the sacred or spiritual.

Facing Minamata disease in 1959, we began to realize that nature had to be respected. In 1970, eighty percent of water pollution came from industry and twenty percent from sewage. Now industrial pollution is one-fifteenth of 1970 levels. This change was driven mostly by public opinion. Until Tokyo's air was polluted, people regarded Minamata as a tragedy that was simply a problem for an isolated fishing village. It didn't relate to their lives.

Ui edited a book about the history of ecological thought in Japan, which collected the words of environmentalists, scholars, and activists.[8] In it, Shozo Tanaka stands out as one of the giants. We asked Ui what Tanaka meant to him.

> For sixty years after his death, Tanaka was basically forgotten. Before the Second World War, he was thought of as very traditional, a conservative leader of a farmer's movement. After the Second World War, he remained in low repute because he was conservative and wasn't respected by the left wing. It was in the 1970s, as the pollution problem became a popular concern, that his name and theories were rediscovered.
>
> Because for sixty years as a society we failed to learn from Tanaka's message, we had to repeat history in the form of Minamata disease. Tanaka's struggle is more relevant than ever today.

Ui feels his challenge is to make a clear, visible example for the rest of Japan. To him Japan's environmental future lies in a kind of localism in which community politics is combined with the initiatives of the common people.

> It's a job of local groups, not the central government. In cities, co-ops of housewives concerned with pollution, food, and safety are sending representatives to local governments. There is a grassroots movement.
>
> There is an air of change in politics. In Yahagi, near the industrial city of Toyota, there is an exceptionally clean river. Its condition is the result of a twenty-year effort. Farm runoff had badly polluted the river, with a major impact on the fish. So a coalition of fishermen and farmers formed to elect a person to visit all of the discharges into the catchment. Now the river is a model.
>
> After 1970 we got an improvement in water quality as a result of local regulations. The central government's laws were too vague and loose. Now eighty percent of industrial water is recycled. Economic and environmental savings came about because of regulations, a fact that is not recognized by economists who argue for deregulation.

Since the 1970s Ui has travelled to Europe, Asia, and North and South

America with his message from Minamata and other cases of pollution. He has visited the victims of Minamata disease in Canada and Brazil, many of whom are indigenous people.

Since Ui had seen the dark side of Japan's economic miracle, it is particularly impressive that his attitude remains optimistic. He believes science can contribute beneficially to the human condition so long as we keep science in its proper place. As we bid farewell, Ui told us, "I'm a scientist, yet I'm well aware that science can be and often is a kind of religion. On the matter of scientific truth, I am a relativist."

Ui is an unusual man: an academic who applied his expertise to a practical problem and then had the courage and ideals to speak out, even though he was up against the wishes of his own university, of government, and of big businesses.

Ever since Rachel Carson's seminal book, *Silent Spring*, appeared in 1962, people have become more aware of the hazards of pollution and have placed increasing pressure on governments and industries to reduce or stop using air, water, and soil as dumping grounds for toxic effluents. And as the residents of places directly affected — such as Grassy Narrows in Canada and Love Canal in the United States — have discovered, there are enormous health and economic consequences of long-term accumulation of toxic compounds. The immediate victims of pollution have fought for compensation for their losses, but in so doing, have found themselves accepting a system in which even a person's life is evaluated in terms of money. In other words, human life, the soul, and nature are reduced to mere commodities on which a price may be settled. People may be paid off to disappear from view and become simply a cipher or statistic, or remain locked in the perpetual role of victim.

In Minamata we met a remarkable man who chose to reject the status of victim. After pursuing compensation, he realized that the very act of setting a price for a settlement merely places the victim on the marketplace, a commodity that can be paid off. Life, health, and dignity are beyond economic valuation, yet in the compensation process, they are reduced to items for sale. He chose to reject this process and seek, instead, recognition of his basic humanity.

Once a week, Masato Ogata would get up before the sun rose and look towards the ocean to see whether it would be a good day. He'd pack his *hibachi*, charcoal, a bottle of *shochu* (local wine), some food, and his four rolled-up mats, then slip quietly out of the house without waking his wife and children. He would walk through his garden to the edge of his property and then down to the ocean. He'd load his stuff into his newly built wooden rowboat, called *The Eternal World*, and push off into the dark ocean. If there was no wind, he knew his journey to Minamata would take him only three hours. He'd stand in the back of the boat and using one oar would paddle out of the bay to the Sea of Shiranui. Looking over his shoulder, he'd see the sky over the mountains getting light. His muscles would ache, and even in the cold, he'd begin to sweat but the rhythm of his movements and the pitching and rolling of the ocean made him feel at one with nature. Ogata's wooden boat was the only one of its kind in the region. When he first ordered it, everyone in the village laughed and ridiculed him. Later he recalled:

> I was beginning to lose my enjoyment of being on the ocean. The water and fish were poisoned by mercury; even my boat was made of plastic, with a high-speed engine. The bow sat so high above the water I couldn't even see ahead of me. I knew in the city people were slaves to time, but even here we were now racing, and worst of all, plastic in Japan was originally made by the Chisso Company. This is the stuff that will never return to nature. Every fisherman knew how the ocean is filled with this garbage. I began to feel so bad about living on Chisso's garbage. I needed a wooden boat. Like the days of my grandfather and my father, free from time, I would be on the boat and think. On this boat I would be able to regain my sanity and know where I belonged.

By the time he'd arrive in Minamata Bay, the sun would be up and the waterfront bustling with activity. He'd tie his boat and retrieve his pullcart from where he'd stored it. He would unload his supplies off the boat and onto the cart. Walking across the dock, pulling his cart behind him, he would make his way to the gates of the Chisso Company. At the front gates he'd politely greet the guards, who often smiled vaguely. As usual he would go over to his spot beside the gates. He'd hang his father's picture on the wall and lay out straw mats to sit on. With his *hibachi* and supplies within reach, he would now be ready to spend the rest of the day at his spot.

The first time Ogata arrived at the factory he was met by suspicion and fear by the arriving workers. But eventually they knew who he was and some even greeted and talked with him. With India ink and a brush, Ogata wrote on straw mats that he hung on the walls for the workers and company officials to read as they arrived to work. The first one said:

"I was beginning to lose my enjoyment of the ocean. The water and fish were poisoned by mercury; even my boat was made of plastic."

MASATO OGATA

> To the Folks of Chisso Company:
> This incident called Minamata disease started when humans stopped seeing other humans as human beings. Isn't it about the time for you to accept the human responsibility? Please . . . answer, respond to my open letter. You, the folks of Chisso, come back soon . . . come home.

Another one said:

> To the Children:
> It was when I was six years old my dad got ill from Minamata disease because of the poison discharged by the Chisso Company. His hands and legs trembled and shook so hard he could no longer walk. He drooled and flew into fits of madness . . . and died. From that time on, I was called by other kids, "Minamata disease kid," and they would throw stones at me. That was so hard. Now, everyone *please think hard about*

Minamata disease; it is trying to teach you something very important.

At lunchtime, Ogata would light his *hibachi*, throw on some fish, and pour some more sake. Throughout the day, curious observers would come by to look and see what his protest was all about. At the end of the day, as the workers left the factory, Ogata would pack up his stuff and make the long journey home.

We had heard about this man and decided it was important to meet him. Ogata greeted us in front of his home. A few steps from his house, across a narrow street, sat a low concrete fence, past which was the ocean. Ogata, a good-looking, slender man with a weathered face, wore a traditional monk's blue working clothes. He seemed to emanate strength, yet his huge friendly smile showed he had another side.

Ogata invited us into a small one-room study and guesthouse; for the next few days, our discussion continued there over tea, beer, and his beloved *shochu*. His words, coloured with a local accent, were very clear and powerful.

About 120 years ago, his grandfather migrated from Ryugatake on Amakusa Island, just across the Sea of Shiranui. The Ogatas were one of the first families to settle in the hamlet of Oki. His mother was from a neighbouring farming village called Akasaki. When she came to marry his father, he already had twelve children; Ogata was born in 1953, the last of his father's fifteen offspring. When he was a small child, he began helping with fishing. He told us:

> There was always work, even for small kids; even as a kid, I liked working on the sea. As a baby of two or three years old, I was on the sea, riding my father's back on the boats. Our family also had some small fields, just enough to feed ourselves growing rice, wheat, and *miso* [soy bean paste]. We had not too many things to buy. The important thing that my father had to buy was *shochu*; he was quite a drinker. He was literally living on the top of *shochu* bottles, stocked underneath the floor. But he never got drunk and lost himself.

To Ogata his father meant everything. He was highly respected as a fisherman and community leader, and was so physically strong that villagers used to say that even death couldn't take him.

> I was always with him and he always wanted to be with me. When I woke up in the middle of the night, my father would be sitting up staring into the fire. I know now that he was in dialogue with nature. As if reading a map, he was visualizing the movements of the tide, the fish, and the wind.

His father had many people working under him. He treated everyone with respect, be they Japanese, Korean, or physically or mentally handicapped. He was respected in return, but his anger, especially if someone treated the mentally handicapped workers badly, made him a truly awesome figure.

This man who Ogata revered so highly died when Ogata was six.

> One morning I was in the garden playing and noticed my father was walking with only one sandal. A few seconds later he stumbled and said to me, "I don't feel good." That was the beginning of the end.

In a few weeks his father developed violent symptoms. His whole body trembled constantly and he couldn't hold anything. He had trouble speaking and was having seizures every few minutes. He visited one hospital after another and nobody could do anything. In two months he was dead.

Right away his death was classified as the thirtieth recognized case of Minamata disease. Within the same year, Ogata's nephew and niece were born with severe birth defects. Neighbours and members of his family began to get severe headaches and numbness of limbs that were typical symptoms of Minamata disease. So did Ogata.

The disease had started years before, when the catch in Minamata Bay was declining rapidly. By the time Ogata was born, people began to witness the "dancing syndrome" among cats. The animals would turn and twist in the air and die soon after, frothing at the mouth. The cats were fish-eaters and, because they were higher up the food chain, the mercury was concentrated in their tissues. The cat population was soon wiped out, and in some areas, rats and mice multiplied to dangerous levels. It was in 1956 that this strange behaviour was identified as Minamata disease. But it took many more years before the cause was publicly acknowledged.

"When my father died," Ogata said to us, "a part of me died too. As a schoolboy, I told myself that I would get revenge on the people who had taken my father."

After finishing middle school, Ogata stayed in the village to fish with his older brother. As the fish declined so did the fortunes of the Ogata family. One day he decided to leave home.

I was on my way to Osaka, but I ran out of money in Kumamoto city. When I was sleeping on a park bench, I was befriended by a young man. He invited me to his home where he was living with his girlfriend. Through them I was soon introduced to a right-wing political organization which turned out to be Yakuza [criminal underworld].

With the Yakuza, Ogata was made to feel like a member of the family. Over a short period of time, he grew close to them.

Once, with a piece of lumber in my hands, I attacked a demonstration of left-wingers protesting against dispatching Self-Defence Force to Okinawa. I got arrested and sent to a juvenile correctional camp. As I look back, there was nothing ideological about what I did, I just wanted to do something wild.

While in the juvenile correction centre, he learned that the Minamata patients in a protest demonstration at the Chisso headquarters in Tokyo were attacked by a group of disguised right-wingers hired by the company.

The correction-centre counsellor came to me and said, "You know what's happening? You may be feeling proud of being a right-winger, but you know what they are doing to the Minamata disease patients? How do you feel, as a kid who lost his father to the same disease?" I couldn't give an answer to this and the counsellor added, "Go home, you don't belong here." I was silent; it was the first time in my life that I found myself unable to talk back.

When he was eighteen he returned to his village but felt very ashamed because everybody knew what he had done.

I went back to fishing. It was a time when the Minamata struggle was approaching a boiling point. It didn't take too much time before I got involved in the movement. Within a year after I came back home, there was a big blockade by boats in protest against Chisso. For me, this poured the oil onto the fire. It was my personal turning point.

In 1968 the Japanese government officially recognized the cause of Minamata disease to be environmental pollution. The following year the first lawsuit was launched by some of the victims. Thus began a series of long legal battles that continue to this day. In 1973 in the Kumamoto district-court ruling, the victims won. While the trial continued, supporters and victims began to protest directly to the Chisso Company. They organized repeated demonstrations and sit-ins. By the end of the trial, second and third outbreaks of Minamata disease were recorded in Ariake Bay and Tokuyama Bay respectively.

The Chisso Company had deep roots in the area, beginning in 1908 with the manufacture of chemical fertilizers through which they made their fortune. The company had its headquarters and main factory complex in Minamata city, where the family ruled like a feudal lord. Minamata was under the umbrella of Chisso's economic and social supremacy. When Japan was waging the Fifteen-Year War (1931–1945), the Chisso Company thrived by manufacturing fertilizers, artificial silks, and synthetic fibres, explosives, oils, industrial chemicals, coals, and oils. Their attitude was "profits first and safety last," and in the pressure to compete with already established business combines, they pushed this policy to the extreme.

In the summer of 1974, Ogata officially presented himself as a member of the movement and faced, for the first time, "the enemy" on whom he had sworn revenge so long ago. Part of his motivation was a feeling of uneasiness at not fighting while other victims were. In the meantime, lots of supporters were arriving in the region and getting involved in the struggle.

The supporters were from all over Japan, and many from the student movement were my age. In this village, too, four young people had come to live and help with daily chores, fishing, and the movement. I liked them. I felt a warmth as fellow human beings. I knew my father was killed by Minamata disease caused by Chisso Company, but other than that, I was totally ignorant about the political and economic structure behind the company. We became good friends and through them I realized the universal significance of this fight. I was growing out of my sense of hatred and revenge.

Ogata's parents, two of his brothers, and five of his sisters were officially recognized as Minamata-disease patients. Three brothers died without applying for official recognition. Having a high mercury level in his hair and symptoms of the disease himself, Ogata applied for recognition and soon became the leader of the organization representing the applicants.

"Since two of my brothers died in their late thirties," he said, "I was quite nervous to reach their ages. Now I feel relieved that I just turned forty."

As Ogata became deeply involved in the movement, he was too busy to be at home regularly, fishing.

My family were losing greatly, having to sell off possessions and live off savings. They always pressured me to keep away from the movement and work harder. It wasn't easy for me. I just wished that one day they would understand me and why I had to do that.

The decision confirming Chisso's responsibility to compensate the victims was in 1973, and a whole bureaucracy had to be set up to screen the applicants and "recognize" the patients.

Before, it was a struggle to get Chisso to admit responsibility; now it became a fight with government bureaucracy. I spent my time arguing with government and court agents about the bureaucratic process of selection, recognition, and compensation of patients.

Over ten years and through this bureaucratic process, Ogata's doubts grew.

> I had this question all the time, which stuck in my throat and bothered me constantly: what is this thing called compensation and why do people sell out for money? I would never sell my soul. So that was keeping me on my feet, but just barely, like a weary scarecrow suspended on a solitary post.

In the meantime, he began to notice that the people recognized as patients tended to become reticent and would stop going out in public. The social pressures of their status as recognized and compensated set them apart from everybody else, and they entered into a state like self-exile. Ogata saw this as a trap.

> I also noticed that our movement began to develop its own bureaucracy. We tried every means, we took every opportunity to fight, but it was all procedures, a huge, constant flood of documents and regulations. The people who dealt with these were lawyers, supporters, and a few of us leaders. The patients who were the plaintiffs had no role to play except signing papers. And I began to detect a sense of induction in this tangle of bureaucratic procedures, into which the patients were being helplessly led.

As he looked backed at those ten years in the movement, these doubts bothered him. At the beginning, it was simply revenge he wanted, but then what happened? He always knew he wasn't fighting for money. Yet he found himself in the position to ask for compensation.

> Finally we were all trapped in the system. We were now dependent on the institution called "recognition." Everybody, the whole movement, was shaped by the system. We had to go to courts with legal strategies, apply for recognition, and negotiate with government agents. In the meantime, where did Chisso go? Since 1978, when they were declared incapable of paying all the money, the government came up with the idea of prefectural bonds to back them up. Which meant that we were

not dealing with Chisso anymore. The system was doing everything. In 1985, Ogata withdrew his application and quit the movement.

To put it very simply, I wanted to quit this money business and find a new direction, break new ground. But if it's not money, what is it?

The voices against my move didn't help either. Some called me a traitor; some said, whatever my motivation was, my move would benefit the enemy anyway. And some asked, "If not for money, then what?" I wish I could have answered more clearly. I was having a hard time emotionally, but now my true mental ordeal began.

There were rumours circulating that Ogata had gone mad. People saw him wandering around in the woods talking to himself.

Yes, I was insane for three months. I began to hear voices as I walked in the hills. I heard the grass, the trees, the wind inviting me to come back. In my mind I was six years old, crying as the voice told me to come back or I'd be eaten up. Then I'd find myself on my father's lap, sitting on his huge Popeye-like thigh. One day I heard the sound of running water talking to me from the earth. But sometimes it was so painful, like a weight pressing down on my brain. I wasn't sure whether I was going to survive. What I hated the most were appliances and machines. One day I went into the living room and threw the television out the window.

Many times Ogata stood on the edge of the cliff looking out over the ocean. At high tide he believed he could step out and walk on water and just keep going to the other side of the world. His family said it was a miracle he got through this time alive.

But those hard days were also a time of enlightenment for Ogata. Then his perspective became clear, and he saw how everything in time and space was connected. He examined all the small and seemingly insignificant details from his past and suddenly they had meaning for him.

Around this time he had his wooden boat made and began his one-man protests at the front gates of the Chisso Company. Ogata laughed shyly and told us that this period caused a lot of problems for his family, but they were thankful about one thing from that time.

Remember when I told you I heard the sound of running water talking to me from inside the ground? Well, I got a company to drill in that spot and they discovered one of the few fresh-water wells on the island.

Another ten years passed. They weren't easy days, but now, finally, I feel much clearer about what I did. *Hosho*, or compensation, essentially includes a sense of oblivion. I'm not denying the merits of compensation as a part of social security and welfare, a common good necessary for social purposes, but in this particular context, money did not mean a thing to me. I'm not saying I don't need money, I'm only saying that the mind and soul cannot be exchanged for money. This is *my* choice; I cannot impose my decision upon anybody, yet this choice is so dear to *me*. You fall into a trap when you think about exchanging your soul for something else.

The next day, May 1, was the anniversary of the official recognition of Minamata disease. It was unusually hot. On our way to the ceremony, we walked up a hill that overlooked the entire Minamata city and the bay. At the centre of our view was the Chisso Company, which seemed to have taken over all the flatlands. Its ominous presence reminded us that the people of the region used to refer to it as "The Company" and envied those who'd managed to find a job there.

Later we attended a small memorial ceremony just outside the Chisso plant. About thirty people, dressed all in black, gathered at the floodgates. Leaning over the fence to the waterway, a group of survivors dropped flowers into the water. The water was thick, green, and sluggish in its apparent stillness. This was where Chisso dumped toxic waste. The ceremony was short and the group dispersed quickly, but the flowers moved very slowly, as if drawing a picture in long, careful strokes, showing that the deceptively solid-appearing water was indeed moving.

Then we all moved to what looked like a vast plain. There had been a contaminated waterway here, where the poisons had accumulated to such an extent that the government decided just to fill it in with land, reclaiming it. On top of those buried poisons stood a massive white circus tent. This was the location of the third memorial ceremony organized by Minamata city for the Minamata victims.

By 11:00 a.m., it was terribly hot inside the tent, but to our surprise, most of the three hundred seats were filled by people in black suits. The only empty seats were in the section reserved for patients and the families of victims. People were surprised to find Masato Ogata in the middle of this section. He stood out among the many older people because of his height and his healthy appearance. It was the first time in many years he had been in an official ceremony. We teased him, saying, "Yesterday you said you wouldn't wear anything formal. Now you look very sharp."

"I realized that I don't have anything else to wear," he replied with a smile. "You guys look good, too," he added, referring to our travel-wrinkled jackets and blue jeans.

As we spoke with him, we soon noticed that a crowd of people had gathered around us, all paying attention to Ogata; his charisma seemed to draw them in. There was a mixture of eager anticipation and apprehension.

Since our visit, Ogata has been the focus of an NHK documentary, broadcast nationwide. He has begun to speak publicly in favour of placing *nobotoke* (popular guardian images found on roadsides) on the reclaimed land where we had stood to console the souls of the victims. In a leaflet announcing his new initiative, Ogata wrote:

> It is time for us to go back to where we belong. Let us return with our souls. Time is calling us. Let me say one more time that the very existence of human beings is solely responsible for Minamata disease and that we humans are all equally responsible. There is no hierarchy of responsibility. Each of us must accept our share and cherish it forever. This is the real message of the Minamata disease incident.
>
> I pray for a heartfelt confession of guilt and apology from the accused and I hope that they will join us in our effort to reveal the real

nature of modern civilization and to learn the meaning of living in the spiritual world. We are native people who must not be separated from the ocean, the mountains, the rivers, grass, and trees.

Minamata pinpoints the terrible dilemma created by modern technology — enormous potential benefits of products, jobs, and profit balanced by ecological and social consequences that usually can't be predicted beforehand and, once recognized, are too expensive to correct or impossible to retract.

Ogata, like Tanaka almost a century before him, saw clearly that victimhood covers over our humanity, that destruction of family and community means destruction of a nation. Poisoning the Earth with our industrial debris eventually poisons all people, their communities, and their ideas. Fortunately, scientists like Ui are willing to speak out even in the face of dire consequences.

CHAPTER 10

GREEN
DEMOCRACY

"If you want change in environmental policies,

don't look to the corporate sector or politicians

like me. You have to go to the grassroots and convince

them there's a problem, make them aware of

what the options are and get them to demand action.

Then people like me will fall all over ourselves

to hop on board the bandwagon."

AL GORE, WHILE TENNESSEE SENATOR

JAPAN is a society in which fitting in is a key social grace. Thus, it is said, "When a nail sticks out, it must be hammered down." Rugged individualism or personal idiosyncrasy is not a highly valued quality where consensus and "face" dominate thinking and behaviour. There is an added feature in Japanese society: it is pyramidal, with power and influence acquired with age and experience. Political leaders tend to be older, and it is difficult for a younger person to gain access to political power.

So the question is whether a grassroots model of social activism can be applied to a country like Japan.

We travelled to Zushi city, fifty kilometres south of Tokyo on the coast, to meet a politician who gave us reason to hope for a different kind of political landscape. Zushi city, with a population of about 57,000, is a bedroom community whose residents commute to white-collar jobs in Tokyo. It is right next to Kamakura, the old city that was the capital of Japan from 1192 to 1333.

Zushi covers an area about one-third the size of Manhattan, but contains a large forest called Ikego, which spans about fifteen percent of the town's area, the size of Central Park. In 1938 the Japanese Imperial Navy forced all people out of the Ikego area to make room for an ammunition depot. The forest was cordoned off and remained virtually untouched, making it the only sanctuary near Tokyo for rare plants and birds, including eagles and falcons.

When the ammunition depot was closed after the Vietnam War, the citizens of Zushi expected Ikego forest to be returned to them. Instead, in 1982 the Japanese government announced a plan to bulldoze the sanctuary and construct housing for U.S. naval personnel in the ammunition depot area. Under the terms of the Japan–U.S. Security Treaty, Japan had to provide U.S. forces with modern, rent-free facilities. Defence Facilities Administration Agency (DFAA) officials told a small delegation of protesting Zushi housewives that the Americans had picked Ikego because it would make a quiet, elite get-away from the small houses and the base in Yokosuka.

Little did the authorities realize that this unilateral decision, just one of many made by the central government without consultation or warning, would create a movement with profound implications for the future of local government in Japan.

Kiichiro Tomino met us at the Zushi train station. He had movie-star good looks, wore casual clothing, and spoke excellent English. Before taking us to his home, he gave us a short tour of Zushi. The small city has a cosy feeling, embraced as it is by hills from behind. It sits on a bay with a sweep of sandy beach.

We reached Tomino's home and were ushered into the living room, which faced a Japanese-style garden with trimmed plants and flowers. Behind the shrubs was a family shrine with a fox as a deity. On the other side of the fence was the Ikego forest. The house itself had a comfortable, warm feeling. Nanako, Tomino's wife, sat with us and took great interest in the conversation. It was obvious that Kiichiro and Nanako were partners not only in marriage but in political activities.

Born in Zushi in 1944, Kiichiro Tomino came from a family that had lived there for three hundred years. He studied astronomy at a doctoral level at the prestigious Tokyo University but had to quit when his father died. He took over the family business and, for more than a decade, was the president of a company producing trash compactors. He had no interest in politics, nor, as he told us, "in human beings and social problems." As an astronomer he preferred to look skyward even during the day. In 1984, when the central government threatened to flatten the green rolling hills of the Ikego forest in front of his house to build 854 houses for U.S. Navy personnel, he realized that if he didn't act, other citizens wouldn't either.

According to Tomino:

The citizens of Zushi are generally conservative and pro-American. At that time, over seventy percent of them supported the Japan–U.S. Security Treaty. However, the issues of why Ikego forest, so precious to Zushi citizens, had to be destroyed while large U.S. naval housing areas in neighbouring Yokohama and Yokosuka are being returned to the Japanese government, and why no rational alternative plan to Ikego was being seriously examined, led to a grassroots movement that was to involve the entire city.

Among those galvanized into opposing the development were housewives, elders, environmentalists, and antiwar activists. The group collected 46,000 signatures opposing the development. But the mayor and council favoured construction and ignored the opposition. Three housewives flew to Washington, D.C., to plead with Defense Secretary Caspar Weinberger, but he refused to see them. So in 1984 the group decided to support a woman who had been a housewife but considered running for mayor of Ikego. Her idealism more than compensated for her lack of experience, but at the last minute she backed out and a reluctant Tomino was recruited to replace her.

The national level of the Liberal Democratic Party (LDP), which supported the base, brought in some influential politicians and businessmen to wage a pro-base campaign. They insisted that the base was important for U.S.–Japanese friendship and called the anti-base group "communists" and "extremists." By taking these extreme actions, the central government, led by the ruling LDP, badly misread the feelings of the citizens of Zushi. Most of the citizens of the normally conservative city were opposed to the construction of the base, and the heavy-handed tactics created a backlash.

Heading towards an almost certain win in the mayoral race, Tomino and his supporters wrote funny leaflets, held warm, community-oriented meetings, and generally ran a "very joyful" campaign. As a result Tomino handily beat Torayoshi Mishima, the incumbent mayor of twelve years, although he still faced a pro-construction majority on city council.

In August 1985, members of two local groups, Ikego Green Operation Centre (IGOC) and the Association for Protection of Nature and Children (APNC), accompanied by sympathetic academics, travelled to the United States to meet with American environmental organizations. Michael McCloskey, chair of the Sierra Club, wrote to several members of Congress on their behalf. He pointed out that Zushi city was not against the base but against the *site* of the base and that the city-sponsored think tank (Working Group to Consider the Ikego Issue, headed by professor Akiyoshi Ogata of Yokohama National University) had eight workable alternatives to building in Ikego. One of the alternatives was to build the houses on land already reclaimed at the Yokosuka base. That would allow naval staff to mix freely with the locals and get to know Japan, rather than dumping them in an elite ghetto.

One of the congressmen wrote to the navy. A senior officer wrote back that the "Japanese government has decided to build the housing complex at Ikego and it is the Japanese side which is responsible for the assessment of its impact on the environment."

In 1986 a pro-construction group forced a recall vote of the mayoral race. Tomino ran again and won. Meanwhile his group collected enough signatures to force a recall vote of the entire council. In the ensuing election, twelve anti-base candidates and fourteen pro-base candidates were elected. When one of the pros died, another anti was elected, which deadlocked the council at thirteen to thirteen. In the mayoral election in 1988 Tomino won easily, and in the 1990 election of councillors, fifteen antis and eleven pros were elected.

In early 1989 Tomino and other city officials went to inspect Ikego forest and were refused entry by defence officials. The Defence Facilities Administration Agency had already started construction of the rainfall catchment basin. The basin began to attract a variety of bird life. Owls — longtime forest residents — were seen. Tomino wanted to keep the basin and incorporate it into long-standing Zushi-city plans to make Ikego a major, walk-through life-science park with a vast seed bank and gene pool. The DFAA wanted to pave it over to make a football field for U.S. Navy personnel.

In September of that same year Zushi officials sought an injunction against construction on the grounds that, under Article 25 of the River

"I did my politics with common sense."

KIICHIRO TOMINO,
FORMER MAYOR
OF ZUSHI

Act, the mayor was in charge of rivers and, in this case, he gave no permission to change the waterways. A protracted legal battle took the case to the Supreme Court where in 1993 the invariably pro-central government court ruled that the city's power over rivers was given to them by the central government and what the central government gives, the central government can take away. Tomino explained what happened next:

> Two other important facts were discovered as a result of an environmental-impact-assessment survey at Ikego forest. A field study led to the discovery of large-scale archaeological remains dating from over 5,000 years ago and to the excavation of a large number of wooden instruments apparently used in daily life about 2,000 years ago. The Defence Facilities Administration Agency made public a report giving the results of research on giant white-clam fossils discovered in Ikego forest. In this report scientists pointed out that for the study of plate-tectonics theory, these giant white-clam fossil beds were of immeasurable academic value. But the national government did not halt the constructon of naval housing, and announced that it would continue in spite of strong protests from the mayor and citizens of Zushi.

The DFAA said that change of local government had no effect on past accords, and the only things local government should be concerned with were matters like sewage and trash disposal from the new housing site.

A third term is the time when a politician's work matures to fruition and he or she can claim credit. But after two terms as mayor, Tomino happily resigned. "If two terms are enough for the president of a large country like the U.S.," he said, "then it is enough for a little city like Zushi. Change is good."

He also wanted to install a female mayor — at the time there was only one other in Japan — in part because he thought it was a good way to introduce ordinary citizens to politics, and in part because most of the members of his party were women. The candidate, Mitsuyo Sawa, won along with six other women councillors. That gave Zushi the second-highest ratio of women in a Japanese government.

By 1993 the first phase of construction in Ikego forest was completed. The building of 300 houses was begun, and the budget for the second phase went up before the central government for approval. It included funds to build 250 more houses.

Tomino drove us to the top of a hill behind his house so we could see the extent of Ikego. The lovely forest right next to Zushi was surrounded by a huge fence and remained off-limits to the citizens.

In the meantime, the Zushi Citizens' Movement has attracted nationwide attention not only for its emphasis on nature conservation, but as a new social phenomenon in Japan. The movement also brought a new dimension into the relationship between the central and local governments. These changes represented a shift to a new political reality, one that included a balance between the defence issue and nature conservation, as well as a reliance on amateur politics and democracy.

Tomino told us that after the war,

> top priority was given to industrial development and economic prosperity. The Japanese government did not seek legislation requiring environmental assessments. When it comes to international cooperation in nature-conservation movements, as opposed to trade matters, Japan is a debtor nation with respect to American and other foreign nature-conservation organizations.

A Japanese member of the Diet who was keen on nature conservation once told Tomino that nature conservation did not attract votes in Japan. But as Tomino pointed out:

> There is now mounting concern from voters who oppose the disappearance from their immediate neighbourhood of natural settings that enrich their daily life. Since I was elected mayor of Zushi, several other mayors have won office on platforms based mainly on nature conservation.

Tomino thought that this trend was growing. He told us:

> Japan has become a major economic power. It must use its power to improve the quality of life of its citizens and to contribute to international society from the standpoint of nature conservation. I believe that the Zushi Citizens' Movement was the first political expression of such a desire.

There are 3,000 local authorities in Japan. In 1991 their budgets totalled $600-billion (U.S.), over forty percent of the U.S. federal budget and more than the Japanese central-government budget. Local authorities were recently given sweeping powers over regional social-welfare needs and were put in charge of administering those budgets.

The Japanese Constitution guarantees local autonomy. The Constitution formally places the central government and local governments on an equal footing. Nevertheless, the prewar concept of *okami* (an inviolable superior existence) with its totalitarian ideology still has very deep roots. I believe that, in the process of pushing so strongly its policy of achieving postwar economic recovery through high-technology industrialization, the central government has been guiding and supervising local governments to the point of making them function as its hands and feet. In this process, the so-called "Japan Incorporated" concept [the notion that all business is represented by a monolithic entity that speaks with a single voice] has penetrated into the area of local government.

In the 1980s the phrase "the age of localism" found an echo in people's hearts. Some forty years after the war, local governments finally acquired adequate staff to formulate their own policies and bring the relationship between the central and local governments closer to the parity specified by the Constitution. Tomino gave us this example:

> Zushi city maintains that it has the proper legal authority to ask the central government to make changes, to cancel projects, or even

to make new proposals in those instances, such as the housing project for U.S. naval personnel at Ikego forest, where the interests of local citizens are gravely affected. Zushi believes it can do so even if such projects are part of a national policy, such as defence, for which the power of implementation is reserved solely by the central government.

The entire nature of local government in Japan is changing. After Tomino's election the city council and the other citizens of Zushi have been in close communication. As Tomino said, "We consult and consult and consult until we reach a consensus. It is a very difficult process, but it is the best way, so we must overcome the difficulties. Direct democracy was a part of our administration." This policy extended to asking children for recommendations for the improvement of city parks and requesting the public to submit designs for public toilets.

At the first city council meeting over which Tomino presided, he declared that every housing development, including the Ikego project, should be frozen until the City Environment Management Plan was completed, in order to protect the total integrity of the city. The council also approved one of the most radical pieces of freedom-of-information legislation in Japan, including a provision for an ombudsman system. The result was fifty-three public-relations boards scattered around the city to let citizens know what was happening around town. They even discussed issues normally handled by diplomats, such as foreign aid (or Official Development Assistance, as they called it) with an eye to carrying out such programs on a human scale by local government. The city officials felt that their experience running a city would be valuable to those in developing countries. At a mayoral conference, Tomino proposed that all Japanese local governments devote 0.1 percent of their budget to help their counterparts in developing nations, especially in Asia and the Pacific. The aid could take the form of advice on things like sewage, social welfare, and city planning.

Tomino took a very progressive stance on the government demand that Koreans submit to fingerprinting every three years (see Chapter 7). He gave the Koreans a choice — they could be fingerprinted, or they could refuse and Tomino, as mayor, would protect them. Of six who came forward, two chose to be fingerprinted and four refused. The police were too afraid to do anything. Other mayors supported the Koreans, and the law was rescinded.

Tomino encountered some resistance from bureaucrats when he proposed that the unused offices in city hall be made available to citizens' groups.

I told them that city hall belongs to the citizens, but they insisted that it had never been done. Since there was no use pushing them, I tried to understand their point of view. I asked what problems they anticipated, and someone said they might write graffiti on the walls. Another concern was somebody might set fire to the building. This was a great lesson to me. I realized that these people feared the citizens and were motivated by an obsession to control an otherwise uncontrollable mass.

Tomino proposed that citizens' committees be established in a number of areas and that anyone interested should come and volunteer. There wouldn't be any selection unless there were too many volunteers. As of 1992 there were 156 city organizations subsidized by the city to take part in everything from delivering meals for shut-ins to outdoor music concerts. These groups were allowed to use space in the city hall.

The city also made a number of changes to improve environmental awareness, such as earmarking ¥5 million for educational pamphlets on the small animals of Zushi to be distributed to schoolchildren, and planting fruit trees on public land. As well, Zushi began to recycle paper, metal, glass, and paper milk cartons; it distributed free home-use compost kits and purchased an electric car for use by public officials in the city.

Elderly Zushi residents got, among other assistance, free medical treatment, bus passes, and word-processing courses. Tomino set up a Public Service Company, which he believed fell between government and private companies. It hired elders to work at jobs like controlling traffic for schoolchildren, working in libraries, and driving school buses. They were paid above minimum wage, and the people expressed pride in serving their community.

Another innovation, painstakingly developed as a collaborative effort between Tomino, Apple computers, Canon, Toshiba, and many scientists and citizens, was a computerized Environmental Management System. One hundred Mac computers were linked to a local area network that divided all of Zushi (except the base) into ten-by-ten metre squares (approximate size of one house). Each square was then ranked from A to D, based on twenty-two factors such as soil quality, drainage, and scenic view. The rankings were then used to determine what should be done to the land to help Zushi achieve its overall goal of sixty percent green space. When building on A-ranked land, twenty percent of the land had to be kept green; B-ranked, forty percent; C-ranked, sixty percent, and D-ranked land had to create an additional twenty percent green space.

Zushi's brand of local government was so unique in Japan that other local councils regularly studied it. But most were frightened by the levels of citizen participation and government openness, fearing such a degree of devolution of power.

We asked Tomino what he was most proud of during his terms as mayor. He answered:

> That I remained a citizen and didn't become an official. What that means is that I did my politics with common sense. When I negotiated with the central government, I always believed the citizens were the most important. I always worked with citizens to make policy.

We asked what "green" meant to him.

> High officials of the central government have maintained an inflexibile position on defence issues, although they recently have been more flexible on questions of pure nature conservation. They

say that a request of the United States government that is based on the Security Treaty must be complied with, and that the highest priority must be given to it. In other words, defence issues take precedence over all matters. One example of this attitude was the statement made by one of the most senior members of the conservative LDP [Liberal Democratic Party] in Zushi's central square during my election campaign. He said, "For the defence of the whole country, I ask for sacrifice on the part of all you Zushi citizens"! The Zushi position, as reflected by me, is that "security guarantees" and "green" carry the same weight for human beings.

The primary objectives of nation building are to protect the lives of its citizens and to create a richer society. I think there are two aspects to this protection of life. One is to protect us from sudden death, namely death from natural disasters and war. But the other is to protect us from slow death, namely death from loss of personality or illness, and our children from the loss of personality because of an inadequate physical and spiritual environment.

These two types of death are of equal gravity to all of us as human beings. So when demands that involve the issue of "sudden death" — in other words, security — clash with those involving "slow death" — in this case, the environment — both sets of demands must be treated with equal care. I therefore maintain that in this instance, the demand for the construction of housing at Ikego forest for U.S. naval personnel — for whom there are alternative housing possibilities — must give way to the other demand, the conservation of Ikego forest, which will be lost forever once it is bulldozed. The Zushi Citizens' Movement has called for the creation of a more peaceful and richer world and has stressed the importance of a better life and social amenities. This path may lead to a Japanese defence policy that would be both wider in scope than the present one — which has been pursued solely in the name of security — and easier for people to understand.

While Tomino talked, he constantly consulted his wife, Nanako. We asked him whether women in politics are different from men, and he answered immediately:

Yes. Women don't lie. Men easily resort to lies and believe that's a natural part of politics. When women came into office, they were shocked by the complexity of politics. It wasn't just a matter of fighting to save a forest or stop a development or speak of the importance of children and nature: there were all kinds of decisions about roads and sewers and telephone lines. And they were often paralysed by the immensity and complexity. But then they come out of the initial shock and some remember the reason they got elected and the issues they believed in and act on them, but others become evasive like male politicians. Japanese think that laws can't be bypassed, but we showed that the mayor and citizens could bypass them.

The events in Zushi city went beyond questions about development and the environment to the very nature of democracy. The city had demonstrated what a community can accomplish when it is interested and active. As a group the residents of Zushi, symbolic perhaps of mainstream Japanese culture, were, becoming environmentally aware: they were starting to think globally, to reconsider their attitudes towards the all-powerful central government, to come to terms with the discrimination of Koreans, and to realize that true democracy was not a right but a responsibility. The awakening of the "sleeping city" of Zushi gives hope, not only to Japan, but all of humanity.

Tomino is a remarkable man, enthusiastic, upbeat, optimistic, and positive. He believes passionately in the power of the grassroots.

To understand what's happening in Japan, don't look at the central government. It's dead. It's all happening at the local level. Right now it's invisible, but in five years, you'll begin to see it.

Tomino's optimism for the future of political activism at the grassroots level is shared by Kazuki Kumamoto, a professor at Meiji Gakuin University in Yokohama. His scholarly work in ecological economics was based on many years of involvement in local movements to protect the environment. Two areas that Kumamoto was most concerned with were Shibushi Bay in Kagoshima prefecture and Shiraho on Okinawa's Ishigaki Island.

In his recent book, *Sustainable Development and Life Systems,*[1] Kumamoto illustrated the issues in those two places. He contended that they offered models for a new type of grassroots localism and environmental movements, in which local residents used a traditional relationship to the land unique to that area to fight against the encroachment of developers.

In Shibushi Bay, officials proposed construction of a crude oil transfer station (CTS) by reclaiming land from the bay. But by dredging and dumping landfill into the bay, its ecological balance would have been destroyed. Local residents were angered and they organized to fight the proposal. They were particularly concerned about the effect of the project on the black pine forest along the beach. The trees protected the village and local farmland against the wind, tide, and the erosion of sand. More importantly, the trees were part of a complete system that ultimately enriched the ocean, a concept expressed by the term, *utsokerin,* or "fish attracting woods."

The forest was also important to the local economy. Once a week the residents raked fallen pine needles into a pile to use as fuel and to sell as fertilizer for tobacco plants. According to Kumamoto, the gathering of pine needles had another ecological effect: to protect against overenrichment of the forest soil, which would eventually result in what ecologists call succession, and allow the black pines to be taken over by other species of trees. In other words, the pine forest was maintained by the local residents, and that environment, in turn, was sustaining the livelihood of the local residents. That subtle balance has been maintained for hundreds of years.

Kumamoto argued this balance was dependent on the traditional notion of *soyu*, or "collective ownership," in which the community owns access to natural resources. This concept, which once existed throughout Japan, has been pushed aside by the modern ideas of governmental ownership, private ownership, and co-ownership. The relationship between the local residents of Shibushi Bay and the forest is comparable to that between the coral reef and the people in Shiraho, whose elders stood together to oppose the airport that would destroy their reef.

The original plan to build an airport in Shiraho by destroying the coral reef was cancelled. In Shibushi Bay, although the CTS was built, only seven percent of the land originally designed for expropriation was actually taken. According to Kumamoto, the notion of *soyu* played a significant role in the legal battles around the disputed areas. When the local residents tried to use textbook legal terms, they were easily defeated by lawyers and government officials. But these same officials and lawyers had no legal definition for the term *soyu*, although they knew that it had existed as a concept for centuries. They found the notion strange, hard to grasp, and almost impossible to deal with. Kumamoto found it exciting that, instead of the local residents having to enter and understand the world of the lawyers and officials, these "experts" now had to enter their world. He told us that Shibushi and Shiraho were just the beginning. We will see many more victories like them in the future.

●

The central figure in the struggle to protect the reef at Shiraho was Setsuko Yamazato, whom David had met years before when he was invited to visit and lend support. It was a classic example of the way grassroots movements grow and exert their force.

When the government had announced its plan in the late 1970s to build a new airport in Shiraho, a fishing community on the southwestern edge of Ishigaki Island in Okinawa, most of the villagers opposed it. For the older people the plan was no less than sacrilegious. The inhabitants of the village supported themselves from the abundance of sea life in the semicircular reef that extended out from the shore. The reef has been designated a world-heritage-class ecosystem yet would be filled in to accommodate the airport runway. The mayor of Ishigaki argued that Shiraho people were only a small group compared to all the other islanders who wanted the airport. The mayor's arrogance made the villagers even angrier. But his decision was firm, and he was already working closely with the pro-airport prefectural governor of Okinawa. Thus began a long struggle.

As the Okinawan musican Shoichi Kina told us, before the name "Okinawa" was imposed by the Japanese and "Ryuku" by the Chinese, people referred to the islands as Uruma, or islands of coral. For thousands of years, the coral reefs around the islands generously supported a community of innumerable life forms of which humans were a part. Since ancient times, the people of Ishigaki Island, about 400 kilometres southwest of the Okinawan main island and only 250 kilometres from Taiwan, called the coral reef the "fountain of fish" and "life-sustaining sea." The magnificent reef near the village of Shiraho was especially renowned for its fish and coral formations, and it was there that the government planned to build the airport.

At low tide, the centre of the reef was like an enchanted lake, crystal clear and filled with multicoloured fish. Fishermen walked along the reef spearing octopus. Underwater were magnificent tangles of blue and grey staghorn coral, schools of large fish that cruised the reef and scooted into deep channels, and along the ocean floor and in crevices, sea urchins and sea cucumbers were abundant.

To build the proposed superport runway long enough to handle the biggest jets, the bay was to be filled in with rock created by pulverizing an entire mountain! Experts and engineers claimed there was nothing unique about the Shiraho reef and offered reassurances the plan was no threat to any important ecosystems.

David recalled his trip to Shiraho in the late 1980s:

At a press conference when I stated my opposition to the airport, reporters told me the government pointed to scientific claims that the airport was no threat to important ecosystems. I replied, "Those 'experts' are either stupid or liars. No biologist can claim to have knowledge that can allow such claim to be made with authority."

Restoration could well be the dominant challenge for environmentalists in the next millennium. The eminent American environmentalist David Brower speaks of the need for CPR — conservation, protection and restoration. Restoration is made necessary because of the massive destruction of ecosystems all over the Earth. But human initiatives can never hope to achieve more than pale imitations of the complex communities that evolve over long periods of time. By far the best thing we can do is protect those ecosystems that remain intact.

Nor was it clear why an airport was needed. There was already a major airport on the island. Several possible justifications for building a second airport were made: construction companies might simply have been creating new make-work projects, political uncertainty in the Philippines might have threatened the security of the American air base there so that Shiraho was to become a new staging area, or it might simply have been the unthinking equation of economic growth and development with progress.

Whatever the motivation of those in favour of the airport, they faced the unflinching opposition of one woman, and after ten years it appeared she might have won.

In early 1980s, Setsuko Yamazato, then living in the countryside of Ishigaki, had come to Shiraho after seeing a television report showing riot police pushing around elderly protesters at a land survey. She had come with no intention of staying, but the battle and the people pulled her in and she has never left.

Yamazato was deeply concerned about many threats to nature on Ishigaki — erosion of the red soil, construction of dams, overdevelopment, tourism, and militarism. But on an island with only 14,000 families and almost two hundred construction companies, it was hard to organize opposition to a project that might employ your relatives. It was a bitter battle right from the beginning.

Yamazato took us on a tour of Ishigaki. There were seven dams on the island and more being built. Some dams were run by the Japanese government, others locally. Invariably the government dams contained more water than the local ones. Islanders, who were the rightful owners of the water, therefore suffered the humiliation of going to the government and begging them for water.

A long tunnel had been built through a mountain, and it revolutionized transportation on the island. As we drove through it, Yamazato told us that it is used by perhaps fifty vehicles a day. Even during times of drought, its walls were wet with leaks. From a ridge, Yamazato pointed out eroding red soil that stained the seawater along the shore and had already choked and killed eighty to ninety percent of the coral in the bay.

Yamazato then took us to Green Park, a newly opened picnic area for city dwellers. The field layout and various structures were highly reminiscent of military training fields, and they made some people suspicious. Toilets were built of concrete, low and round with glassless slit windows, looking for all the world like army pillboxes; one very small area contained five of them. At the highest point in the park was a three-storey observation tower built to look like a massive boulder. It had holes in the walls about eight inches off the ground, too high to drain rainwater and too low for a child to look through, but perfect for a gun emplacement. Were the people paranoid? Perhaps. But on his last visit, the director of the Economic Development Agency was brought in to tour the site; he landed at a helicopter port built nearby, even though there was already one a few miles away. If not a potential military installation, it was a case of rampant overdevelopment.

Yamazato's English was so good we kept forgetting she came from a family of farmers on Ishigaki and was not born in North America. Her father and mother got married in Tokyo, where they lived for twenty years. Yamazato considers herself Okinawan because she was born and grew up on the island. She was left with her grandparents as an infant when her mother became ill and had to return to Tokyo. When the final stages of the war reached Okinawa, the Japanese authorities forced the Ishigaki Islanders to evacuate their homes. Yamazato and her family fled into the jungle where malaria was the biggest enemy and claimed the lives of her mother and grandfather. After the war she was raised by her father's mother.

"*We asked again and again for environmental assessments of the new airport.*"

SETSUKO YAMAZATO,
ACTIVIST

Yamazato never finished high school, but as a teenager, she got a job with a U.S. geological survey of the islands for the military. Her hope was to learn English, but she also learned valuable information about water sources, vegetation, and soil. To complete the reports, she lived for three years in Tokyo, then got a job with a small airline company. It took her to Honolulu and San Francisco.

After moving back to Tokyo she became an office worker. But nostalgic for Okinawa, she began to meet with a circle of islanders to listen to and study Okinawan music. She started a traditional dance group.

We had come to appreciate the music only after leaving the islands. That made me want to come back to learn more from the elders. In 1963 I returned to Ishigaki city. I came back to a seven-month drought and it was quite a shock after Honolulu. The pineapple industry had just gotten started and I became concerned with the *kogai* [pollution] of the red soil from the plantations that was washing into the sea.

Yamazato went back to her native village and began to collect music.

I was especially fond of unaccompanied work songs, lullabies, and farmer's field songs. My cousin put me to work in his rice fields. I was so happy to go into the fields, but I found myself surrounded by other farmers listening to *sumo* [traditional wrestling] or baseball or European classical music on their radios. It was not the way I imagined it would be. Before we used to do all the work to songs and chants. I still remember hearing those songs when I was young.

Soon she began weaving instead of farming.

I love it here in Shiraho because I have elderly friends with so much to teach me. I feel more relaxed with older people, perhaps because I was raised by my grandmother. She was born in the early Meiji and could speak no Japanese. She was not Japan oriented like most of the younger generations have become. For her the war didn't end until she died because she had lost her husband, daughter-in-law and grandchild.

Moving to Shiraho proved to be a major turning point in Yamazato's life. At the time she had no idea that ten years of intense political activism were about to begin. As she got involved in the movement to stop the proposed airport, Yamazato began to see the political and economic structure behind the problem. The cost of the proposed airport was said to be ¥38 billion, 95 percent of which would be paid for by the central government. Proponents of the airport suggested the island farmers and fishermen would find new markets and top prices for fresh products shipped directly to Tokyo. As well, big-spending tourists would flood the area. Thus, the prefectural government supported the airport for its claimed potential. The mayor and the governor worked together, using political manoeuvres to ram the airport through. Yamazato told us:

We asked again and again for economic and environmental assessments of the new airport. But they totally ignored us, until finally they said, "As long as the local and Japanese governments admit a need for a new airport, there is no need for an assessment of its impact."

Yamazato and other anti-airport villagers feared that the new airport would devastate their environment and local economy by attracting major resort developers and multinational agro business. But their greatest concern was the impact on their traditional lifestyle and values. The elders were afraid that their children and grandchildren would be forced into the larger economic system imposed from outside and would be severed from their cultural and spiritual roots. They also feared the militaristic implications of the new airport. With a weak smile, Yamazato added:

> Japanese people tell us we are paranoid, but we have a different sense of reality. Originally the Shiraho harbour site was started by the U.S. Army Corps of Engineers and handed over to the Japanese at reversion.

After twenty-seven years of American occupation and the subsequent reversion to Japan in 1972, Okinawa still remained the military keystone of the U.S. presence in Asia. One-fifth of the major Okinawan islands was covered by U.S. bases, and that represented seventy-five percent of all bases in Japan (see chapters 1 and 2).

> There were young people in the movement against the airport, but we kept losing them because they were put under enormous pressure. Kiyoshi Mukaizato, a sugarcane farmer, was the head of the committee opposing the airport. He was arrested twice. I lost a lot of friends. The pro-airport people cut themselves off from me. Somebody threw stones at my house and broke my windows.

It was after that incident that she got a dog.

> I did everything. I did posters, made announcements, held meetings. At traditional events like weddings, festivals, and dances, men are expected to be master of ceremony and that's fine with me. But at these political meetings I didn't limit myself to the traditional roles for women. A lot of other women didn't either.

It is remarkable to see the parallels with other grassroots groups that have sprung up independently and spontaneously all over the world. It takes someone who becomes concerned enough to act on an issue, be it a dam, pollution, a new road, or pesticide spraying. A small group of concerned people then begins a process of informing themselves, often encountering duplicity, bribery, and threats from government and industry opponents. As support builds, media events such as demonstrations, marches, and pickets serve to inform people about the controversy. Pressure is put on vulnerable points. It may seem as if the wheel is being reinvented, but each new group adds to the public's scepticism of political and business claims, its ecological awareness, and its criticism of the claimed benefits of economic progress. It's all part of what future historians might recognize as the beginnings of a global mass movement.

Although Yamazato downplayed her role in the movement, it was obvious that she had been largely responsible for the international recognition the Shiraho case has earned. With her excellent English and her experience working overseas, she played a central role in organizing a worldwide campaign from this tiny village. Since the late 1980s, the World Wildlife Fund (WWF) has been actively involved in this campaign. She travelled to Thailand in 1987, to Costa Rica in 1988, and to Australia in 1990 to present her case in international conferences. In Costa Rica, Tokyo, and Australia she met Prince Philip of England, an active patron of the WWF. These meetings resulted in the prince's visit to Shiraho in March 1992. The villagers welcomed him with a traditional lion dance. He stayed overnight and saw the reef firsthand. He said in his speech that it was not his decision *where* to build an airport, but *how* to build it should be given very careful consideration.

When we visited, the struggle continued, although the pressure on Shiraho appeared to be alleviated, since Japanese authorities are hypersensitive to international attention and criticism. Yamazato told us:

> It has been a very long fight, but support from the outside has given us energy. So far it has been a success, but they now want to build the airport on another part of the island. The proposed site, near the community of Miyara, is right between two streams. The Miyara community is fighting the site.

From our inn we watched the fishermen bring in the morning catch: two baskets of large black tai to be sent to market in Naha, a large crab with beautiful red spots on the carapace, a two-kilogram spiny lobster, four porcupine puffer fish prized for medicinal use and many different small reef fish. The reef that people call Ryugujo, or sea god's palace, still seemed to provide generously for the village.

Later that afternoon we sat on the wooden floor in Yamazato's house, drinking tea and looking out at the fields. The house was so close to the beach we could hear the waves gently lapping the shore. Yamazato's solace came from weaving. In one room was a loom, surrounded by coils of coloured silk. She eked out a living weaving silks for kimonos, and she and a few friends had formed a co-operative to buy silkworms to make their own thread. The other room was a library and sleeping area dominated by an exuberant black puppy. We sat in the weaving room, which was bare of furniture except for a single table. From hanging lines, naturally dyed threads dried in the summer heat. Behind these lines sat a mountain of boxes filled with documents for the movement. The young woman who refilled our cups and acted as Yamazato's assistant turned out to be a visitor from Tokyo who'd arrived only the day before to get acquainted with Yamazato. Our host was calm and relaxed and talked easily about her personal problems and dreams.

As an outsider, Yamazato was vulnerable to criticism and suspicion. Throughout the struggle, her health was precarious, with periodic crises her doctor couldn't diagnose. Finally after ten years, she went to the hospital for extensive tests and discovered she had tuberculosis. The high drug resistance of the disease demanded a strict regime of multiple drug treatments for a prolonged period. While reluctantly following the prescription, she also turned to traditional Okinawan medicinal plants.

However, what concerned Yamazato more than her physical condition were the scars left in the minds of the people. Political conflicts divided communities and not infrequently families.

We must rebuild relations in the village, reconcile those who were anti- and pro-airport. We need healing. The last ten years I have lost many friends. But now I'm finally getting some back.

For Yamazato the effort to heal human relationships was similar to the attempt to heal the natural environment that human beings have damaged. The process would not be mechanical, but spiritual. Visibly weary from the struggle, Yamazato felt firmly sustained by her friends and the sense of community of which she was a part. *Shima shakai* (island society) refers to a communal bonding that Okinawan people still retain, a sense of identity based on a common feeling of rootedness. Yamazato told us about a traditional mutual-aid society called *moyai* or *moai*, which she believes embodies the communal bonding.

Once a month we gather in someone's home to drink and talk. There are usually twelve to fifteen members. We pay in a certain amount and members can draw out money, which is then repaid at low interest. I think the business part is an excuse to have a party. I am happiest when I have a shot of *awamori* [local wine] with friends who like to sing and dance.

Yamazato is also happiest when she is weaving. When she weaves she forgets the whole world.

Weaving, singing, dancing, eating — these things came into me when I was small. Being raised by my grandparents really formed my foundation. Lots of other things entered and accumulated in me since then, but recently they have become less and less relevant, and I feel more and more confident that I can live without them. What is essential to me is what I had originally. I can no longer deceive myself. After all, that is me. Recently there was a blackout that lasted a few days. I discovered I was quite calm about it. I even started to appreciate life without electricity. I was struck by the beauty of candlelight.

Yamazato taught us a beautiful expression, *tinupana* which literally means "flowers of hands," and refers, in the local language, to handicrafts. She recently organized a crafts group and named it Society. It is primarily an educational organization in which the younger generation can continue with traditions and learn from the elders. But it is also an economic basis for the local residents. Yamazato is therefore trying to develop a market for their products through her network of supporters all over Japan.

But Yamazato has never stopped thinking about the broader implications of the Shiraho struggle.

> I am still very impressed with the sea here and with nature. But now over ninety percent of the water and coral reefs have been destroyed by development. I want to break out of the wall of Shiraho and establish an island-wide analysis of the environment.

She also believes that the whole chain of the islands between Japan and Taiwan share a common ecological and cultural basis on which she envisioned an economic and political territory.

"I even have a name for it," she said with a shy smile. "Urumania." The name stems from the ancient term *uruma*, meaning coral islands. Urumania is Yamazato's utopia. Studying Okinawan history, she found important clues in the traditional economic practices, such as a communal system of ownership and distribution appropriate to the local ecology.

We asked her what drove her to continue, after her sickness, the alienation from old friends, and all the hardships of the battle. She answered:

> Something spiritual. I was raised by my grandparents from the premodern time. Imagine, the old men would wear sarongs! I grew up worshipping gods at the local *utaki* [sacred places]. The world of gods, spirits, nature, and festivals is what my upbringing was. And now I realize that I inherited something spiritual from my aunt, a *noro* [shaman]. That's why I can't tolerate when the harmonious relationship between the gods, humans, and nature is disrupted. Then I am hurt as well.

On our last night in Shiraho, Yamazato took us to a meeting place so that she could introduce us to the people who fought on the front lines, braving arrest and injury to save their coral reef, the heart of their village. As they walked into the room, they seemed like fragile relics from another time. As these elders pass away, a long lineage of language, customs, and memories comes closer to being lost forever. Yamazato, at almost sixty, was one of the youngest people in the group, trying to absorb what the elders had to pass on.

Yamazato, in her blue kimono, sat on the floor holding her *sanshin*. Her face glowed with excitement. When she began playing her instrument, a seventy-year-old man joined in with his beautiful tenor and an eighty-year-old woman with her lively dance. Every one of them turned out to be excellent singers and dancers. Mukaizato, the chairman of the protest committee, led us in a celebratory dance — a fitting end to our visit. Out of their successful opposition to the airfield in Shiraho, the villagers have regained a feeling of community and asserted the importance of their traditions.

Like people of the First Nations in North America, Tomino and Yamazato have acted out a deep feeling of attachment for the land. In building a base of popular support and keeping pressure on politicians, they are being political in the most profound way. Their success confirms the power of grassroots support to bring about change.

Once the environment — air, water, soil, other living things — is central to any worldview, it becomes inseparable from people's lives, culture, and history. Modern science and technology and telecommunications have fragmented the world into bits and pieces disconnected in time and space. This shattered world cries out for a renewed sense of interconnectedness.

tHe fooD
coNNectIoN

"It's a cycle. One life produces another and another and

one life eats another and another.

We are born and die and born and die.

That's why there are no enemies. Everything is

balanced. To live is to eat. To eat is to involve

death because we are eating something's life."

YOSHIKAZU KAWAGUCHI

tHE Japanese preoccupation with food is obvious to foreigners almost from the moment they arrive in Japan. Concession stands hawk all manner of specially prepared foods, box lunches, and desserts. And a visit to the basement level of large department stores is a gustatory delight as one samples the mouthwatering tidbits offered as enticement. A special treat on a visit to Tokyo is a morning spent at Tsukiji, the largest commercial fish market in the world. Kilometres of stalls display sea life of amazing variety. The aesthetic presentation and the absolute freshness of the creatures, many still alive, attest to the central role of food for the Japanese.

Global ecological degradation should be a major concern to a country that sits so high on the chain of predators. It is ironic that Japanese place a great premium on high-quality food yet the high-tech agriculture so widely used makes it impossible to avoid residues of pesticides and industrial toxins in that very food. Furthermore, the unsustainable harvesting of highly prized fish such as eels, tuna, and cod is decreasing their numbers while pushing prices skyhigh. Environmentalists are not highly visible here, and there's little sense of emergency or alarm. However, there is a movement in agriculture that has at its base a recognition that industrial agriculture, with its heavy application of chemicals, use of widespread monocultures, and dependence on machinery, is not sustainable.

We visited one of the leaders of a radically different agriculture that looks to nature for inspiration and guidance.

Yoshikazu Kawaguchi lives fifty kilometres south of Kyoto in Nara prefecture, the traditional heartland of Japan and birthplace of the first Japanese nation, called Yamato, which emerged in the fourth century. His fields are probably among the oldest in the country, and his "new" way of farming and living is an attempt to rediscover the original methods used by the first farming populations.

We turned off the main road into a small alleyway with a stream beside it. Black tiles adorned the roof of the traditional-style house. Yoshikazu and Yoko, his wife, greeted us exuberantly. Kawaguchi, a thin man with an almost childlike build, wore a white cap and blue work clothes.

Over the entrance to the house was a cloth curtain, which we parted, then walked through. The packed earth floor in the front hall was our first indication of the house's age. Most of the farmhouse complex, we learned, was 150 years old and had housed the Kawaguchi family for more than a century. Behind the house was a courtyard crowded with small plants. There was an old-style toilet and bathhouse, with a little wooden door that barely kept out the cold of the early morning or evening. Beyond that was the guest house, a new building very simply built with aluminum windows and wood walls. Inside, it was bare except for a *kotatsu* (a low table covered by a *futon*, which holds in the heat from an electric heater under the table, under which people put their feet to keep warm) in the middle of the floor, a table by the door with some books for sale — Kawaguchi's and others — and a Yamaha organ by the wall. Despite the main uses of the building, Kawaguchi confessed that his favourite pastime was to play table tennis with his children.

We used to have a TV, but when my eldest son entered kindergarten, we decided to get rid of it. My son would sit very close to the screen and his eyesight was suffering. After we stopped TV, the children started reading passionately. At first I was happy but now I am worried about their eyes again.

We all nestled into the *kotatsu* to eat lunch, which was served by Yoko. The table filled up with small dishes of spinach, cucumbers, *daikon* (white radish), carrots, and rice, as well as meat dishes. Grinning brightly and sitting perfectly straight, the inquisitive, slightly bashful Kawaguchi explained to us that the rice was actually a mixture of three different varieties, one of them an ancient strain that was reddish in colour. Almost everything on the table was from his fields. He began his story.

I was born in 1939. My family has always been farmers. We had a small plot, about seven hundred square metres. I wanted to be a painter or a photographer. But since I was the eldest son, from about the age of sixteen, I was a farmer. At the beginning we didn't have chemical fertilizer or big farming machines. But they came. I used them for more than twenty years. Then I got sick. My liver was breaking down.

While sick with a chronic liver disorder, Kawaguchi came across a newspaper series by Sawako Ariyoshi entitled "Fukugo Osen" (Complex Pollution).

Suddenly I realized that it was the herbicides and fertilizers I had been using for years that were the main cause of my illness. I then knew that my whole form of agriculture had been a mistake.

From that starting point, he discovered the seminal books of Masanobu Fukuoka, *The One Straw Revolution*[1] and *The Natural Way of Farming*,[2] both of which were originally published in Japanese in 1975 and 1976 respectively.

It was impossible for me to go back to those forms of farming that poison our earth and bodies. I knew that no matter what obstacles or difficulties I might face, I had to start practising natural farming.

For the first two years of natural farming, Kawaguchi lost his entire rice crop. But he learned from the experience and, in the third year, adopted transplanting methods of inserting young plants into small holes in the ground.

Many farmers are still getting sick from pesticides without realizing the cause. It is very difficult for a farmer to get out of his routine. Enjoying nature is not part of mainstream farming. It has become an enterprise designed only to make a lot of money. Farmers are removed from the philosophy of raising life. They are surrounded by nature but they are also removed from it at the same time.

The vegetables and rice we were eating were all naturally grown in Kawaguchi's fields. They had a fresh, rich taste missing in many industrially grown foods.

The farmers think they are making more money by using machines and chemicals because their harvests have increased. But actually it is an illusion. They have to buy the machines, pay for the fuel, and constantly purchase more and more fertilizers and pesticides. Their vegetable and rice harvest may be large, but their crops lack nutrients and are quite tasteless. Worst of all, these farmers are destroying the earth and harming people's health.

In grade five here, students learn about farming. But the

textbooks all talk about highly mechanized farms. When children come here, they find there are no machines. When they first pull a plant from the soil, they are afraid of the dirt clinging to the roots, so they hold the plant with their fingertips as far away as possible and hold their noses saying, "It stinks." But out of a class, there are two or three who absolutely revel in feeling the soil and have to be rounded up to leave.

The enjoyment of the soil, the foods it produces, and the life it gives is an important part of Kawaguchi's philosophy.

I don't like the word agri*culture* because "culture" implies human interference. That leads to moneymaking and enterprise. The main purpose is not money or enterprise but to improve people's health. The yield is smaller with natural farming, but the food is real, it has more life. It's not artificially pumped up. You need less of it to live.

After our lunch, Kawaguchi took us on a tour. As we walked through the fields, it was obvious that Kawaguchi's fields were nothing like his neighbours'. The rice paddy felt more like a nature preserve than an agricultural concern.

The biggest practical difference between natural and organic farming is whether or not you till the land. That is also a fundamental philosophical difference. I think the basis of tilling is scientific, western thinking. It puts Man and nature in conflict. It says nature can't do it properly without man. In natural farming, Man is part of nature. Farming is a practice in nature; it is a part of nature. It is the difference between producing and growing.

Kawaguchi makes a distinction between the standard agricultural practice, which focuses on fruits and vegetables as products, and natural farming, which views the growth of life as the goal from which humans may derive a living.

Organic farmers believe that humans have to do something. For example, they use fertilizer, albeit organic. Natural farming says we don't have to use fertilizer, we don't have to till. We don't see insects and weeds as enemies. There are no definite rules for natural farming. It depends on the place and season. Instead of memorizing rules, however, we will always be fine as long as we have wisdom.

Between twenty-eight and forty days after germination, the rice plants need some help. They are forming their bodies. After forty days in September, the plant works on making the seed. So between twenty-eight and forty days, I help by cutting back the competition. Winter grass can be left because it will die anyway. Summer grass is cut and let lie. The soil forms the way a forest floor does, by the vegetation that piles up. Early November is harvest time. Other life forms are coming out of the carcasses of old life. We get an overlap of one season's life with the next.

When North American aboriginal people saw European settlers ploughing for the first time, they looked on in amazement. Realizing the plough was turning the top under, they said, "You are doing it upside down." The Europeans laughed at the ignorance of the "savages," but today's massive crisis of soil erosion suggests the native people may have been right.

As a natural farmer, Kawaguchi does not plough the soil or use chemical fertilizers or pesticides. If the ground has to be partially cleared, he cuts rather than uproots the offending plants, leaving the tops where they fall to decompose and reinvigorate the earth's life cycle.

He plunged his hands into the soil to show us its overtly healthy composition, handling it not with pride or disdain, but naturally. His soil was black and sticky with decaying plants, and we agreed that it smelled like the soil and farmland of our childhoods. Kawaguchi called it "the smell of life."

Natural farming was developed by Japanese agricultural philosophers, not farmers. One of the main proponents was a member of a religious order. Natural farming was a pillar of their religious thought. Because these people were not really farmers, the practical techniques needed a lot of experimentation. Within two or three years, most people who tried to implement it gave up and went back to other methods. Only a few of us still practise natural farming.

According to Kawaguchi's philosophy, nature is a complex community of living things, which humans do not understand. It is impossible to define one or a few species of plants or insects as good or bad when we have so little knowledge about their role in the entire ecosystem.

When we looked more closely, we realized that the variety of plants on his fields was reminiscent of a bog. Bogs don't appear as impressive as a majestic stand of trees in a forest, but when you bend down and examine the tiny plants closely, you discover a stunning variety of species. In contrast to his neighbours' biological deserts, Kawaguchi's field was a virtual wilderness. There was a profusion of plants, many small ones flattening out along the ground and others forming fuzzy clumps and thrusting strawlike stems upwards in a bouquet. Indeed, he called them "my forest" and the area actually smelled like a forest.

In a normal rice paddy, the water is devoid of life. Methane is produced by decaying vegetation, and the soil is like clay. Many people want my rice. People know it is good. But there is more demand than product. Nature is designed so that one farmer cannot make enough food for many people.

Rice is a profoundly local product. It is not heavily traded on the stock markets because more than ninety-five percent of all rice in the world is consumed where it is grown. Japan-grown rice is heavily subsidized by the government, which also imposes steep tariffs to keep out foreign competition. There is a widely held belief that Japanese rice is superior to imported rice in nutrition and taste.

We asked Kawaguchi what he thought of the 1993–94 "rice crisis" in Japan, which many people felt was fabricated to cause panic among the population. A group of political parties used it as an opportunity to promote free trade, with the backing of the United States. The opposing group reaffirmed the nationalist sentiment arising from the "rice is sacred" ideology, even resorting to racially slanted attacks on the quality of Thai rice.

The ideal situation is to grow what you eat and to eat what is grown in your area. Free trade *sounds* good. We say we should go beyond state borderlines, but we are still talking about what is profitable for consumers or producers. We have to go beyond that, too, and talk about life forms. From that point of view, I don't think life forms should be transported long distances. Health should be maintained by eating things grown locally. Otherwise, you are disturbing regional interdependence. If you eat things grown far away, it won't fit perfectly into your local system. It can be detrimental. But I am not rice-centred like some Japanese farmers. In Japan, rice happens to be our staple. Elsewhere, it could be wheat or corn. Rice is not sacred.

As a local product, rice could be a model for other crops. Like rice they should be kept diverse and locally grown and consumed. There should be a strong move away from monocultures of highly inbred stocks. Inbred strains can become extremely vulnerable to disease, insect predation, and climate change, because they lack the genetic flexibility to adapt to new pests or environmental conditions. Growing diverse local crops is the best way to maximize land use and productivity while minimizing vulnerability to environmental surprises.

Kawaguchi showed us over every inch of his three fields. He cut off a few flowers of broccoli, which we put straight into our mouths and happily munched. Then he yanked out two *daikon*, which we polished on our pants and bit into. Along the way, he pulled *satoimo* (Japanese taro) from the soil and tore off a leaf for us to sample. Food should be eaten this way, we remarked, directly from the field with no fear of poisons. These days the word "dirt" is equated with uncleanliness, but dirt is part of soil, the giver of life itself.

Although Kawaguchi walked gracefully and lightly, he had an unassuming self-assuredness, as if he was very comfortable in his world. From time to time he exposed small patches among the vegetation and revealed potatoes and onions sprouting. He showed us the wheat that he'd sown over the rice paddies. (Wheat was harvested in early June, then rice was planted in the same area and harvested in November.)

It was mid-spring now, and as we moved through the fields, we came in contact with crickets, frogs, and dragonflies in the underbrush. Kawaguchi told us that we might even find an eel in the rice paddy. Going against the modern farming practices of his own family and neighbours hasn't been easy, he told us.

> We have been seeing other life forms as our enemies. But if we see them as friends, it changes how we act. The more we learn about what's happening in soil, the more we learn about life.
>
> After ten years, professional farmers realized what was happening and that my rice was wonderful. But they still didn't change. These days, they are informed by television of what is happening, so the level of understanding is higher. On every level, people are realizing that natural farming is good, but they can't shift. I guess they are afraid of changing their habits, but they say, "We are shy to try something different." We need about three out of ten people to overcome this inertia. After that, when five out of ten are doing it the rest will be shy about being left out.

When weeds and insect pests are allowed to grow freely without imposed control and the fields are contiguous and small, neighbours are understandably upset. In a country where conformity and harmony are high priorities, the pressures on Kawaguchi must have been intense. He explained calmly with a small smile playing around his lips.

> Fifteen years ago, they probably thought I had gone mad. They accused me of letting weeds and insects get into their fields. I didn't say anything about what their insecticides were doing to *my* fields. In a natural system, deadly mutations don't break out. That happens

when there is a monoculture and we spray chemicals. When I began, other farmers were afraid my fields would become hotbeds for pests. When they came around five or ten times a year, I would listen. I never tried to tell them my way was better or argue with them. Then when they stopped, I would thank them, tell them I heard their concerns, say I would do my best, and carry on the same way. When they complained that weed seeds spread from my fields to theirs, I cut the weeds in a small area. But the important thing is to continue my way of farming, and not to compete with others.

We have long been conditioned to look on neatly groomed fields as desirable and aesthetically pleasing. But as we walked back to the guest house, we looked over at the neighbouring fields and realized our perception had changed. Now the carefully groomed rows seemed sterile and empty.

At this point we expected that our visit was at an end, but suddenly we were presented with another meal, this one comprising even more dishes than the one at lunchtime. After spending the day in the country air, it felt good to eat and enjoy ourselves. Unfortunately for Kawaguchi, we kept peppering him with so many questions he hardly had time to eat. His wife, Yoko, told us not to worry. Kawaguchi, she said, doesn't eat much normally. Kawaguchi agreed, saying that when you find something that is so much fun and that you can be so passionate about, you don't have to eat. Eating shouldn't be a rule or an obsession. We should eat as it pleases us. He smiled and told us that on that day eating was not his number-one priority.

We asked how Kawaguchi selected his plants. Did he breed for specific traits, as farmers have done since the agricultural revolution began some ten millennia ago?

It's a difficult problem. It's true that we can go back to the very early plants, but they wouldn't feed us. Now the more we select, the weaker the plant becomes. Some people are against that. They say it's discrimination against other plants. But how far do we go? We eat other life, that's a form of discrimination. I accept that, but with respect. We don't become greedy. Selecting healthy plants is not from a greedy mind. Yes, I do select in that sense.

But if pesticides are not used and biological controls are not deliberately encouraged, what stops predators from exploding like a plague on his fields?

All kinds of life forms thrive. Some small animals survive in the soil. Dead life forms accumulate and many things live on them. Some insects will eat rice and their droppings nourish the soil. This will be absorbed into the rice and the rice will survive. Rice will die and become a part of this cycle too. The accumulation of dead plants and animals becomes the stage for new life to grow. Actually, I learned dead bodies are more important than the soil itself. There are rice eaters and eaters of the rice field. It's a killing field. There's territoriality — the strong ones will win. That, too, is a fact of life. So in the real world, animals and plants are helping each other live and also killing each other. Those two aspects make one big totality.

We were so inspired by Kawaguchi's knowledge and enthusiasm we hardly noticed the passing of time. Keibo asked Kawaguchi about EM (effective micro-organisms), a technique of spraying large quantities of micro-organisms onto fields.[3] EM was developed by Professor Teruo Higa at the University of the Ryukus. Its premise is the notion that oxidation, the process that causes rust and corrosion, is the basis of environmental degradation. Its adherents claim that micro-organisms that check oxidation can enrich soil, purify water, and deodorize barns. The theory has received a lot of publicity as a way of significantly increasing crop yields. Its advocates believe it will solve the problem of world food production. Kawaguchi replied:

EM is still not free from trying to apply a scientific way of thinking. What science can find is part of something, but just a part. So the person working with EM found a part and is drawing on that part. But in the totality of soil, air, water, and living things, it's too simplified an approach. First, he distinguishes between "good" and "bad" organisms. That is wrong. Each micro-organism has a much wider range of activities than just the one he's looking at. So you can't pull out just one function; there are many more micro-organisms than science knows, and each one is complete in its existence and part of a totality. So to find just one wonderful function of one organism and bring it into the field disrupts the harmony of the field. The basic thing is to trust life and let it live in the natural world.

Kawaguchi's insights are simple but profound. Scientists are understandably enthusiastic about how much has been learned in this century. But in their exuberance, they lead us to believe that the curtains of ignorance have been pulled back to reveal nature's deepest secrets. The application of knowledge to create powerful technologies creates an impression of understanding and control. But it is illusory because the time reference is so short. Chemicals that will kill insects can be synthesized, thus giving the impression that pests like mosquitoes and flies can be controlled. But our ignorance is so vast that "biomagnification," the process whereby chemicals are concentrated hundreds of thousands of times up the food chain, was discovered only when birds began to go extinct after DDT spraying.

Kawaguchi continued:

The rivers, the soil, the Earth are polluted. We did it. People using EM think we can solve the problem. But this, too, is wrong. The diseased Earth must be allowed to live. This is the quickest and best remedy.

Kawaguchi's sage advice is a striking contrast to the "technological fix" beloved of engineers and experts. He makes us realize that so little is known about the workings of nature, new technologies inevitably create unanticipated problems, whether from dams, petrochemicals, antibiotics, or cars. The tendency then is to carry on with the offending technology because it has become so deeply integrated into our economic and social systems. Instead of halting the troublesome technology, we try to create another technological solution to the problems created by the technology in the first place.

Certain proposed "scientific" solutions to global warming illustrate this tendency. Instead of doing the obvious, which is to cut back on greenhouse-gas emission and hope nature can recover, some scientists propose, among other things, seeding the upper atmosphere with sulphur dioxide from a fleet of jumbo jets; putting huge amounts of iron, a limiting growth factor for algae, into the Antarctic Ocean to stimulate carbon-dioxide-consuming plants; and spreading a massive plastic sheet in space to partially shield the Earth from the sun. These proposed megaprojects indicate a mentality that fails to acknowledge our ignorance or show respect for the complexity of the biophysical features of the planet and, instead, has faith in human inventiveness and creativity to control our destinies.

We asked Kawaguchi what was wrong with using our intellectual ability to increase yields and quality of products. He replied:

> EM and organic farming are variations of technique. Each one has a sense of wonder over one aspect of nature. But they have no idea of the wonder of the totality. So EM shows wonderful effects, but once it is applied in nature, we have no idea what it will do. EM might be effective in the short term, but its effects will disappear because nature is always changing and will overwhelm it. If they use a lot, I am sure it will cause problems in plants. Every life form is based on so many elements that they can't be reduced to one or two. You can never say one micro-organism is good or bad; that can be possible only in one environment.

Australian scientist Bill Mollison has recently successfully promoted an indigenous agriculture called "permaculture."[4] It involves using plants specifically belonging to that area for farming. We asked Kawaguchi how it differed from natural farming.

Mollison's approach is almost there, but it's not there. Permaculturists understand ecosystems very well and speak of sustainable lifestyles within this ecosystem. But Mollison's followers are trying to use locally found plants in standard farming. It's like a garden. It's still human controlled. They are still trying to apply science. But natural farming philosophy attempts to follow nature. We don't try to make nature do what we want.

When we interjected that Mollison does make a step forward by showing respect for local flora and fauna, Kawaguchi continued:

But he hasn't taken the big step of acknowledging that he doesn't know everything and that we must live within nature. The land lets you live. The seasons give you the food from the land.

The belief that scientific and technological knowledge is so powerful that nature can be "managed" finds its most striking expression in the language of industrial forestry. Foresters and the forest industry refer to the tree plantations that grow up after the "liquidation" of old-growth or "wild" forests as "normal" forests. Forests are assessed in terms of "harvestable timber." Trees are called "stems" while noneconomic species are "weeds." An ancient forest is called "decadent" and, if allowed to fall down, will "go to waste." The complex community of living and nonliving things that make up a forest is described simply as a potential crop. The idea that an ecosystem like a forest is analogous to a farmer's field is a bizarre rationale for modern forestry practice. Kawaguchi agreed.

We never touch forests and mountains with our knowledge. We never bring our knowledge into the mountains. Of course, natural farming is not nature. We have our goals. We want crops. My farm looks like a forest but it is not. I have an objective — I want a crop — but we never do that with forests and mountains. All living forms are dependent on mountains and forests. They are sacred. Here in the fields, the most basic component is not rice, it is air and water.

The intimate connection with the Earth and dependence on water, seasons, and natural rhythms provide a constant affirmation of the cycles of our own life and death, as Kawaguchi reminded us again:

Life and death are just different forms of life. In the field, the maximum life span for a rice plant is half a year. You can't go beyond that. Human life, too, must end. Some people try to find medicine that will cure death. They see death as an enemy. I won't say that I am not afraid of death, but if I don't accept it, I can never really live or accomplish my work. Life cannot exist without eating other life. One life produces another and another and one life eats another and another. We are born and die and are born and die. That is why there are no enemies. Everything is balanced. To live is to eat. To eat is to involve death because we are eating something's life.

"All living things are

dependent on mountains

and forests.

They are sacred."

YOSHIKAZU KAWAGUCHI,

NATURAL FARMER

As Kawaguchi puts a fresh vegetable into his mouth, he smiled. "But I don't think about that while I eat."

Natural farming, as Kawaguchi stressed repeatedly, is more than just a way of growing fruits and vegetables. It is the practical embodiment of a worldview that sees human beings deeply embedded in the natural order and subservient to it. Natural farmers accept the enormity of their ignorance but trust the generosity of nature when approached with respect and humility.

Natural farming methods are not fixed. The natural farmer should be constantly flexible and must learn intimately about the soil, insects, and natural conditions of the area. We must acknowledge and work with these variables and thus adapt our methods to encourage growth with minimal interference in the natural cycle.

This philosophical outlook extends to every aspect of Kawaguchi's life. He is deeply absorbed in traditional Chinese medicine and treats family members and about fifty friends and neighbours, much to the consternation of his wife; she fears he'll be prosecuted for practising medicine without a licence. In many ways, he is an indigenous person, his knowledge and way of life derived from his body and the earth.

> I use medicine from China that is 8,000 years old. I regard it as wisdom of humanity. Everything is from nature. Synthetic things are not used. Two or three thousand years ago, China had a superb, well-rounded, integrated system of medical knowledge. It would be impossible for me to come to that knowledge by myself. I am only beginning to understand through reading.

The development of mainstream medicine has paralleled the development of mainstream agriculture. Modern technological medicine attempts to cure sickness the same way modern agriculture tackles farming problems.

> In medicine and in agriculture alike, there must be a true way that respects life as it is. Unless we discover it, there is no future. We must go back to our original state and regain lost knowledge. Aboriginal people remind us of what we have lost. I am not denying scientific knowledge, but we must go beyond that and reach knowledge that can grasp the nature of life. I believe we all used to have that systematic body of knowledge. Each place, each locality, each ethnic group had a system of medicine. In India and Thailand it can still be found.

The basic principles of farming and health are the same, Kawaguchi believes. We cannot comprehend nature, only assist it as best we can. Nature re-creates and heals itself. "As I learned how to grow rice," he said, "I learned how to heal myself after twenty years of mechanized farming."

Twenty years ago, when Kawaguchi's liver stopped functioning, he went to hospitals, but no one could help him with the cysts growing on his face and body, his inability to urinate, and the yellowing of his skin. So he turned to Chinese medicine.

An acupuncturist introduced me to ancient Chinese traditions. I learned that my health and my family's health had to be dealt with by ourselves. Since I changed to natural farming and ancient wisdom eighteen years ago, no member of my family has been to a hospital. In modern medicine there is no cure for the common cold or for cancer, but in this system the answers are there. The body and mind cannot be separated. It is almost impossible to have a sick body and a healthy mind. Both must be healthy.

Kawaguchi believes that being self-sufficient in food and health is essential.

The more I learn, the more I understand that ancient people had a deep understanding of life and that we know little about it. Sometimes I am scared about practising my medicine because, strictly speaking, it is illegal. But we must realize human laws don't apply to nature. There is a place beyond human laws. As long as I am not making any money and limit my patients to my friends, I don't think it will be a problem.

Kawaguchi feels he is evolving towards an understanding of our complete immersion in nature. We must trust in nature, both outside in our surroundings and within ourselves. We need respect, awe, and humility.

As we helped Kawaguchi's wife put the dinner dishes away, he set up his slide projector. We settled in for the show. Like a quiet missionary with a magic lantern show, Kawaguchi used stunning slides, which he himself had taken, to illustrate his philosophy. There was no preaching, just explanation. The pictures were mostly of his fields and his travels. His logic, like his writing, was simple, original, poetic, relentlessly cohesive and persuasive. Towards the end, the pictures showed a shocking contrast between natural life and the concrete paved world most of us live in. It was almost as if he was showing us the approaching autumn and winter of human existence.

The most remarkable movement in the twentieth century has surely been the shift of people from agrarian societies to cities. From fewer than fifteen cities of more than a million people in 1900, humanity now occupies more than four hundred! More than half of our species now resides in cities, and the flow of people into them has become a raging torrent. But in such human-created environments, in which the only contact many have with food is at the supermarket, we become increasingly alienated from the biological world that supports us.

It has been suggested that the profound alienation and loneliness within the highly pressured city life in Japan has caused a search for other values. The shocking discovery that well-educated young people were attracted to the doomsday cult Aum Shinrikyo has led to a radical re-examination of Japanese values.

Almost all the people who tried natural farming were urban dwellers, salarymen who decided to change their way of living. Some people come to learn a philosophy of life, others child-rearing, education, or medicine. But some move from cities to the country and start farming. A few use natural farming, but many are landless. So we rented a piece of land that was unused and practised on it. There are 200 to 250 people learning there. There are now about five natural farms where we learn together.

To Kawaguchi the next stage of civilization will be based on the value of life.

You can see this feeble sprout coming out. In the natural world, everything starts out weak, forests or fields look feeble. It starts under the shade of the trees or in the leaf litter, and with light it can grow and replace the forest.

As Kawaguchi walked us to the train station, the moon was high over Miwa Mountain. Our day should have been exhausting, but we found ourselves still energized by Kawaguchi's spirit.

It was only after I started natural farming that I felt happy to be a farmer. Before, I felt as if I was standing in a deadly world. My rice and vegetables were growing, but I watched insects dying in agony and my fields become silent places devoid of any other forms of life.

The natural, almost spiritual way that Kawaguchi has lived his life left us with a feeling of timelessness. It confirmed for us that he was on the threshold of something almost religious.

I've tried many forms of spiritual discipline and meditation, but ultimately I realized I am a farmer and have accepted the Earth and nature as my teachers. After all, the goal in life is to discover how we can be truly happy and saved from fear and uneasiness. Actually in this sense, farming is secondary for me. My biggest motivation is to find peace of mind and to become more aware of the cycle of life and nature. In natural farming, we can never be an expert; everything is a succession of discovery and surprise as we come to realize that nothing is permanent or fixed but is always in a constant state of change. As my understanding of life and nature grows deeper, so my mind becomes more and more peaceful.

As we said goodbye to the Kawaguchi family, we reflected on the transformation in society in the past century. With lightning speed, humanity has undergone a fundamental shift in our connection with the Earth. Large parts of the population now work in factories and offices far removed from the life-sustaining activity of growing or gathering food.

Natural farming signals a shift from large-scale industrial farming based on the notion of our ability to control food output. Kawaguchi uses a fundamentally different mindset, beginning with respect for the complexity of nature and humility about the extent of human understanding of that complexity. From that position, he has created a way of life built around nature's ability to sustain it. It is an important lesson in a world in which our lifestyle and demands contribute to clearing of forests for land, depletion of soil fertility, and chemical pollution of water and air. For Kawaguchi the change was mandated by practices that threatened his life. We wondered whether humankind has to be pushed to that brink before we will seriously begin to alter our agricultural practices.

The Japanese, like the citizens of all industrialized nations, are an urban people. Tokyo, Osaka, and even Kyoto are dominated by concrete, glass, and asphalt, the hallmarks of modern cities. And to city folk, food is what is available in shops and restaurants. Often highly processed and manipulated, it is hardly recognizable from its natural state. But some young people are finding new meaning in life, one that springs from a different attitude towards food.

We travelled to Kamakura, the old city that was the capital of Japan in the thirteenth century, to speak with Shonosuke Okura, a "modern" *noh* drummer. The house belonged to friends of Okura's, but we agreed to meet him there because it was close to where he was performing that evening. We had already had dinner, but when we got to the beautiful old house, we found the dining table filled with different and unusual types of seafood. Okura encouraged us to eat. He explained that he'd received the food for a performance he'd given earlier that day in Ibaragi prefecture. In the traditional world he inhabited, food was often the form of payment. Again he urged us to dig in, saying:

> When I was eighteen years old, I ate naturally grown vegetables for
> the first time. I was shocked because I never knew vegetables could
> taste like this. The vegetable itself had this flavour. I began to see that
> vegetables sold in stores were not real vegetables. At the time I wasn't
> sure I wanted to go on with *noh* drumming.

Noh is traditional Japanese theatre with at least six hundred years of history. The dancer-actors wear masks and move slowly and subtly to the accompaniment of musicians and drummers. The most important instrument is the drum called *tsuzumi*. Okura was a direct descendant of a family that has kept the tradition of *noh* drumming alive for centuries. *Noh* theatre is extremely stylized and formal. The people involved in *noh* theatre tend to be very conservative and traditional in their outlooks. We wondered about Okura.

> I felt I had to carry on the tradition, but there was always a gap between what I wanted to do and what I had to do. When I encountered natural food, I realized there was an animal in me. Until then, I had thought food was something people bought at the store, but now it is something I grow myself.

At first Okura learned from a religious group that grew natural food. Later on he became an apprentice to a farmer who showed him how to plant and tend vegetables.

> I took up farming full-time. The second year I became independent as a farmer and leased an orange field in Issu to grow vegetables and rice. I sent the products to my family and others outside. They couldn't believe the flavour. My father, who had been depressed by my decision to quit drumming, realized what I was doing once he ate my food.
>
> They were so happy that they bought a piece of land in the mountains. I cleared the forest, cut trees, and began to farm, but it didn't work because the soil wasn't ready. So I had to use organic fertilizer and learn how to make soil. It was very depressing. I'd plant seeds, young shoots would stick up, and then they'd disappear. But I learned from these experiences, and the next year, I got a crop.

As our conversation continued, we were concerned that Okura might have forgotten about his performance. It was already close to midnight, but he told us not to worry, that we still had plenty of time.

> While I was struggling, I found a *daikon* that was growing where I had dropped it accidentally. And it was huge and beautiful. It was perfectly shaped and had a beautiful symmetry of leaves. When I cut

it open, the insides were beautiful. And it had grown without any help from me. So I realized that the idea that *I* am making these was simply not true. Ninety-nine percent is grown by nature. What I do is a tiny part.

As he became more involved in farming, Okura found that agriculture was a tightly organized industry. The farmers' co-op would even establish the amount of fertilizer to be used. He was familiar with this kind of tight control from his experiences with *noh* theatre and drumming.

I realized in the world of agriculture, the situation was such that young people had no future, no chance to succeed their parents in the work. I met farmers who were surprised to see me working in the field. They told me, "It's great you are farming. My kids don't want to."

It was then that Okura realized that many of the problems plaguing the farming world were similar or parallel to what the world of *noh* was experiencing. This insight allowed him to think back to the world he was ready to give up. The drum and its rhythm have their roots directly in the heartbeat of human beings. It is rooted in our souls. While he was living on the farm, music slowly came back to him. One day it became clear that he was back in the world of *noh*.

Finally Okura told us it was time to go to the Full Moon Gathering, an event Okura organized once a month at Chojagahama beach. Considering the dinner we had eaten earlier and all the seafood we had consumed since, it was surprising we were able to get through the door.

We looked up into the sky to see a bright full moon, which was occasionally eclipsed by fast-flying, dark clouds. At around midnight, motorcycle riders began arriving in large groups. Okura was a well-known rider and had travelled all over the world on his bike. In North America he'd crossed the continent with Native Americans, playing his drum while they played theirs.

At last, around one in the morning, Okura began to play his *tsuzumi*.

He was dressed in formal attire, a black kimono with family crests and loose pants called *hakama*. As he beat the drum, he chanted in a low voice that rose slowly to a high-pitched yell. It was not a familiar sound to us, but he was obviously very well trained. A modern dancer in a loose and colourful traditional kimono danced wildly on the sand. As the dancer flew around him like a butterfly and as the drumming became more furious, suddenly with a loud crack the skies opened up and rain began to fall. But Okura's expression and drumming didn't change. The motorcycle riders who were standing watching the performance, their jackets shining slickly from the rain, hardly seemed to notice the downpour. Everyone's attention was riveted on Okura and his partner.

Once the performance was done, even though the rain had turned to a torrential downpour, the ceremony continued. The leader of the motorcyclists welcomed David as their guest of honour. Women in kimonos sat on the sand. As the guest of honour, David was asked to participate in a traditional tea ceremony. Until recently, breaking tradition and performing *noh* like this on the beach in the middle of the night was unthinkable to the traditionalists in Okura's family. By the end of the ceremony, Okura appeared beside us in leather motorcycle gear.

Now I know that my playing is expressing my experiences as a farmer, but at the time I didn't know that. The full-moon ceremony shows our relation between wind, the beach, sand, and the moon. These are part of my music. I can always go back to these things.

We asked Okura if he had been inspired by indigenous people.

Yes, but instead of seeing indigenousness as something special, I see it as something normal. It's in all of us. We must not resist the effort to keep indigenous culture going. We can learn from it. Instead of seeing it as foreign or special, even we modern people may have a kind of wisdom, so we have to work together.

He then mounted his "wheels" and with his unlikely group of biker friends, disappeared into the misty curtain of light rain.

In all parts of the world, human beings are undergoing a dramatic shift from rural village life to urban city living. In Japan's rugged landscape, this transition is especially striking as cities spread out to cover over rice paddies and farmland. In cities, people buy their food packaged, often highly processed, with little to remind them of the food's source or origins as farm produce. Okura took us back to the wellsprings of life, our nutrition from the Earth, while Kawaguchi went even further to an appreciation of the natural world's incomprehensible gift of bounty.

CHAPTER 12

teaching for a future

"I get them to imagine being soil, becoming water.

They imagine all kinds of things, water in a cup,

the ocean, rivers. They travel through the water. They

move their bodies or they sleep and listen to music.

Sometimes I show pictures and lead them. Other times

I let them imagine on their own. Sometimes I use

just words. I get them to imagine being a pig. They are

in the womb, they grow, they are born. Life then

begins as a pig until it is finally killed."

TOSHIKO TORIYAMA, TEACHER

tHE global degradation of the environment is a consequence of human activity that springs from a *mindset* — beliefs and
assumptions that shape our priorities and the way we perceive our surroundings. For most of human existence, our brains were our critical
edge for survival, conferring an ability to organize information and to use

this knowledge base to exploit our surroundings. But for most of our history, we lived in small family groups of hunter-gatherers or small-scale agriculturists with limited technologies and minimal consumption. The human imprint on the Earth was light.

Today we are the planet's most numerous large mammal, with the added gift of science and technology muscle power, and an insatiable appetite for more and novel consumer goods. Driven by a global economy, we are perceptibly altering the biophysical makeup of the Earth to the detriment of much of its biodiversity and our own societies.

In this human-dominated world, education plays a crucial role. In the past, each new generation acquired life skills by observing and copying their elders — an apprenticeship system. In modern society, formal education has replaced the elders in transmitting social, economic, and historical values of the dominant institutions. State-controlled education has played a seemingly contradictory role, reinforcing social standards and beliefs while simultaneously encouraging young minds to explore ideas at the leading edge of human thought. It is not an accident that universities have often been the most volatile foci of radical and revolutionary fervour.

In Japan, education is the dominant means of imposing expectations and socially acceptable behaviour. Beginning with preschool, there are strong incentives to gain admission to the best schools and to do well, because at every level, performance will shape a child's career options in the future. North American educators compare their student performances with Asian students and suggest the country's postwar economic success is a reflection of its educational institutions.

But critics like Katsuichi Honda (see Chapter 2) accuse Japanese education of producing hardworking automatons who parrot back what they've memorized. He characterizes Japanese people as *medaka*, fish that cluster in schools and seem driven by an overriding need to stay within that group. Environmental journalist Hiroshi Ishi (see Chapter 2) claims that industrial Japan is driven by a rigid underlying militarism. Japanese learn to approach their work with military dedication and go to war with their competitors. Others informed us of the growing phenomenon in schools of *ijime,* schoolyard bullying that seems to persecute children who fail to conform to schoolyard standards and can be cruel enough to drive such children to suicide.

Given the enormous parental, teacher, and peer-group pressure on Japanese schoolchildren, it takes an exceptional child to do something extraordinarily different. Aika Tsubota was one such. She created a comic book, *Secrets of the Earth,*[1] just before she died in 1991 of a brain hemorrhage at the age of twelve. When her teacher assigned an elective project, Tsubota spent two months drawing and creating a guide to the Earth. Her main character was Earth, which had the head of a blue globe and the body of a human. Throughout the book, Earth explains to a sixth-grade boy and girl about the history of the Earth and the equilibrium of the ecosystem. The children talk with Earth about the problems of environmental destruction and learn some practices such as recycling and conservation to curb these problems. On the last page of the book Aika wrote:

"If everyone helps one

another to create a beautiful

world, it will be wonderful."

AIKA TSUBOTA,

AUTHOR OF

SECRETS OF THE EARTH

> While writing this book I was thinking about the people in Africa and Southeast Asia. In these places children even younger than I am are working. I feel sorry that they can't study. To correct such problems we must first get rid of wars. I am so lucky that I have a home and am able to go to school and learn. I'd like to study hard and work to help eliminate the gap between the rich countries and the poor countries. I want to become a doctor and save lives. To improve our environment I decided to stop being selfish and do something about it. If everybody in the world thinks selfishly, the Earth won't last long. If everyone helps one another to create a beautiful world, it will be wonderful.

It has been many years since Aika's sudden and tragic death. In that time "Secrets of the Earth" has been translated into five languages and read in more than sixty countries. It has been made into a musical, and two theatre groups in Japan are presenting plays based on the book. The white paper put out by Japan's Environmental Agency, textbooks, and educational videos now feature the characters Aika created. Aika's parents travelled to Beijing in 1993 to accept a certificate of her posthumous election to the prestigious Global 500 Honour Role of the United Nations Environmental Program. Despite her brief life, Aika has left something to inspire future generations.

In education, a teacher's influence on children is often second only to that of parents, and in Japan teaching is one of the nation's most honoured professions. Although *sensei* means teacher, the title carries far more reverence than its English translation conveys. In Japanese society, teachers have an obligation to live up to this respect. In a rigid state education system where the emphasis is on rote memory and correctness of performance and behaviour, few teachers dare to be idiosyncratic or original. Toshiko Toriyama is one of those rare individuals who have survived within that system while bringing a fundamentally different approach to teaching.

The day we were to meet Toriyama was bleak and rainy. As we entered the coffee shop in the Tokyo headquarters of Sony, we saw her looking expectantly in our direction. She had a bright smile, a simple haircut, no makeup, and despite her age looked like a teenager. We had barely finished greeting each other when she dramatically recited a well-known poem by Kenji Miyazawa.

neither yielding to rain
nor yielding to wind
yielding neither to
snow nor the summer heat
with a stout body
like that
without greed

never getting angry
always smiling quietly . . .[2]

As other patrons in the coffee shop stared in our direction, Toriyama seemed completely unselfconscious. Perhaps sometimes overly dramatic, but always concise and passionate, Toriyama stands out in a crowd. "I read this famous poem for the first time when I was ten years old," she said.

The poet, Kenji Miyazawa (1896–1933), was a teacher of farming and a philosopher who wrote children's stories. Although he died at thirty-seven, he had such a full life that Toriyama thought if she could achieve just half of what he had, she, too, could die at thirty-seven and be happy. Kenji's philosophy was that without the world becoming happy there was no personal happiness. He had a vision for a new kind of education:

We are all peasants; very busy, our work gruelling

We wish to discover a way to live with the zest and vigour of our ancestors

I wish to discuss this within the context of the proofs of modern science, the experiments of truth seekers, and the unity of our intuitions

Individual happiness is impossible until the entire world gains Happiness

The awareness of Self will gradually evolve away from the individual to the group, society and the cosmos

Is not this direction the path trodden and taught by the saints of old?

The new era is to be found in a world which has become a single consciousness and a living thing

Living properly and strongly means having an awareness of the galactic system within oneself, and acting in response to it

Let us seek the world's true Happiness

The seeker's path is already a path.[3]

After we sat down together, Toriyama told us about some of her unique teaching methods.

We would take children to a slaughterhouse to see pigs actually killed and butchered. Then we take them to a pig farm and see how piglets are grown under crowded, dark conditions. Children are shocked to see how different it is from what they imagined. It is dark and the rooms don't even have windows. Every hour the piglets are showered with a horrible antiseptic solution. There is no family life. All the pigs are separated. Everything is controlled. The children begin to see from the pig's point of view. For the children, pigs were nothing but meat that they saw wrapped in cellophane in the supermarket. Suddenly everything is connected in a very immediate fashion.

Under Toriyama's tutelage, children learned to appreciate animals and see that life comes from other life, and for that, they should have a deep respect and appreciation. When she began teaching, she was surprised to find that some of her pupils thought that fish were born and lived in what they were packaged in at the supermarket. Toriyama told us a story about the parents who gave their child a beetle as a pet. When it died, the boy looked at it and said, "The battery has run out." After Toriyama's lessons, her students approached life differently.

The children taste more carefully what they are eating. One boy said, "Now I realize how precious life is because that animal is the only one of its kind in the whole world." A girl said, "My mother is surprised because I began to eat a lot of fish. I feel I must eat more fish than meat because a fish is whole with eyes." A boy wrote, "Before this, I didn't know how pigs were feeling, so I ate meat without a thought. But now I can't treat food in a careless way that would match the sadness of the pig."

After a turbulent career teaching in the formal education system, Toriyama quit and decided to strike out on her own.

I want to start a Kenji school based on his ideas. In his world there were all kinds of creatures and they all talked — even acorns and foxes. He used to quote the Buddhist teaching that everything in the universe is connected with a fine thread that extends out in all directions. At the centre is a precious stone, and everything in the web is like a crystal. All over the universe from one end to the other are threads extending in all directions. Wherever they intersect, there is a crystal, and every entity, every grain of sand, raindrop, bird, insect — not just on Earth but everywhere in the universe — is represented. Then light enters and hits every crystal and reflects back onto every other crystal.

We told Toriyama that this seemed reminiscent of astronomer Carl Sagan's work. He wrote that the latest ideas in astrophysics tell us a big bang occurred fifteen billion years ago, when there must have been a brilliant flash as matter itself was being formed in this unimaginably hot and dense cauldron. As the universe exploded outward, different states of particles formed, gradually cooling and forming the different elements of the universe. Today, through the history of stellar and biological evolution, we, like all other things in the universe, are made of the same *stardust*. Toriyama agreed.

"So if one crystal is destroyed," she said, "it affects every other one. It means if we lose dragonflies, we lose human beings. It is urgent to put Kenji's ideas into practice."

Throughout human history, people have understood the interconnectedness of everything — the past, present, and future, the rocks, stars, trees, and ourselves. Therefore everything we do has repercussions that ripple throughout the universe. Modern science has tended to fragment our view of the world, but now physics is restoring the notion of interconnectedness. The chaos theory suggests that a butterfly's flight or a stone tossed into the ocean reverberates around the Earth.

Toriyama was the editor of *Hito* (human being), one of the leading magazines for teachers. She had been using that as a voice to advocate her ideas. When we spoke to her, she was planning to launch a new magazine called *Kenji's School*.

As we looked at the animated, vivacious woman sitting before us, it was hard to believe she was born in 1941, the eldest of five children in a family living in Kure in Hiroshima prefecture. During the war, her father worked as an engineer in a bullet factory on a large naval base. After it was bombed by the Americans, the family was forced to move away. If they hadn't moved, they probably would have been in Hiroshima when the atomic bomb was dropped.

> When I was a child, I loved making flower gardens. I planted seeds and watered them every day and would watch them grow. I started when I was four years old and have never stopped. Seeds were my playthings. If I ate something that had a seed, I'd plant it.

In 1960 Toriyama became active in a student movement that opposed resigning the U.S.–Japan Security Treaty. Her parents asked her not to take a prominent role in the movement. She could still be involved, they said, but they wanted her to stand in the back, out of sight. Instead, she stayed active in the movement but decided to move out of her parents' house.

> I worked for four years as a tutor while going to school. I was not living well. I had very little money and was eating very badly. By the time of graduation, I was critically ill. My teachers liked me, so they eventually helped me find a job. I ended up in Tokyo prefecture, far enough away that my background in the student movement wouldn't be known.

She took the job on condition that she be surrounded by good air, good water, and good earth. She spent five years teaching at a school in a remote part of Tokyo prefecture right next to a national park. There were sixty-three children in the whole school. It was "so remote that some families still didn't even have electricity. Our classroom was the mountains and the rivers."

This location suited Toriyama. As a girl she'd spent her time swimming in the mountain streams, and she recalled swimming alongside snakes and having fish nibble at her feet.

I gathered mountain vegetables and mushrooms. We would collect wood and dead leaves for making cooking fires. Even today, when I see piles of dead leaves, I want to pick them up and take them home.

Eventually she moved to a school near the American military base in Yokota, Tokyo. The Vietnam War was raging at the time and there were always jets flying overhead. "I used to cry because it was so noisy. I couldn't hear the dripping rain on the roof. I made a rice paddy in the corner of the schoolyard and planted a vegetable and flower garden."

Every two months, she took her pupils and their parents to the mountains where they fished and the parents composed *haiku* poems.

I loved fishing. When I was a girl, I'd make my own rod and line and tie hooks on. In rice paddies, there were lots of fish in the irrigation ponds and ditches. I would use a screen on a bamboo frame and scoop things in the ditches. My grandmother often told me, "If you collect those living things they'll come back to haunt you at *obon* [the day to welcome souls of the deceased]." So I was afraid of *obon*, but I continued.

The school itself was a surprise to her. She told us:

It was the first time I saw a school with more than one section per grade. The problem was that in the Japanese system, one section can't stand out or get ahead of another. So each week we were told exactly what pages to cover in the books.

As a result she was always fighting the school officials and only lasted three years at Yokota.

She married when she was twenty-four. The couple soon had two daughters, and Toriyama continued to teach while raising them.

While still a teacher in conventional schools, Toriyama used a variety of teaching methods, most of which didn't conform to the subscribed curriculum of other Japanese schools and teachers.

We taught about the Ainu and North American Indians living harmoniously with nature. Throughout the year we had a theatre on

Okikurumi [the god that is said to have descended on the Ainu community of Nibutani in Hokkaido] and the devil. We learned how the Ainu lived. I also had what I called Imagination Class. I had children act out being a praying mantis. They'd feel themselves born out of an egg mass, seeing the world for the first time, wriggling out of the shell, eating each other, sleeping, catching prey, laying eggs, dying. When they were tired, children asked for an Imagination Class. It energized them and stimulated them to do lots of writing.

Not only did Toriyama have the children imagine they were animals and experience what they were feeling and what they must go through, she included inanimate objects. She had one Imagination Class where the children became pencils. She asked them how many people it took for them to become a pencil. The trees began to grow, people have to cut them down, transport them to the factory. There are ships built for transportation, iron to make the ships, and miners to get the iron. Through this process they realized what it takes to make a pencil.

One kind of pencil is made from incense cedar from North America. I had the students therefore become a seed buried in the soil in the mountains of the American West. It begins to rain. We feel the moisture drenching us and feel the water as it seeps into our seed coat. We sprout. Then comes spring, summer, autumn, winter. One year, two years, three years. One metre, two metres, three metres. Finally twenty metres and one day we see a man coming towards us, he puts a chain saw on our trunk — oh, we're being cut. We're being cut down and it hurts.

They also learned the history of pencils. That a hundred years ago a Mr. Yamazaki saw pencils being made in France. He studied the process there, then returned to make them in Japan. The children became Mr. Yamazaki. Toriyama took them to a pencil factory. Afterwards, the children really appreciated each pencil.

Toriyama once took her grade-three class on a field trip to the countryside, something almost unheard of in Japan. By midday all the pupils were all hungry and asking to be fed. As they gathered around, Toriyama produced a live chicken. As they studied the chicken, touching its feathers, feeling the sharpness of its claws, and looking into its beady little eyes, she announced that this was their meal. The children were horrified, some even began to cry, and all of them begged her not to hurt the chicken. Toriyama began to tell them about food and where it comes from. For the first time they realized that the cooked meat they ate so often at home had once been a live animal.

Eventually hunger overcame their reluctance and the children agreed to eat the chicken. They participated in killing the bird, plucking it, cleaning it, cutting it up, and eventually cooking it. Hearing about this field trip, the school authorities were furious. But the parents were astounded to see a marked change in their children's attitude towards food. The youngsters had become deeply aware that they depended on living things for their own nourishment.

> We invited a "nuclear gypsy," a person who goes from one nuclear plant to another to work in the reactor, to come and talk in the classroom. We had all heard about nuclear plants but had no idea what they were or what the wastes were about. We have always been led to believe that we never have enough electricity. So we started asking, "Are we making the best use of electricity?" We learned that electricity is sent by people who work with and are exposed to radiation. Since all these plants are built in the countryside, we in cities get all of the advantages while these workers are affected. If it's really safe, why not build them in the backyard of the president of the electric company or in the middle of a big city? The children were shocked that adults would act like this.

> If we chose a theme like ocean, river, or forest, the students came up with ideas. They imagined they were plankton, the fish, the trees. They had to study what was in it. They learned how everything is interconnected. They looked at the life of coral, dinosaurs, the birth of the Earth. Children get very interested in nature. Their bodies

come into resonance with the Earth. We learned how Ainu lives were destroyed by the Japanese. The ways Ainu and North American Indians were treated are so similar. The aboriginal people presented different ways of thinking; they didn't think about possessions. Imagination is very important in the way we teach.

Toriyama produced three films. *Body, Life, Food*, subtitled "One Month of Children with Toshiko," was done in 1985. The second film, *The Teacher Who Jumped into the Universe with Joy*, is about the former students of Kenji Miyazawa. According to his students, when he saw a beautiful sky, the poet would jump with joy. He would fly with the birds or he would come in and say that he had been swimming in the flowers.

The third film is called *Everyone Is a Monkey King*. Monkey King is the hero in a Chinese folk story who resisted the teaching of Buddha and was imprisoned in rock for five hundred years. When a great monk came by, the Monkey King became a disciple and followed him to India. The moral of the story is that only by good teaching could he see the way. Toriyama saw a direct link between this story and some of the problems that children face now.

We are imprisoned in rocks. How can we come out and find a way of life? Children's bodies today are being destroyed both physically and mentally. Both the body and the soul are sick. They have skin problems and allergic reactions that didn't exist twenty years ago. Reactions to pollen became so bad that one study stated that up to forty percent of all children have problems. As well, there is asthma, children who refuse to go to school, anorexia, violence, bullying, and suicide. Parents and teachers don't know what's going on. In Japan everyone has to conform or they become a target. How can they be made healthy? I think the education policy went wrong, but it's mainly the parents.

One night she showed *Everyone Is a Monkey King* to two hundred parents. "After watching the film, some of them were crying. I told them that destroying the Earth is the same as destroying your children."

The last stage of the destruction of nature is the health of our bodies and those of our children. Without healthy children to grow into contributing members of society, the future looks bleak. But Toriyama refuses to give up. "Look at the story of the Monkey King," she said. "He was released from the rock after five hundred years, and there must be a way for us to come out of our rock." The solution may not be in a faraway place, but within ourselves: the body may be the final battleground. Like the Monkey King we have the ability to find the answers, find the way out. We just have to look in the right places.

Toriyama held a workshop for parents whose children were sick. She showed them films and magazines and discussed alternatives and solutions. Parents were challenged to face their problems and begin to heal themselves as a first step to helping their children.

When Japan was poor, people had to work hard together, but now they seem to have lost their purpose. They need something that binds human beings together in a profound way, or we can't go on. Until now, parents blamed the minister of education or the school or the teachers. But they need to face themselves. Some of the best teachers have left because they're burned out or discouraged. This film urges parents to change themselves.

After seventeen years, Toriyama and her husband parted. Then, after thirty years, she resigned as a teacher in the formal education system.

At my farewell, I asked the children, "Eight years from now, who thinks the air will be cleaner?" No one put up their hands. "Who thinks it will be worse?" Most put up their hands. Then I asked about the water, soil, trees, oceans, rivers. Everyone responded negatively.

We human beings have never gone through this kind of environmental crisis. So our children are having to go through it without being taught what to do. How painful it is. I want to tell adults to wake up. I tell children, "Don't give up. We have to work together. Will you work with me?" Soon it will be the next century. I'll be sixty years old. It's my target to reach that age.

Since childhood, Toriyama has been interested in Kenji Miyazawa's ideas. One of the poet's dreams was to create a school, but he died before he could realize it. Today Kenji is one of the most popular poets in Japan, but Toriyama wonders how many people understand what he was trying to accomplish: an environment where young people could learn the values of nature and farming. A Kenji school doesn't have to be confined in permanent buildings, she explained. The school could be freely spread by individual supporters — teachers, parents, even students — all over Japan. The ideas could be applied in different forms. For example, children going to public school could attend classes by taking breaks from public school, or they could attend after school. The Kenji way is not a passive form of education; Toriyama had already tested it while she was still teaching.

> We would participate and become things — we would be rivers, trees, flowers in Kenji's world. And a Kenji school is not just for children, but also for the parents. It is crucial for parents and youngsters to think together about their lives and about nature. The schools would form a network of people in which everybody would be connected.

Toriyama's radical approach is much more than a way to educate children about the facts of life. It is an attempt to reconnect these children to their biological roots. To her, nourishment, sexuality, and death are natural and must be accepted and appreciated. And it's important, she feels, to reach the source of the children — their parents. Through her magazine and films, she is slowly gaining support for her message that somehow we have to look at and repair a world that is sick and dying.

> People seem to be giving up, but we have to do something about the environmental crisis. The rate of destruction is so fast there is no

time to waste. So we need lots of people doing something. Adults work hard to send children to good schools and to get good marks, but what are they studying for? Is there anything more important than working for the health of the Earth and the health of people? I'm happy that children have told me, "I'd like to do something about it."

We reflected on the enormity of the challenge Toriyama has accepted as we bid farewell and entered the subway station. Many of the large, industrialized cities of Japan are ecological nightmares, biological deserts entombed in concrete and asphalt, with rivers choking on industrial sludge and garbage, air thick with exhaust fumes and factory emissions. The pollution became more intense the closer we got to Tokyo. The problems here can be seen as much a failure of education as of politics and business.

Our investigative journey began in Okinawa at the southernmost tip of the Japanese archipelago and over two years took us through the country to Hokkaido, the northernmost major island. Everywhere, after we penetrated the curtain of ritual greetings and politeness, we found an amazing array of diverse, creative, and original people, which suggests a massive potential for innovation. The blanket of social expectation and approbation that restricts individualist behaviour and nonconformity is pierced by those who somehow find the strength and courage to think and act on their own observations and beliefs.

Around the world, social structures are collapsing under the weight of explosive population growth and massive shifts in where this population lives. There are enormous pressures of widespread poverty, ecological collapse, civil strife, and the increase in new and old diseases — AIDS, malaria, tuberculosis. Highly industrialized countries like Japan, which depend on global resources and markets, are beginning to confront the reality of their dependence on renewable and nonrenewable products, of the planet's finite limits, and of the ecological and social unsustainability of our high-consumption lifestyle. It is from the turmoil within the Japan that we now see that new paradigms, priorities, lifestyles, and goals are emerging. They provide an important source of new ways of perceiving, thinking, and acting for all of us in the global village who strive to find ways to achieve social, economic, and environmental balance.

epilogue

by Keibo Oiwa

OUR journey has come to an end. On the way, we encountered many remarkable individuals who showed us the unfamiliar faces of a complex society. Their unique ways of thinking and acting, their ethnic, cultural, historical, and ecological diversity, challenged our image of the Japanese monolith, a people all conforming to a single identity.

Some might argue that the people we met are nothing but dots scattered throughout Japan. And that, for us, finding the dots was often more a personal and instinctive act than a scientific and methodological one. Both of these suggestions are true. But when we connected the dots, we were astonished to see a meaningful shape emerge.

These idiosyncratic individuals share some common traits: they are remarkably uninfluenced by the thoughts and ideologies that dominate the Japanese intellectual world, both left and right, liberal and conservative; they have a special relationship to a particular place, whether a remote Okinawan island or a crowded neighbourhood in Osaka; and they enjoy a sense of connectedness to their natural, cultural, and communal environment.

They also seem to share a different sense of time. The process of swift modernization has left most Japanese with a profound contempt and disgust towards their own cultural tradition. Such an atmosphere of self-hate, supplemented by an inferiority complex towards Americans, successfully drove the nation towards the postwar economic reconstruction. But the people we met in our journey somehow survived without losing their roots in the past; they still make good use of cultural tradition, as if, to use a Japanese expression, drawing fresh water from the well.

They are not traditionalist in the narrow sense of the term, however. Their imagination and creativity have not been restricted or hampered by the past. Rather, their connectedness and rootedness drive their imaginations and creativity. They are radical in the original sense of the term.

None of the people in this book is merely a dreamer or a thinker, for all are traditional in the sense that they live up to the old teaching that thoughts and action are inseparable. They are practical, yet sensitive to spirituality. They are humble, yet proud of who they are. And, probably most importantly, they are fun to be with.

Every journey has a personal side. Ours was no exception. Travelling together, David and I rediscovered Japan through each other's fresh viewpoint. In March 1994, as we started a trip to the western part of Japan, we began to talk about our individual pasts. In hotel rooms across Japan, at my home, and on a boat to Okinawa, David told me how uncomfortable and sometimes unbearable it had been for him to grow up with a Japanese name and an Asian face in a racist society. His stories about Japanese-Canadians who struggled with their own sense of identity were moving, some funny, some sad. While he found their loss of identity and assimilation tragic, he also felt that trying to identify himself with ethnicity was artificial and strange.

David was most comfortable when he spoke about one Japanese-Canadian in particular: his father, Carr Suzuki. At the time, Mr. Suzuki, who lived in Vancouver, was critically ill with cancer. I cherish the memory of David's wonderful stories about this man whom, it turned out, I would never meet.

Also at that time, I began to talk about my own father, but soon realized I didn't have much to say. What was most curious to David was that, until I turned thirty, I hadn't known for sure that my father was Korean, and I had grown up with no Korean cultural background. David asked me, "So, is he ashamed of being Korean?" I responded, "Are you kidding? He's so proud he's almost racist." Another thing that perplexed David was my delight with my newly discovered Korean background. "But you're not Korean," David pointed out, "so how can you be pleased?" To this I said, "It's like securing a foothold," but I could not clearly explain what it meant to me to be connected with my father and his experiences as part of a minority.

For David, a Japanese-Canadian *sansei*, travelling in his grand-parents' homeland was an odyssey into a foreign culture, but in many ways it was the same for me. I had been away more than fourteen years. That absence and discovery of my Korean background made Japan look exotic to me. Moreover, as I met people in minority communities, I increasingly realized the strength that came from a minority position. I even thought it was better to be a minority.

The vast majority of people rarely question their identity, nor are they conscious of it. Their understanding of the past and their imagina-tion about the future are limited. The oppressed minorities of the Ainu, the Okinawans, the *burakumin*, and the Koreans often stand on the crossroads where the crisis of humanity meets with the crises of animals, plants, oceans, rivers, and mountains. Because they are restricted to these critical places, their environmental understanding becomes deeper and their vision of the future clearer.

In April 1994 David returned to Canada and moved into his father's home to care for him. Carr Suzuki's final days passed rapidly, and in brief faxed messages, David told me what those days were like. His descrip-tions struck me as strangely joyful, a son sharing a final sacred ritual with his father: "My father is becoming rapidly weaker, but his mind and his spirit are so strong that he is hanging on. Last weekend, I drove him up to our cottage on Quadra Island. I thought he might die, but he became stronger and I wheeled him around in a wheelchair. He kept saying,

'This is paradise,' and was so happy to have seen it once more."

Soon I received another fax. His father had passed away. David wrote in his father's obituary:

Carr Kaoru Suzuki died peacefully on May 8th. He was eighty-five. His ashes will be spread on the winds of Quadra Island. He found great strength in the Japanese tradition of nature-worship. Shortly before he died, he said: "I will return to nature where I came from. I will be part of the fish, the trees, the birds — that's my reincarnation. I have had a rich and full life and have no regrets. I will live on in your memories of me and through my grandchildren."

Two weeks after his father's passing, David decided to come back for another trip to the eastern part of Japan. I asked him to meet my father. I was deeply moved by David's relationship with his, and I wished to begin a new relationship with mine. I had a hunch that, in David's presence, my father, who had always been painfully reticent when speaking to me, might be more comfortable talking about himself.

And I was right. In a meeting with David and me, my father eloquently told us about his personal history: his childhood in North Korea under Japanese rule, his voyage to Japan, and his youthful aspiration to fight for the emancipation of his nation. He told us that he got stuck in Japan after the end of the Second World War and had never been back to his native country. All his family members were wiped out during the Korean War. At the end of our meeting, my father added that he would return to his homeland to spend his last years there.

Much of what he said then was new to me and my family. The taped record of the meeting has since become an invaluable part of his legacy. He passed away one and a half years later in Japan, without fulfilling his dream to go back to Korea.

The period during which David and I travelled, interviewed, and wrote this book was a time of caring for our fathers, parting from them, and mourning for them. I feel that our journey has given me an opportunity to explore my own sense of identity, an area my father left behind for me to explore. In this sense, the journey, to me, is continuing.

For Japan, also, change is ongoing. After so many years, the myth of a monolithic Japan is crumbling. Signs of change may still look small and feeble, yet they are everywhere. Diversity is surely the key to a better future for Japan. And for me, it is also the key to a new self, one that is no longer lost and disconnected. Our journey and the people we met taught me that Japan has much more to offer than I used to think. With their wisdom, we still might be able to regain our connection to our own past and to our future.

chapter 1: the Legacy of war

BOOKS OF INTEREST

Chibana, Shoichi. *Burning the Rising Sun: From Yomitan Village, Okinawa, Islands of U.S. Bases*. Translated by South Wind. Matsuyama city: South Wind, 1992.

Field, Norma. *In the Realm of a Dying Emperor*. New York: Pantheon Books, 1991.

Maruki, Iri, and Toshi Maruki. *The Hiroshima Panels: Joint Works of Iri Maruki and Toshi Maruki*. Saitama: Maruki Museum, 1988.

Tsurumi, Patricia E., ed., *The Other Japan: Postwar Realities*. Armonk, N.Y.: M. E. Sharpe, 1988.

chapter 2: remembering the past

[1] *Japan Times*, 10 June, 1995.

[2] *San Francisco Chronicle*, 20 June 1994, and *New York Times*, 23 January 1994.

[3] Hazel O'Leary, letter to U.S. Secretary of Energy, to the President of Power Reactor and Nuclear Fuel Development Corporation, 7 February 1993.

[4] *The Impoverished Spirit in Contemporary Japan: Selected Essays of Honda Katuichi*, ed. John Lie (New York: Monthly Review Press, 1993), 1.

[5] *ibid.*, pp. 50–51.

[6] *ibid.*, 54.

[7] *ibid.*, 55–56.

[8] *ibid.*, 56–57.

[9] *ibid.*, 95.

[10] *ibid.*, 171–73.

[11] *ibid.*, 174.

[12] *ibid.*, 178–79.

[13] *ibid.*, 180.

[14] *ibid.*, 179.

[15] *ibid.*, 158.

[16] *ibid.*, 129–130.

[17] *ibid.*, 143.

BOOK OF INTEREST

Japan's Plutonium: A Major Threat to the Planet. Berkeley, Cal.: Plutonium Free Future, 1992.

chapter 3: Life is the treasure

[1] Shoko Ahagon, *The Island Where People Live*, ed. and trans. C. Harold Rickard (Hong Kong: CCA, 1989), vi.

BOOK OF INTEREST

Ahagon, Shoko. *Inochi koso takara* (Life Is the Treasure). Tokyo: Iwanami-shoten, 1992.

chapter 4: a sense of place

[1] Jun Ui, ed., *Yanaka-mura kara Minamata Sanrizuka e* (From Yanaka Village to Minamata, Sanrizuka: Sourcebook of Japan's Ecological Philosophy) (Tokyo: Shakai-hyoron-sha, 1991).

[2] Gerard Piel and Osborn Segerberg, Jr., *The World of René Dubos* (New York: Henry Holt, 1990).

[3] Michiko Ishimure, *Paradise in the Sea of Sorrow*, trans. Livia Monnet (Kyoto: Yamaguchi Publ. House, 1990).

BOOK OF INTEREST

Higa, Yasuo. *Kamigami no koso* (Gods Underneath). 12 volumes. Okinawa: Nirai-sha, 1989–92.

chapter 5: the original people

[1] Shigeru Kayano, *Our Land Was a Forest* (San Francisco: Westview Press, 1994).

[2] *ibid.*, 18.

[3] Shin'ichiro Takakura et al., eds., *Ethnography of Ainu* (Ainu Minzoku-shi) (Tokyo: Daiichi Hoki Shuppan, 1969).

BOOK OF INTEREST

Exhibition Organizing Committee. *Exhibition of Ainu Pictures to Promote Human Rights*. Sapporo: Exhibition Organizing Committee, 1993.

chapter 6: shared blood, different futures

[1] Norma Field, "Beyond Envy, Boredom, and Suffering: Toward an Emancipatory Politics for Resident Koreans and Other Japanese" in *Positions* I:3 (winter 1993) Durham: Duke University Press.

Byung-Lo Chung, *Childcare Politics: Life and Power in Japanese Day Care Centres* (PhD thesis, University of Illinois, Urbana-Champaign, 1992).

BOOKS OF INTEREST

Buraku Liberation League, ed. *The Road to a Discrimination-Free Future: The World Struggle and the Buraku Liberation Movement*. Osaka: Buraku Liberation League, 1983.

Buraku Liberation Research Institute, ed. *The Literacy Work and Discrimination in Japan*. Osaka: Buraku Liberation League, 1990.

Hane, Mikiso. *Peasants, Rebels and Outcasts: The Underside of Modern Japan*. New York: Pantheon Books, 1982.

Tanaka, Hiroshi. *Zainichi gaikokujin* (Foreigners in Japan). Tokyo: Iwanami-shoten, 1995.

chapter 7: the korean mirror

[1] *Japan's Subtle Apartheid — The Korean Minority Now* (Tokyo: Research and Action Institute for Koreans in Japan, 1990).

[2] *ibid.*

[3] *ibid.*

[4] Hiroshi Tanaka, Report in *Shosusha kara mieru nippon* (Yokohama: Meiji Gakuin University, Institute for International Studies, 1995).

Seisanareta rekishi o tou, Zainichi no sengohosho o motomeru kai (Tokyo: 1994). Pamphlet (in Japanese).

[5] *Time* magazine, 12 September 1994. *The Australian*, 28 November 1994. *The Australian*, 12 December 1994.

[6] *Japan Times*, 6 June 1995.

[7] *Japan Times*, 7 June 1995.

[8] *ibid.*

[9] Shijong Kim, "Mienai machi" (The Invisible Town), in *Gen'ya no shi* (Poems of Wilderness) (Tokyo: Rippu-shobo, 1991).

BOOK OF INTEREST

Tanaka, Hiroshi. *Zainichi gaikokujin* (Foreigners in Japan). Tokyo: Iwanami-shoten, 1995.

chapter 8: voices from the belly

[1] Shunsuke Tsurumi, *Amenouzume-den* (The Legacy of Amenouzume) (Tokyo: Heibon-sha, 1991), 145–64.

BOOK OF INTEREST

Tsurumi, Shunsuke. *A Cultural History of Postwar Japan: 1945–1980*. London: KPI, 1987.

CHAPTER 9: **POISONED WATERS**

[1] Kenneth Strong, *Ox Against the Storm: A Biography of Tanaka Shozo* (United Kingdom: Paul Norbury Publications, 1985).

[2] *ibid.*, 122.

[3] *ibid.*, 119.

[4] *ibid.*, 201.

[5] *ibid.*, 206.

[6] *ibid.*, 211.

[7] *ibid.*, 211.

[8] Jun, Ui, ed., *Yanaka-mura kara Minamata Sanrizuka e* (From Yanaka Village to Minamata, Sanrizuka: Sourcebook of Japan's Ecological Philosophy) (Tokyo: Shakai-hyoron-sha, 1991).

BOOK OF INTEREST

Ishimure, Michiko. *Paradise in the Sea of Sorrow*, trans. Livia Monnet. Kyoto: Yamaguchi Publ. House, 1990.

Ui, Jun, ed. *Industrial Pollution in Japan*. Tokyo: United Nations University Press, 1992.

CHAPTER 10: **GREEN DEMOCRACY**

[1] Kazuki Kumamoto, *Jizokuteki Kajhatsu to seimeikei* (Sustainable Development and Life System) (Tokyo: Gakuyo-shobo, 1995), 18.

BOOK OF INTEREST

Tomino, Kiichiro. *Gurin Demokurashi* (Green Democracy). Tokyo: Hakusui-sha, 1991.

CHAPTER 11: **THE FOOD CONNECTION**

[1] Masanobu Fukuoka, *The One Straw Revolution: An Introduction to Natural Farming* (Emmaus: Rodale Press, 1978).

[2] Masanobu Fukuoka, *The Natural Way of Farming: The Theory and Practice of Green Philosophy* (Tokyo: Japan Publications, 1987).

[3] Teruo Higa, *Chikyu o sukuu dai-henkaku* (EM: The Revolution That Will Save the Earth), vols. 1 and 2 (Tokyo: Sanmaku shuppan, 1994–95).

[4] Bill Mollison and Reny Mia Slay, *Introduction to Permaculture* (Tyalgum, Australia: Tagari Publications, 1994).

BOOK OF INTEREST

Kawaguchi, Yoshikazu. *Taenaru hatake ni tachite* (Standing in the Godly Field). Hirosaki: Yasosha, 1990.

CHAPTER 12: **TEACHING FOR A FUTURE**

[1] Aika Tsubota, *Secrets of the Earth* (Tokyo: Chikyu kankyo heiwa zaidan, 1992).

[2] Hiroaki Sato and Burton Watson, eds. and trans., *From the Country of Eight Islands: An Anthology of Japanese Poetry* (Seattle: University of Washington Press, 1981), 505–6.

[3] Mallory Blake Fromm, *Miyazawa Kenji no riso* (The Ideals of Kenji Miyazawa) (Tokyo: Shobunsha, 1984).

BOOKS OF INTEREST

Kogo, Motohiko. *Midori no boken* (Green Adventure). Tokyo: Iwanami-shoten, 1988.

Miyazawa, Kenji. *Winds from Afar, Stories by Kenji Miyazawa*. Translated by John Bester. Tokyo and Palo Alto: Kodansha International, 1972.

Toriyama, Toshiko. *Shizen o ikuru jugyo* (To Live Nature in the Classroom). Tokyo: Bansei-shobo, 1991.

Toriyama, Toshiko. *Minna ga songoku* (Everyone Is a Monkey King). Tokyo: Taro-jiro-sha, 1994.

PERIODS IN JAPANESE HISTORY

JOMON Pottery Culture (8000 B.C.–300 B.C.)

    Rice Cultivation introduced

YAYOI Pottery Culture (300 B.C.–A.D. 300)

YAMATO State (A.D. 350–7th century)

    Buddhism introduced

NARA Period (710–794)

HEIAN Period (794–1185)

KAMAKURA Period (1192–1333)

MUROMACHI Period (1338–1573)

        1543 – Portuguese arrived on Tanegashima Island and introduced firearms to Japan

        1592 – Hideyoshi invades Korea

EDO TOKUGAWA Period (1603–1867)

        1633 – First stage of policy of isolation from world

        1639 – Portuguese ships banned from Japan

Genroku Era (1688–1703)

Bunka-Bunsei Era (1804–1829)

        1853 – U.S. Commander Perry arrives

MODERNIZATION Period (1867–present)

Meiji Era (1868–1912)

        1889 – Promulgation of the Imperial Constitution of Japan

        1894 – Sino-Japanese War

        1904 – Russo-Japanese War

        1910 – Annexation of Korea

Taisho Era (1912–1926)

1914 – Japan declares war on Germany (First World War)

1923 – Great Tokyo earthquake

Showa Era (1926–1989)

1931 – Mukden incident, Japan occupies Manchuria (beginning
the Fifteen-Year War)

1937 – Japan invades China

1940 – Tripartite Pact signed by Japan, Germany, and Italy

1941 – Japan attacks Pearl Harbor

1945 – Atomic bombs dropped on Hiroshima and Nagasaki, war
ends as Japan surrenders

1946 – Promulgation of the Constitution of Japan

1950 – Creation of National Police Reserve, renamed the Self-
Defence Force in 1954

1950 – Korean War begins

1951 – San Francisco Peace Treaty and Japan–U.S. Security
Pact (Anpo) are signed

1960 – Anpo Movement against the renewal of the Japan–U.S.
Security Pact

1972 – Reversion of Okinawa

Normalization of relations with People's Republic of China

Heisei Era (1989–present)

1995 – 50th anniversary of the end of Second World War

(Source: Japan Almanac 1994, Tokyo Asahi Newspaper)

acknowledgments

This book is a chronicle of the four trips we made over a two-year period. During that time we crossed Japan from the southwestern islands of Okinawa to northeastern Hokkaido and interviewed more than sixty-five people known for their grassroots activities. The interests of our interviewees fell into three broad areas — peace, civil liberties, and environment — and this is essentially how we have organized our book.

All these people gave generously and freely of their time and interest, and we are very grateful to them. Many of them were sufficiently fluent in English to allow us to carry out our entire interview in English. When interviewees spoke only Japanese, Keibo translated. We hope we have presented all those we have quoted faithfully and respectfully. That is our way of thanking them for their generous gift of time and ideas.

As well, there were others we interviewed but could not fit easily into this format. They included Jung-do Bae, Konosuke Fujii, Akiko Fujimoto, Susumu Fujimoto, Miwako Kaizawa, Kazuto Kato, Shinya Kim, Shokichi Kina and the Champloos, Reiko Ko, Motohiki Kogo, Shigeru Koyama, Shigeyoshi Matsumoto, Miki Matsuo, Kazuko Murata, Kiyoshi Mukaizato, Kinhide Mushakoji, Keiko Nakamura, Tadao Osawa, Luis Toguchi, Sumio Yamamoto, and Sogil Yan. We are grateful for the time they spent with us and regret their exclusion from the final product.

Some who went beyond the bounds of hospitality and courtesy deserve special mention. We thank the incredible generosity of Shigeki Takeo, Yumiko Horikoshi, Yuriko and Masamitsu Takiguchi, all of whom accompanied, guided, and hosted us at different points along our journey.

Shun Oiwa was an excellent chauffeur who navigated some terrifying streets and also served as a photographer.

We were fortunate to have journalist Cleo Pascal as a research assistant and Thom Richardson as an editing assistant.

We have no idea how we could have pulled things together and kept focused on what we were writing without the heroic efforts of our editor, Jennifer Glossop.

We also thank the Institute for International Studies at Meiji Gakuin University in Yokohama and the David Suzuki Foundation in Vancouver for providing us with the space, staff support, and materials as we were working on this book. We are grateful to the authors who generously gave us permission to quote from their work.

Finally, without the enthusiastic support and hard work at home of our wives, Tara Cullis and Mari Sato, while we were travelling and working on the book, it would not have been written.

INDEX

THE DAVID SUZUKI FOUNDATION: WORKING TOGETHER FOR A SUSTAINABLE FUTURE

The David Suzuki Foundation was established to create a world of hope in which our species thrives in balance with the productive capacity of the Earth.

Our mission is to find solutions to the root causes of our most threatening environmental problems. Then, we work with our supporters and their communities to implement those solutions for a sustainable future.

Our mandate is broad, ranging from projects on climate change, air, soil, water, fisheries, forestry, energy, and liveable cities, to defining the foundations of sustainability, how social change occurs, and the potential of new economic models.

We can only accomplish this with the support of concerned citizens who care about the environment. We invite your help.

JOIN OUR PARTNERSHIP… JOIN THE FOUNDATION!

Name ———Address ————————————————

City/Province ———Postal Code ———Telephone ——————

Here is my donation of:

——$30 ——$50 ——$100 ——$500 $ ———————

——$1000 National Sponsor ———$5000 Founder

——Cheque ——Money Order ——Visa ——MasterCard

Card No. ———————Expiry Date ——Signature ——————

Yes, I'll become a Friend of the Foundation.

I authorize the Foundation to receive the following amount from my Chequing Account on a monthly basis. I understand I'll receive a tax credit and the benefits of becoming a Foundation Supporter.

——$10 a month ——$15 a month ——$25 a month $ ———a month

I understand I can change or cancel my pledge at any time. I enclose a sample cheque marked VOID for bank coding.

Signature ————————————————————

Please return this reply memo with your tax-creditable donation.
Cheques can be made payable to The David Suzuki Foundation.
Thank you very much for your support!

THE DAVID SUZUKI FOUNDATION, 219 - 2211 WEST FOURTH AVENUE, VANCOUVER, B.C., CANADA V6K 4S2 Phone (604)732-4228

Fax (604)732-0752

Canadian Charitable Registration No. 0873299-52

U.S. Charitable Registration No. 94-3204049